WITHDRAWN

"*From Landfill to Hallowed Ground* is a compelling saga, detailing the events following the horrific attack on America on September 11, 2001. Marra details how many first responders, filled with sadness and disbelief, selflessly acted with courage, love, and dignity in what became a massive recovery operation. The heroic efforts of these public servants helped restore our faith in the human spirit in the face of monstrous acts perpetrated upon so many. We shall never forget what they gave, and the victims will never be forgotten."

—Anthony J. Marra
Retired Assistant Chief, New York City Police Department
On September 11, 2001, as Commanding Officer of all police services,
Patrol Borough Staten Island, Marra established the crime scene at the Landfill.

"A gripping account of September 11, 2001, through the eyes of one who served there. Lt. Frank Marra, NYPD-Ret., artfully, adeptly, and sensitively takes us through the most horrific experiences of his honored career, leaving no stone unturned. The Staten Island Landfill, 'that sacred and hallowed ground,' became the world's largest 'movable' crime scene, where the debris was picked apart to find anything that might identify victims who had perished, from human form to dust. This book is a must-read for those who were there, and it is an excellent resource for undergraduate and graduate students, as well as researchers in mass disasters, terrorism, psychological trauma, and the resulting stressors. I urge you to read it."

—Richard L. Levenson, Jr., Psy.D., CTS
NYS Licensed Psychologist
Certified Trauma Specialist
Police Surgeon, NYS Troopers PBA

From Landfill to

Hallowed Ground

From Landfill to
Hallowed
Ground

The Largest Crime Scene in America

Frank Marra
Maria Bellia Abbate

BROWN BOOKS
PUBLISHING GROUP

From Landfill to Hallowed Ground:
The Largest Crime Scene in America

Brown Books Publishing Group
16250 Knoll Trail Drive, Suite 205
Dallas, Texas 75248
www.BrownBooks.com
(972) 381-0009

A New Era in Publishing™

ISBN 978-1-61254-243-0
LCCN 2014955699

Printed in the United States
10 9 8 7 6 5 4 3 2 1

For more information or to contact the authors, please go to
www.FromLandfillToHallowedGround.com

To all the victims of the 9/11 attacks
and their families.

To the First Responders who perished that day
and those who gave so much of themselves post-9/11
in a tireless effort to bring normalcy to a very
dark period in our country's history.

To the fallen NYC skyline,
a one-of-a-kind view that will never be again.

Contents

Author's Note

Calm before the Storm

I remember clearly everything I did on September 11, 2001, and wish I didn't. I wish I had no memories of that day and wish that day had been different. Like so many thousands of others, I wish it had never happened, but it did, and my thoughts over a decade later are still too clear and too real.

I woke early, put on the coffee, and got my son Anthony up for school. Anthony was five years old and in kindergarten, and my daily routine was getting him ready, fed, dressed, and on the bus. My wife normally worked from home, but on this day, as luck would have it, she had to go to the office.

My son Dominic, who was one and a half, was up early as well, so I put him in his high chair. Dom and Anthony ate breakfast while the three of us watched television. Suddenly their cartoons were interrupted by a local news flash. The next thing I saw on the television was the south tower of the World Trade Center on fire. As the smoke billowed, I became mesmerized by what was happening. I assumed that this was some type of terrible, tragic accident, at which time I put Anthony on the bus.

Dominic and I continued to watch television, showing the tower smoking. I decided to call my father, Anthony Marra, who was the Borough Commander of Staten Island. I asked him if he was aware of what was going on at the World Trade Center. He said he had started to receive calls from his office about what was happening. I thought at first a small aircraft had crashed into the tower, but then I saw the second plane strike the North Tower with such force it almost came out the other side of the building. I said to my dad, "This is not a coincidence. These are not small planes but commercial airliners. This has to be some kind of attack." My dad was silent and then agreed that, in his forty-year career, this would be a day that no one would be prepared for. As we said good-bye, we both knew what had to be done.

As soon as I hung up the phone, I knew I had three calls to make. The first was to my office at the Brooklyn South Gang Unit. I spoke with my Lieutenant Joe Cardinale, who instructed me to get my personal business in order and to make my way to the office. The second call was to my wife, Laura. I told her to tell her boss she needed to leave. She had witnessed the second tower being hit on television at work, so she knew what I meant.

The third call was to my in-laws who lived around the corner to ask them to come and stay with my youngest son Dominic so I could get my son Anthony from school. He was my main concern. I needed to see him, to know he was safe. When my mother-in-law arrived, I headed straight for P.S. 32.

When I pulled up to my son's school, the street looked like a parking lot. The outside of the school screamed the word "panic" with cars parked on sidewalks and grass. I had to block someone's driveway to park a block away. The inside was jammed with people, and I could see the fear and panic on the other parents' and teachers' faces. We all had the same thought: *Just get my child and go home*. Phones were ringing, someone was talking over the loud speaker, and I heard someone say, "Mr. Marra, do you want me to get Anthony?" After what seemed like an eternity but was probably five minutes, we headed home. I gathered my work bag, told my mother-in-law I would stay in touch, and headed into Brooklyn around 9:15 a.m.

I was secure in the feeling that my children were safe and my wife was on her way home. Eventually my dad had to send a police car into New Jersey to get her. Laura was stuck in traffic so deep that she would not have gotten home unless this bold move was made. What I realized at a later moment was that despite all the craziness that was happening around us, all the fear, all the panic, this moment was truly the "calm before the storm" because what would follow in the next forty-five minutes would change all of us for the rest of our lives.

1

Field of Death

The body bags were piled up on the ground, a morgue in the making. There was no particular formation, just piles waiting to be used. Eventually the body bags would be spread out right next to one another in a military formation like soldiers going into battle. The bags would cover the outfield of the Staten Island Yankees Stadium, located in Richmond Terrace, in Staten Island, New York. The stadium for the class A affiliate of the New York Yankees is located on the waterfront directly across from Manhattan, a ferry ride away.

On a normal afternoon, this stadium would provide one of the best views of any stadium in New York, a picturesque landscape of the New York City skyline. On this day, it would be the backdrop of a temporary morgue. It would provide a view of devastation and astonishment for its onlookers. On September 11, 2001, the outfield was something it was never intended to be.

About four hours after the devastation had begun, I looked around and saw a sunny, perfect September day with a mild temperature, blue sky, and no clouds in sight. It quickly transformed into a sky engulfed by heavy dust and debris that could be seen from space. The best and iconic part of the New York City skyline had fallen. The assumption was that there would be an endless stream of body after body that would have to be removed from an area later identified as Ground Zero.

As the day went on, we learned that the bodies from both fallen towers would be removed from Ground Zero and transported to private ferries. The ferry boats would then transport the bodies to staging areas throughout the city: Yankee Stadium, Shea Stadium, and Staten Island Yankees Stadium. At the staging areas, NYPD detectives and police officers would begin to try to identify bodies that had no identifying documents. The deceased would be fingerprinted. DNA swabs of their mouths would be taken. Dental molds could also be done if needed. For the deceased who could not be identified at that time, they would be categorized with a missing persons report. Those who were identified were to be labeled homicide victims.

Later in the day, it became clear that there would be no bodies arriving at these staging areas. The search effort for people would be too arduous of a task manually. The seemingly endless piles of twisted steel and cement would have to be moved by machinery. Initially all the adrenaline we were working with seemed to be enough strength and hope that we would recover someone, anyone. As time passed, it became increasingly real that there would not be anyone to recover.

Word had worked its way through channels that the private ferries that were to be used to transport the dead would now become transportation for the living. It was becoming difficult, at times almost impossible, for people to get off of Manhattan; therefore, the ferries would run from Manhattan to all five boroughs and New Jersey in an effort to move people out. Everyone was extremely eager to get home to loved ones, especially since most people were unable to contact their families as a result of the downed cell towers.

At the time, my detectives and I were on the Manhattan side, and I decided that for traveling purposes, it would be easier to take one of the ferries to Staten Island rather than to fight through the cars and buses left on the bridges and the tunnels. From Staten Island, I figured I could get a ride back to our office in Brooklyn.

We began to help load the first ferries. I stood on the ferry going to Staten Island to help with the people on-board. Many of these people looked dazed, confused, and scared, as if they just survived a fifteen-round fight. Their faces were dirty and covered with dust, but it couldn't disguise the expressions on their faces—sheer tragedy and fear. I had a hard time looking at them, but an even harder time not wondering what must be going through their minds. Were they relieved they survived, confused and in shock still by what they saw, distraught because they may have lost someone or left someone, or maybe all three? Not only their faces were disturbing; many were covered from head to toe with a whitish gray dust of cement. Several had torn and ripped clothes. Some people were missing one shoe or even both. Women were walking with broken heels. A small group had superficial wounds that they had sustained as debris fell from the Towers, as these people ran for their lives.

The most bizarre group I witnessed were those covered in jet fuel. They wore an awful odor; their clothes were soaking wet as if someone had sprayed them with a fire hose. I approached one of the women and asked her if she could tell me how this happened. She said that she was standing in the lobby waiting for the elevator. She explained that she heard a loud crashing sound above her that had caused the whole building to shake. For a second, things quieted down, which offered only brief relief, and then all of a sudden she said that she began to hear a loud thundering noise like a herd of buffalo headed toward them. She and her coworkers began to panic and headed toward the elevators. The doors began to buckle, and gasoline flooded out from the elevator. Her expression was so memorable, as she continued to explain that the gasoline came from above with such force that it shattered all the glass in the lobby and knocked down everyone who was waiting for the elevator. She paused for a moment and almost breathless, shaking her head in disbelief, said, "I was in the South Tower."

I would learn days later that when the planes hit the Towers the fuel compartments on board the planes that housed the jet fuel had immediately ruptured on impact. This rupture caused the jet fuel to shoot down the elevator shafts and into the lobbies. The fuel traveled roughly eighty to ninety stories downward, cracking the elevator doors and flooding into the lobbies.

Thankfully the ferry boats were stocked with water and various food items, prepared for a day of business. We began to distribute these items to the people on board, and paramedics attended those injured. Many of the people who had jet fuel on them began to complain that their eyes were burning and they had trouble seeing.

When we arrived on the Staten Island side, we decided to stay on board to continue to help with the transporting of all of these people. There were still thousands of people on the Manhattan side who needed to get off the island. One gentleman in particular asked me if he could help out in any way and said that he would not mind making the return trip to help with the crowds of people. He introduced himself as John and said he lived in Staten Island. He worked on Wall Street, and his daughter worked in the South Tower. He explained that he was hoping that on the return trip he would see his daughter. He had spoken with her earlier, and she said she was fine. He called home to his wife, but she had not heard from their daughter. Rather than say the wrong thing, because clearly this gentleman was nervous and scared, I replied, "No problem, we will take all the help we can get."

During our trip back to Manhattan, John and I made small talk to pass the time and distract each other from the reality of what was going on. At some point, he asked me about what it was like trying to get into the city with all the craziness.

I told him that as I headed to Brooklyn to meet with my team I was greeted with scenes of chaos and confusion. It looked like the end of the world. I crossed the Verrazano Bridge, and it was completely empty of all traffic. At the toll booths, everyone had to show identification to proceed. When my team and I left to go to Manhattan, we experienced the same protocol, but the scenes were so much worse. Cars were left abandoned on the Gowanus Parkway. As drivers entered the Brooklyn Battery Tunnel, they had to swerve in and out of traffic. People had just stopped and abandoned their vehicles.

On the Manhattan side, the cars had layers of thick dust on them caused by the fallen Towers. Everything was pulverized and created a huge dust cloud that billowed into the tunnel. As drivers emerged from the tunnel and drove toward the World Trade Center, or what was left of the World Trade Center, they could go only so far. The mounds of debris and of twisted steel and cement poured onto and covered all of the West Side Highway, taking down everything in its path, including a Marriott Hotel and a good portion of the Winter Garden, a large building in the Financial Center across the street from World Trade Center.

We continued to talk, and I asked John what he saw when the planes hit the Towers. He said that he could hear the impact from his building on Wall Street. It was incredibly loud and disturbing. At first no one overreacted to the sound, but then the rumor began to spread about what was actually going on. He said his secretary told him that she had heard that a large plane hit the South Tower. "I then left my building to find out what was going on, and I could see a large hole in the South Tower and flames coming from the inside," he said. He went back inside to get his coat and call his daughter. Then his face grew drawn and sullen, his eyes stared into the sky, and he said, "When I came back outside, that's when I saw people jumping from the South Tower. This is an image that I will never forget. I can't imagine how bad it was inside that building so that the better idea was to jump to your death."

When we arrived back on the Manhattan side, the large crowds had lessened, and additional ferries, as well as private boats and various vessels, were still in service helping to transport people out of Manhattan. I could see people walking across the Brooklyn and Manhattan bridges. My team and I took additional trips back and forth, and John stood with us helping out. I would see him attempting a cell call every once in a while. I figured he was trying to call home or his daughter, but I did not ask. He told me on our last trip back to Staten Island that he had not heard from her but he remained hopeful. I tried to be supportive. I said that the cell phone service in the area was severely damaged when the Towers fell. John nodded, walked away, and began handing water to those in need.

When we docked in Staten Island, I told John that my team was going to stay. It was about 7:00 p.m. I explained that we were going to try and get a ride back to Brooklyn because a new shift was coming to relieve us. John said he was going to take one more trip over in the hopes of seeing his daughter. He said that maybe the cell service was improving and that maybe he would hear from her soon. I agreed with him, I thanked him for all his help, and we shook hands. In that moment, we both must have felt the same. Shaking hands just didn't seem to be enough, and in a moment of raw emotion, we embraced. I wished him and his family well. I thanked him again. He told me that I helped keep his mind off what could possibly be the inevitable. "If I don't hear from or see my daughter in the next hour or so, I have to come to terms with the fact that she is dead and then explain that to her mother." John began to break down and sob. I was utterly speechless.

Here was a man who for five hours displayed an act of selflessness by putting his own feelings aside to help others. Who does that in today's society that is filled with such selfishness and hatred? At that moment, reality slapped me hard, and I called my family immediately to tell my wife and three boys how much I loved them. John walked away and got on the ferry. That was the last time I saw him.

September 11, 2001, was the longest day I have ever experienced. The sights and sounds that I heard and saw will haunt me forever. As I think back and reflect on that time, there are two thoughts that stand out about that day. The first is seeing the devastation and horror that was the World Trade Center and saying to myself that the best part of New York City was lying on its side. The second thought is of John, the man I hardly knew who made such an impact and impression on me that day. I hope everything worked out for him. I hope and pray that he found his daughter and together they took a ferry ride back to Staten Island just as we had done that day so many times.

2

Landfill to Crime Scene

I arrived home on September 11, 2001, about 10:00 p.m. When I thought about how fortunate I was at that moment when my wife Laura greeted me at the door with a comforting hug, I felt my body slump into hers in both relief and sadness. I know she said something about our boys being asleep, but it all seemed mumbled. I was in a fog. I had gone on adrenaline the whole day, using up every ounce of mental and physical strength I had, and I was ready to share with her all the chaos and tragedy I witnessed. We sat and talked, almost at a whisper, still trying to comprehend the reality of what took place. Even as a cop, and as much as I have seen on the job, I had not been immune to pain and emotion, and I gave her the best description I could about what I saw and heard.

The calmness was shattered by a call from my father, Anthony Marra, NYPD two-star chief and Borough commander of Staten Island. He explained, in his authoritative, all-business tone, that all the staging areas that were origNally set up were never utilized, nor would be. He said that the tons of twisted steel and cement were going to be moved from lower Manhattan to the Staten Island Landfill. From that point on, since there wouldn't be any survivors, the Landfill would now be the main staging area.

There was no longer search and rescue, strictly a search and recovery. He told me that the crime scene, all that was left at and around Ground Zero, would be moved by truck and barge to the Staten Island Landfill. It would now become the largest movable crime scene in American history. All individuals currently involved in the Brooklyn South Gang Unit, which was my current assignment, as well as other detective units from within the city, would be reporting to the Landfill. Initially patrol officers needed to stay at their present assignments for continued public safety, but everyone throughout the New York City Police Department eventually ended up at the Staten Island Landfill and worked into the search and recovery rotation.

On September 12, 2001, I was off to Staten Island. Because this was a crime scene, most of the detective bureau would be part of this operation, and what an operation it was. All detective units ranging from the Gang

Unit to the Organized Crime Control Bureau would be utilized. Narcotics, Public Moral Units, and detectives from seventy-five different detective bureaus throughout the city were also heavily involved.

The Landfill was so vast that it had its own water access that connected to New York Harbor. Who could've imagined that the "dump," as we islanders referred to it, was going to house all the debris and remains of one of the most tragic and largest attacks on US soil?

Two white trailers were then brought in for temporary headquarters, one for the NYPD and the other for the FBI. Then like an atom bomb exploding or the "big bang," different tents and trailers began to spring up. After only three weeks of operation, there were two temporary headquarters, a cafeteria, and a supply tent, where anything from gloves to heavy coats could be obtained. There was also a tent assembled for "mustering," where the members of service would meet to get daily assignments and a trailer for medical attention and various medications/antibiotics. The dump turned into a small city. Frank Tegano, NYPD retired crime scene detective, recalled his experience:

When we first started at the Landfill, I remember there was a pizza truck that came every day with donated food, and caterers from Staten Island sent food. We even had barbeques. Later OSHA [Occupational Safety and Health Administration] and the Board of Health said that we could not cook or eat any food in this area. We were cooking and eating in clouds of asbestos and debris.

I was assigned to the auto pound. Others were assigned to the doctors' trailers, the cafeteria, the crime scene trailer, and the sifters. Many civilians from privately owned construction companies with sifting machines were assigned there as well. Vice President Dick Cheney's construction company from Texas was among those companies from out of state.

The Landfill was a crime scene but not a traditional crime scene. A normal crime scene is roped off, and the only people allowed in are the crime scene detectives. Evidence is removed that could help in solving the crime, and the area is then guarded by a police officer until there is no further evidence that can be found. At the Landfill, the evidence from this crime was not only the bodies and body parts. There was the visual evidence of the planes striking the buildings, and the evidence from these planes was recovered at the Landfill. I remember there were areas designated for plane parts such as tires, landing gear, engines, seats, framing of the plane structure, and numerous other small pieces that could be seen and identified. I always expected to see more, but the planes were pulverized when the Towers collapsed, a lot like the office furniture and computers. I was at the Landfill for over five months, and I never saw office furniture or computers. Not only was this the largest crime scene in American history, but it was also the longest ongoing crime scene. Every day some form of evidence was found.

The Landfill was set up for search and recovery. In the early stages, the mounds of debris would be raked through by detectives and first responders and then eventually by sifting machines. The use of the sifting machines expedited the search and recovery process. The Crime Scene Unit was all set up and ready to go. Detectives worked in pairs. One detective had the arduous task of taking photographs of body parts, and the other detective would be in charge of documenting all the information. There would be some days that detectives not assigned to the Crime Scene Unit would have to help in the crime scene tent because a crime scene detective had court or took the day off. Some could handle this assignment, but others could not. There were times that a detective would become overwhelmed. During those instances, they were removed from the tent and replaced by others who could handle the assignment.

Frank Tegano was assigned to the crime scene tent to handle the bodies and body parts that were recovered. He later spoke candidly about his experiences at the Landfill and moments that were difficult to forget. During his time there, he recalled moments in the crime scene tent that were very difficult because of how the Landfill had been perceived:

They didn't categorize it as a morgue; they just called it the Landfill. Once we got there, we were set up with a tent with tables and plastic on the tables. Detectives and first responders would go sifting and then bring the body parts to us and just dump them in piles on the plastic tables. Then we would carefully go through the evidence. We had anthropologists with us who were there teaching us how to determine whether the bones we saw were human or animal. The reason for this was that the two Towers had three restaurants, so there could be steak or pork or even chicken bones that could be taken for pieces of human flesh or bone. We had to know the difference. By the time we were finished at the Landfill, we had recovered and tagged over 3,500 pieces of bone or flesh.

Detective Tegano worked at the Landfill from September 2001 to January 2002. He emphasized that this was a crime scene and documentation was important:

These bodies were often wrapped and covered in cement, mud, and different materials. They had been exposed to the elements, and the decomposition process had already begun. Every day a refrigerated morgue truck would arrive at the Landfill to pick up the body parts to be brought back to the City Morgue in an attempt to identify who these people were from the list of the missing.

In the beginning, all the bodies that were coming in . . . you'd get a body, and it would have an ID tag on it. That was the hardest part. I remember seeing a girl at the Morgue. I could barely make out that this was a woman. . . . But as I am going through her identification, I could see that she was a twenty-six-year-old gorgeous blonde working for Cantor Fitzgerald. And I was angry, just angry. I remember she lived in the Rockaways, and I just became so angry. The job suddenly became personal.

DNA testing through hair, skin, and saliva swabs, if possible, along with fingerprints and dental records, would all be utilized to identify the body parts and the victims. The crime scene detectives at the Landfill were all issued dental cameras, used to photograph the jawbone and teeth with close-up photos of fillings. The trick with the fillings was that we needed to get three fillings together in the same mouth to enhance the identification process.

The identification and notification processes were bittersweet. Many families were looking for that phone call, for closure, or for some sort of finality that their family members had been recovered. They weren't waiting for a phone call claiming their family member survived. When they received a call, they would have to be told how we verified the identity. We would have to explain that through DNA testing we were able to make an identification but explain that we are sorry to say that we had only his or her hand, foot, or maybe a finger. The families would then be allowed to pick up the body part for burial. Unfortunately, this scenario was common at the Landfill or City Morgue. There were also chunks of flesh too ground up to identify what body parts they were because of all the dirt and cement mixed into the flesh. These parts would be sent to the Morgue for DNA testing. All body parts eventually made their way to the Morgue to be frozen until testing could occur.

Remembering this was a crime scene would always hit home when first responders working the sifters would bring police officer equipment like hats, gun belts, shields, weapons, and firefighter equipment such as gloves, jackets, or helmets to the crime scene tent. Each day at the Landfill became like almost any other job. We would go through the motions, perform our assignments, and fulfill our duties for the day on our twelve-hour rotation, until we were reminded of the reality of the situation and why we were there. The NYPD lost a total of 23 members, the Port Authority 37, and the NYFD 343.

I know that all the equipment was kept in a special place, bagged separately, and sent to the Morgue to be examined closely for anything that could lead to whose equipment it was. They would look for a serial number or shield number. When a police officer or fireman was found at Ground Zero or at the Landfill, the body was transported immediately to the Morgue in Manhattan. When evidence was determined at the Morgue, whether it was a police officer or fireman, a procession would be formed, and everyone in the procession would stand at attention and salute until the body was inside. Normally this would also be done once the family arrived at the Morgue to view the body, remains, or evidence.

Items brought to the crime scene trailer made this a special crime scene. One day, one of the sifting machines broke down, and there was something stuck in the sifter, preventing it from turning. A large piece of cement appeared to be wedged into the sifting mechanism. Because of its size and awkwardness, workers took a couple of hours to pry the item free. Then they had it picked up by a backhoe and put on the debris pile. When the backhoe operator dropped the item from his bucket, it hit the pile, causing a piece to break off. The operator saw something shiny. After more chipping away, investigators found pounds of gold that had melted together. Because the gold was mixed with so many different materials, at first we could not identify what it was.

Apparently the Treasury Department had leased floor space in the basement of the World Trade Center. When the Towers collapsed and were on fire, the impact coupled with the jet fuel that burns at 1,200 degrees melted everything in their paths. But not all the gold housed in these sub-basements melted. Later we learned that much of the gold survived and had to be taken by subway from where it was located to an undisclosed location. The gold that was found at the Landfill was given to the FBI.

Many different items were recovered, including narcotic safes and the copper from the elevators that were priority in the first two weeks. The Drug Enforcement Administration (DEA) also leased space at the World Trade Center. There were safes housed in the sub-basements where evidence was being securely kept for narcotics cases. The retrieval of these safes was of grave importance to the DEA and was imperative to court cases. No evidence, no case. Amazingly these safes were all found prior to using the sifting machines. They were located by rake and shovel and a lot of luck.

This small working city became a grave, a burial ground, for people who perished on that day. Tegano speaks for those who served at the Landfill when he said it should be seen and perceived as holy ground:

One day there will be a mass grave site for all the World Trade Center victims that could not be identified. Early into this crime scene the recovered bodies had identification on their persons. As time went on, it became hard to identify someone or even what you were looking at. By the end, it was almost impossible. Bodies and body parts had been exposed to winter and decomposition and were unidentifiable. I take with me many thoughts and memories.

3

Personal Effects

By the middle of October 2001, rake and shovel were put down at the Landfill, and the sifting machine was front and center, making evidence retrieval at least four times faster than raking through the debris fields. The sifting machines all came from Texas. At least ten sifting machines operated at the Landfill. These conveyor belts were welcomed pieces of machinery that increased work capacity and took less of a toll on the detectives and first responders working there.

Throughout my time at the Landfill, we often came across personal effects from victims, whether at the auto pound or at the sifters or even in the crime scene tent. Personal effects came in different forms: jewelry, identification tags, briefcases, or credit cards. Every once in a while, we would receive a call from the main headquarters at "The Hill," a nickname given to the Landfill, that a family member or members were here to take personal belongings from a loved one's car. I would send one of my detectives to drive the family to the auto pound or escort them personally. These situations became emotional and created memories that stand out more than others.

One day, a family showed up, mom and two children, which was unusual, because typically only one person would come to retrieve some items and then leave. We always asked for identification from the person and proof of registration for the auto to make sure this was one of the registered owners. We never had a problem with people providing the proper identification and information requested.

I greeted the woman, a tall brunette with a forced smile. She introduced herself as Michele: "I am here to look through my husband's car for anything that might have been left behind. He died in Tower 2; he worked on the 85th floor." I asked her what kind of vehicle. She responded softly, "A white S500 Mercedes Benz." We walked Michele over to the car. Normally we would let the people take as long as they wanted while they were there. We knew this was all part of their grieving process.

We told them that they could take any effects from inside the car but that they could not take the car itself. I explained that all of these autos were part of a crime scene and told her to notify her insurance company that we had the car. Michele understood the procedure and opened the rear passenger door and told her children to get in. She closed the door and took out an 8 x 11 framed photo of a man. We assumed it was her husband. She placed the picture on the driver's seat facing the steering wheel. When I looked at her, she reopened the door just a little and said that if we didn't mind, they were going to sit here for a while. She seemed as though she was trying to recapture moments when he was alive. I nodded to her and told her to take as much time as she needed.

I asked one of my detectives to keep an eye on them and make sure this did not get any more bizarre because she had the keys to the car, probably her set. I wanted to make sure she did not try to drive this car out of the auto lot. We locked the gate to be sure. After about thirty minutes, I went back to the car, and I could see that Michele had been crying. She was holding a cigarette lighter; it was chrome with a Harley-Davidson insignia. She rolled down the window and told me that her husband's passion was riding motorcycles on weekends with his friends from work. Michele then whispered to me, so her children could not hear: "I hope to bring some form of closure. His body has not been recovered."

With that, she got out of the vehicle and carefully let her children out. She told me she was also there to see if she could retrieve his briefcase and asked if she could look in the trunk. I told her she absolutely could and offered her my help. Michele opened the trunk with her remote, and the briefcase was there along with what looked like some birthday gifts wrapped in a colorful paper. Michele closed the trunk and said, "My daughter's birthday was September 13. Those are her gifts, but I don't want her to see them. She is only five. Do you have a large garbage bag I could put them in? I will give them to her for Christmas." I answered her and heard my voice crack as I spoke. We grabbed some garbage bags, reopened the trunk, and put the gifts into the bags without the children noticing. She grabbed the briefcase, and we closed the trunk.

Michele put the briefcase on the hood of the car and opened it. Inside were paperwork and a birthday card. She began to read it and cried uncontrollably. I tried to comfort her. The children became upset seeing their mother crying, so I closed the briefcase and began to walk Michele and the children to the temporary headquarters.

One of the detectives brought the closed briefcase to Michele. "You have been more than kind," she said, "but I am going. Could you have someone drive us back to the top where my car is?" Her children got into the van first, and then she did. Michele rolled her window down: "I left the picture of my husband on the seat. I have others. He loved taking family rides and just talking with the kids. He worked all week and would get home late. Sometimes they were sleeping, so weekend drives were our best times together." The van pulled away.

As the crime scene trailer began to see more and more evidence, the effects told their own stories. Some of the body parts wore identification tags; others wore jewelry. There were all types of jewelry, from earrings to bracelets to necklaces. Some of the hands still had rings on their fingers. The jewelry was removed and separated from the body, but everything was marked with a serial number so we could match the body part with the jewelry. So much jewelry was being recovered through the sifting machines that the commanding officer of the Landfill, James Luongo, came up with a process that the jewelry would be photographed and then sent to all the New York newspapers. This was done so that the entire tristate area—New York,

New Jersey, and Connecticut—could view the jewelry on a daily basis. The hope was that someone would recognize the jewelry and help in identifying the bodies and body parts recovered.

This process definitely had some success, and I remember people would come to the Landfill to get a closer look at a ring that they thought belonged to their loved one. There were wedding bands, engagement rings, and even college or high school rings. In addition to the recovery of jewelry, identification cards were being found through the sifting machines, in particular from Cantor Fitzgerald. When Flight 11 crashed into Tower 1, the plane hit right below the Cantor Fitzgerald offices, making escape impossible. The plane took out a large portion of the stairwells and damaged the elevators. When Tower 1 collapsed, 658 of 950 employees in the Cantor Fitzgerald offices died.

The Staten Island Landfill World Trade Center Recovery Site sifted through over 1.45 million tons of debris. Over the course of the operations, the sifting machines and personnel working those machines were able to retrieve over 600 Cantor Fitzgerald identification cards, but not all belonged to the missing. This was an astonishing endeavor, and I could only hope these identification cards found their way to the families of the people who were lost. I know that pieces of jewelry were still not claimed when I left the Landfill to go back to the Gang Unit, and I believe there are still over 600 pieces of jewelry unclaimed in possession of the NYPD.

The crime scene yielded many different items in addition to jewelry, watches, and identification cards. There was also an abundance of house and car keys. I don't know what happened with those items. The house keys would be tough to track. The auto keys were quite damaged and not usable. In total, 54,000 pieces of property were recovered and 19,000 returned. All 1,200 victims were identified either through DNA, fingerprints, or identification.

I would always read the missing persons sheets while my detectives made rounds at the auto pound. The sheets would keep us up to date about those who were missing from the World Trade Center. As time went on, those missing persons became homicide victims. There were two men on the list that I went to high school with. I was able to verify this through different publications like the *Staten Island Advance,* which is the local paper in Staten Island. The *Advance* ran continuous stories about Staten Island residents who were reported missing after the Towers fell. The *Advance* would also publish individual stories about people presumed missing or even dead. Between the *Advance* and our missing/homicide sheets, I was able to verify that the two people whom I had graduated high school with were victims of the September 11 attacks.

Anthony Starita, a graduate of St. Peter's Boys High School Class of 1984, an employee of Cantor Fitzgerald and a former Staten Island resident, was living in New Jersey at the time of his passing. Paul Barbaro, a graduate of St. Peter's Boys High School Class of 1984, an employee of Cantor Fitzgerald and a former Staten Island resident, was also living in New Jersey at the time of his passing.

I knew both men but had not spoken to either in over eighteen years. Seeing their names on those sheets made me feel so connected and sad that it is hard to describe. One day while at the Landfill, on break during a familiar rotation at the auto pound, I happened to be looking at one of the local newspapers and was viewing the pages where the jewelry was displayed. I noticed a high school ring. I looked closely at it and saw that it said St. Peter's, but I could not make out the entire insignia. For the next few weeks, I would look in the paper to see if there were any other rings with the St. Peter's insignia. I did this daily because I was hoping that maybe one of the rings could have been Paul's or Anthony's.

The search became personal. I began to look at the jewelry before it was photographed. I began to look through everything that was recovered to see if I could be lucky enough and find one of their rings, providing they were either wearing that ring or even got a high school ring. It felt good to try to find out if the ring belonged to either of those two men. Using my time to try to help a family bring closure to an extremely difficult time helped me to deal with what had happened. I think that is one reason I spent six months at the Landfill. Being there made me feel I was helping, contributing in some way. Anyone who worked there felt the same way.

I continued my search up until the time I left the Landfill but had no luck. There were St. Peter's rings but not St. Peter's Boys High School in Staten Island. I hope that Paul's or Anthony's identification cards from Cantor Fitzgerald found their way back to their families. There was more to looking for a connection to Paul and Anthony, and it wasn't just that I knew them and we went to high school together. We had our prom at the Windows on the World restaurant. Whenever I tell people where my prom was, I always say that it was at the highest location you could have been in New York City with the best view of the city. Windows on the World was located in the North Tower 1 on the 106th and 107th floors. Windows on the World was a catering hall/restaurant and all four sides of the restaurant were windows, which allowed us to look at all five boroughs and New Jersey as far as the eye could see. I remember at my prom everyone was leaning on a window and just looking down. I remember getting that sick frightening feeling of being so high up. Imagine those people trapped up there, with no chance of being saved, and either staying and accepting their fate or desperately jumping.

The prom, by my best recollection, was the last time I saw Paul and Anthony and a lot of others. Here I was, eighteen years later, looking for their school rings, rings that could be mixed in with the steel and cement that was Tower 1 along with Windows on the World. I dedicate this chapter to Paul and Anthony.

4

World Trade Center Vehicle Pound

The Landfill was a crime scene like no other. Each area was separate and distinct, but all shared a common goal—search and recovery. Each told many stories, and this investigation spread far over 2,200 acres. One of the components of this crime scene became the World Trade Center Vehicle Pound, also referred to as the "Auto Pound."

After about a month, the Staten Island Landfill, a location known as the drop-off point for household waste, began to take its place in American history. Its strong bright lights at night shone across the Staten Island sky as the "city" took its shape there. A comfort zone began to build for those assigned to the recovery site. I ventured out into the Landfill to get a close-up tour of something that in the past I could see only from hundreds of feet away. The auto pound was my steady post. From the first day I was there to my last, I saw hundreds of cars delivered to the Landfill from Ground Zero.

As things had begun to settle down at the Landfill from the initial chaos, Commanding Officer James Luongo called a supervisors meeting to bring together all the sergeants, lieutenants, and captains who were assigned to the Landfill to give permanent assignments. This was a way to lock down responsibilities and secure all loose ends. I remember being at this meeting and trying not to volunteer for something that I would regret, especially knowing this was going to be a long, ongoing recovery endeavor. One of the things we were always reminded in the NYPD was not to volunteer for anything. Volunteering never worked in our favor, only the Department's. I stood there trying to say nothing, trying not to break the "Golden Rule." Then as if someone took possession of me, like a faucet my mouth just poured out, "I'll supervise that!" I was now in charge of the auto pound at the Staten Island Landfill.

I had volunteered, but over time I realized that I had scored. I had to speak with Lieutenant Bovino for my assignment and had to gather an understanding of what the responsibilities of the auto pound were. For starters, the auto pound would be located about one mile from where all the sifting would be taking place. It was stationed close to the highway for easy access. The main objective of the

Staten Island Landfill World Trade Center Auto Pound would be, over time, safeguarding autos that were left behind.

The cars were brought to us from Ground Zero and the surrounding areas by barge and on trailers. These cars were either abandoned on the streets or left in parking garages. Most were damaged, some more than others, when the Towers fell.

Resembling a used car lot, the auto pound ran twenty-four hours a day. The shifts were twelve hours, 6:00 a.m. to 6:00 p.m. and then 6:00 p.m. to 6:00 a.m. I worked mainly the 6:00 p.m. to 6:00 a.m. with Tony Brognano and Matt Eadiccio. The conditions we worked under at the auto pound were similar to the other designated recovery areas around the Landfill. No matter where I was, I could feel the dust from the fallen Towers in my throat, and the wind just continuously whipped it around even more, at times making seeing difficult. The cars were covered with it. As a result, we were required to wear surgical, protective masks because of the increasing winds at the Landfill. The cement dust and debris particles whirled through the air constantly and created a much bigger health issue than any of us could have imagined.

Our job at the auto pound was to accept the vehicles that were delivered. We would log them in and then voucher or tag them to maintain inventory. Once a car was accounted for, we would park it until the next step was figured out. Sometimes in the beginning, we would pick a car from the auto pound where the keys were left, and my detectives and I would use that as our transportation to drive around the Landfill. Heavy in our minds were thoughts of the owners of the car and who and where they were. We wondered if these people ran for their lives when the Towers began to crumble, were trapped inside and never came out, or were safe at home and had yet to go look for their cars.

I estimate that at one point we had 250–300 vehicles. They would come to us by trailer. Some were in great condition and some in just good condition. The main problem with all the vehicles was the appearance of the heavy cement dust and asbestos, which not only was visible on the outside but also made its way into the climate control centers on all the cars. This condition deemed these cars unfit to be returned to their owners, so almost all cars were paid for by the insurance companies. The ramifications that could result from returning any vehicle that could negatively affect the health of the car owner could prove to be more of a financial burden for the insurance companies in the long run.

Over time I was given a temporary headquarters vehicle from our communications division, and we were able to utilize this vehicle to complete our paperwork and to eat our meals away from some of the harsh elements outside. We were also able to hook up a microwave, coffee machine, and other basic necessities. The temporary headquarters made life at the auto pound manageable. We also had a television, and I vividly remember being able to watch my beloved New York Yankees and the Arizona Diamondbacks play. Most important, it kept us out of the elements. We were there for the winter, so it was a place to keep warm and a place to keep us from the smell of the crushed cement and asbestos that the vehicles had on them, the circulating dust and debris, and the smell of methane gas that the Landfill produced from the decomposing garbage.

Once all cars retrieved were accounted for, we were required to safeguard them until we were instructed otherwise. Every once in a while, we would get a call from the main headquarters located up by the sifters that a family member was here to take personal belongings from their car or to pick up their family member's auto. Other than that, we just made sure the autos stood intact and nothing additional happened. As time went on, we were told that the insurance companies were paying the owners off for all vehicles taken from Ground Zero. "Total them," we were told.

The nights and days were long, but the memories were even longer. I think by just being there we felt we had a sense of doing something to help the situation. In the end, all the cars that we had vouchers for were crushed. They were deemed unsuitable to be given back to the owners. Ironically, the cars were crushed because of the toxic elements on them, which presented a threat to the owner, yet the first responders were initially told that the air around Ground Zero was safe.

On one particular day, Tony and Matt, detectives in the Gang Unit, were conducting their usual procedure of inventorying the autos. I was in the temporary headquarters vehicle assigned to the auto pound reading the newspaper and supervising. Suddenly Tony darted into the trailer yelling, "Frank, you have to see this. You are not going to believe it!"

Unaffected by his abrupt manner, I replied, "What's up, Tone? Did Rauer sneak up here and you found him sleeping in one of the cars?" Detective Rauer was another Gang Unit detective.

Tony just looked at me like a deer in headlights. "I wish it was that. You have to take a walk with me." There had been a lot of talk of weird and unexplainable sightings up at the Landfill during these months, so I have to admit that Tony had me real curious.

I followed him out into the chilly, cloudy night air to the back of the lot where we parked all the trucks or SUVs. He brought me to one particular truck, a late model Chevy Suburban. At this point, I was confused and wondering what he was really up to and what had spooked him. Then I thought, *maybe joke's on me.* "Tony, we have five more suburbans just like this one."

"Not like this one, take a closer look at the hood."

As I peered closer, I could see about a six-inch pile of cement, the entire length and width of the hood. At first, it looked like a tiny pre-poured concrete foundation like a mold made out of cement. Then I finally made out what it was and realized what had shaken Tony. Embedded in the hood, encased in cement like a prehistoric fossil, was a full ribcage attached to a spinal column, and encased in the ribcage was an assortment of organs still connected to hip bones.

There was complete silence as we looked in amazement at the hood of the truck. I reported this to the main headquarters and requested that crime scene come down to the auto pound. An anthropologist came with them. The crime scene detectives decided the best course of action would be to remove the hood from the truck and transport the hood to the crime scene trailer. There, along with the anthropologist, they would be able to chip away at the cement so they could remove the bones and organs without too much damage in an attempt to identify this person.

That day at the auto pound was a clear reminder, not that you needed one, of why we were there. This Chevy Suburban told stories of its own, a few in fact. Did the owner just run and abandon his vehicle while running for his life when the Towers fell? Who was this individual whose last moments on this earth had to be nothing short of tragic? Was this a police officer or a fireman? There are so many unanswered questions that I hoped could be resolved, especially for the family of this person. One thing

I did know was that this crime scene, this Landfill would be a part of me for years to come.

In the first three months we were there, the vehicles would come in a steady stream of six to ten at a time. The autos would get the once over, we would spray paint a number on the windshield in orange paint, and that number would then be placed on the voucher. This was the way we could keep track of the autos. We were required to look through them for personal effects and to see if there was anything out of the ordinary. Much of our job was "babysitting" to see what would happen with these autos. We would conduct an hourly walk-through in pairs to make sure there was nothing out of the ordinary going on and that no vandalism had occurred. Basically we made sure the autos stood in the condition they came.

The nights and days at the auto pound were long and at times emotional, but the memories were even longer. In the end, all the cars that we had vouchered were crushed. The owners had received notices from their insurance companies that they would be paid for their cars. The autos were deemed unsuitable to be given back because of the toxic elements they were exposed to. These elements had gathered in the autos' climate control systems, which presented a threat. The first responders, the detectives and police officers who handled these autos from day one until they left our possession, were initially told the air at Ground Zero was safe by the Department of Environmental Protection. I think they got that one wrong.

5

Vending Carts

Cars and trucks weren't the only form of autos that we came across during my time at the auto pound recovery site at the Landfill. I was sitting in the headquarters trailer when I received a phone call. Someone from the main headquarters was calling. I was told that we had a delivery coming and that we should get prepared. Although some days were relatively monotonous, some days were full of surprises, sadness, and weird experiences. So when they called and emphasized for us to be prepared, I couldn't imagine what it would be. Some days, things just couldn't get any stranger.

In response to the main headquarters' request to be prepared, we immediately designated an area and awaited the arrival of our incoming autos. When the delivery came, it was not autos we were retrieving but vending carts. Initially I was somewhat surprised to see them, but it wasn't all that strange to encounter vending carts in

Manhattan. They were like permanent fixtures on every other street corner. Many of these were the carts that could be seen in New York City in front of office buildings or on street corners. Vendors sold everything from a cup of coffee to a small meal.

We had spent about three to four hours with these carts when they slowly began to tell their own stories. We would scratch our heads and wonder yet again what we were really getting involved in.

At times, a cart owner or two would make their way to the Landfill to retrieve or claim ownership of their vending carts. The first person I encountered trying to retrieve a cart drove up in his own car. He asked if he could look at a specific cart. There were seven lined up all together. It was hard to tell them apart because they looked like carbon copies of one another. I gave the gentleman his cart and watched closely as he began to give it a close inspection. He looked at the inside and then the outside. Then he actually walked inside the cart and really gave it the once-over. He approached me, "Can I take the cart?"

The procedure for allowing the owners to retrieve the carts required some red tape. Even though this was part of a crime scene, the hierarchy had determined that these carts were used to produce income for the individual. Coupled with the fact that we could use the space, we were allowing the owners to take commercial vehicles back. The stipulations were that the owners had to wash the cars, or in this case carts, before taking them, and they had to provide us with proper documentation. I told the man that he could have the cart, explained the proper protocol, and emphasized that I needed to see proper documentation to prove this cart was indeed his.

The gentleman, whose name I assumed was Mr. Moussad because that was the name that was on the registration he showed me, was pointing to the cart he had just inspected. He said in a heavy accent, "That is mine." I took his paperwork and tried to match his registration with something on the cart, but I couldn't find any type of documentation in the cart or on the outside. The permit from the outside appeared to have been removed. There was nothing to identify this cart on the inside. I told him, "I cannot properly identify this cart as yours. Your paperwork does not match anything, and actually, there is nothing to match it. Did you notice that when you were inspecting the cart there was no documentation on it?"

He responded, "Yes, but I know it is my cart, and you have to give it to me." I apologized and told him that I absolutely could not give him the cart without proper paperwork and that the cart produced none.

The man just looked at me puzzled and staring. I could see that he was becoming agitated. He began to raise his voice and started to make demands. "You don't know who I am. You don't know anything," he shouted. I reminded him that he was in no position to make demands and that he would have to leave. He started to walk away; "I will be back, and I will bring paperwork for all of these carts."

"Great, if you bring the proper paperwork you can have them all. Trust me they are taking up valuable space." He gave me a long hard stare, mumbled something that I couldn't make out, and left. That was the first of many of my encounters with these vending carts. The whole situation became more and more peculiar.

After this individual left, my detectives and I began to look through these carts for paperwork. Out of the seven carts, five had registrations in the name "Moussad." The registrations were in a drawer inside one of the carts. None of the carts had permits we could see. We could see the residue outline on the front windows where they would be. It looked as if they were ripped off, possibly in a hurry, because on some of the carts' front windows small pieces of the permits were still there. The permit allowed vendors to sell food products on the street. The permit had to face out so it could be easily seen for inspection by the New York City Health Department. My thoughts at that point were that if Mr. Moussad returned and the carts were his, we would help him look them up to get them out of the lot quicker. I told my detectives to let me know when he showed up and also to make sure the front gate was locked.

I would enter the Landfill off of Victory Boulevard, a secondary more nondescript entrance that we would use to get to the auto pound, which was more convenient than the main entrance. On a Wednesday afternoon as I entered the Landfill driving to the auto pound, I spotted a car about one hundred yards ahead of me driving in the same direction. I don't think the driver saw me. When I pulled into the auto pound, the car was outside the gate, and I realized it was the same man from two days earlier trying to take the cart.

I parked my car and went inside the trailer. I told one of my detectives to greet the guy and explained that he was the man from the previous day who wanted to take a cart. Mattie went outside and after about ten minutes, came back and said, "Definitely the same guy as the other day. He claims to have paper work for at least five carts." Tony, Mattie, and I went to greet our visitor.

He was all smiles, significantly less agitated from our prior meeting. He said that he had the proper paperwork for five carts. He then handed me a folder. I saw right away that the name on all the paperwork matched what I saw in one of the carts: "Moussad." I continued to look through the paperwork and said, "I saw you come in the back entrance. That is for police and sanitation only."

He looked straight at me. "Sir that was not me; I came from the entrance off the highway."

"Did you go up to the main headquarters to let the personnel there know what you needed?"

He shook his head nonchalantly and responded, "No, I just drove straight here."

I pulled Mattie and Tony off to the side and told them that this guy was lying because I had followed him in. He had come in from the Victory Boulevard entrance.

"I'll tell you what, my friend, if you legitimately are Mr. Moussad, you can take your carts and go." I handed him back his paperwork.

"I am not Moussad; my name is Sam. Moussad is my Uncle." He produced a driver's license with a name on the license that I could not pronounce, but I know for sure it did not say "Sam." I asked him who Sam was. He said that was his nickname.

"You're not Moussad," I said. "I really don't know if you are Sam, but either way I can release these carts only to the registered owner. "Sam" became so irate that he threw all the paperwork in the air. The wind blew it throughout the lot.

I looked at him and said, "Here is what will happen next. You are going to pick up every piece of paperwork, and when you're done, you are going to walk to your car, get in, and drive out toward the main entrance, not the way you came in because that was you I saw. If you don't know where the main entrance is, these two nice detectives can escort you. Tell your uncle that if he wants these carts, he needs to come here himself. He can ask for me. I'm Sergeant Marra. If I ever see you here trying to get these carts, I will kick your ass all over this lot, OK, Sam?" He just looked at me and began to pick up his paperwork. When he was done, I had Mattie and Tony take him to the main entrance. After that incident, we requested that sanitation close off the Victory Boulevard entrance. Unfortunately, sanitation said that was not possible, so we began to block it off the best we could with some of the autos we had in the auto pound.

I never heard from the uncle, we never saw Sam again, and that was the last time anyone tried to claim the carts. Rumors began to fly about the carts, but they did not start at the auto pound with that incident; they started at Ground Zero where the carts came from. These stories were unsubstantiated. Separating rumor from fact had us scratching our heads and wondering what the truth was.

Rumor: The people who owned the vending carts were aware of the attacks and began to move the carts away from the Towers approximately thirty minutes before the first plane hit the Towers.

Fact: The vending carts that were delivered to the auto pound were undamaged. In fact, a very good friend of mine, Andrew Buonantuono, who was working for a construction company at a job downtown, spoke to me about going to work that morning and trying to get a cup of coffee but couldn't seem to find a vending cart in or around the area of the World Trade Center and Battery Park City. He said that on that particular morning, he took a train to Bowling Green in Battery Park and walked up from the train only to see no carts. "As I walked to the job, I noticed that all the carts that would normally be at specific locations were gone. I walked around to different spots, but nothing. So strange. It didn't make any sense."

Rumor: All of the food, beverages, and cash registers were seen being removed from the various carts surrounding the areas around the Towers and placed into vans.

Fact: The vending carts at the auto pound had no signs or traces of food or beverages, plates, coffee cups, or stirrers, nor did they have any cash registers or money.

Rumor: There were claims that the vendors/owners or workers were seen removing the permits the morning of the attacks.

Fact: All the carts received at the Landfill were missing their vendors' permits, and they appeared to have been removed.

Rumor: The vending cart owners knew about the planned attacks, were of Middle Eastern descent, and would not pick up the carts themselves.

Fact: The vending cart owners never showed up to retrieve their carts. I know that one person attempted to take five carts, and he was not the registered owner.

Whether these situations were coincidental or not, I don't know. It would be hard to prove any of these rumors. I know that the carts we received at the auto pound told their own stories. This was a tug-of-war scenario between fact and fiction that went on quite a bit at the Landfill. Perhaps it was a coping mechanism, trying to make sense of so many things that had transpired during these tragic days. People wanted to be able to piece together all of these unanswered questions.

I stand behind the facts that I presented based on personal experience. I was at the Staten Island Landfill. I saw the carts that were delivered to the Landfill firsthand. It was odd enough that the vending carts were completely undamaged considering the destruction that took place. Even odder was the fact that there was no sign of food or beverages, no paper plates, forks, knives, spoons, not even a cash register. There weren't any permits on these carts.

As with many uncertainties about the events of September 11, the aftermath raised intriguing questions that will likely never be answered, including many about the carts. The destruction came so fast; when was there time to empty these carts? People left their autos, some valued at over 100,000 dollars. If the autos could not be saved, how could the carts be moved to a safe location so quickly? At that critical moment, what was a safe location? Did first responders clean the carts after the devastation occurred? Would that have been a priority? Why no permits? Was there a perfectly logical explanation? If so, what was it? Granted there was about one hour between the time that the first plane hit and the first Tower fell. No one expected that Tower to fall. I'm sure that in the spirit of business the cart owners would have just relocated and continued selling. Why did they flee and take everything. How did they move to a safe location?

As odd as the facts were and how much people may have wanted answers to justify what they saw and experienced, my goal is simply to record what I saw and heard at the Landfill. Most of these rumors would be almost impossible to prove, and at that time, we were trying to pick up the pieces of the devastation, not make sense of it. That would be someone else's job. The vending carts, just like so many other pieces of evidence, would become part of the crime scene that took us in many different directions. Like all of the vehicles that were brought to the auto pound from Ground Zero, the vending carts were eventually destroyed.

6

Red Cross Worker

In addition to the mysteries surrounding the food vending carts, I remember hearing many different stories of other strange and unexplainable occurrences. The Landfill, with all its lost and fallen civilians as well as the city workers who also perished, was a vulnerable and spiritually exposed place. It never dawned on me that of all the different stories and rumors at the Landfill we would also hear "ghost stories."

There is so much to speak of regarding my memories of the six months I spent at the Landfill. So many years have passed, and I am finally able to put together all those memories. When I began to piece together my thoughts and experiences and combine them with all the information that Maria, my co-author, and I collected, I never expected someone to recount what he believed to be a paranormal experience which triggered a memory I had long forgotten.

The largest movable crime scene in American history had ghost stories to tell. I had encountered my own odd experiences, and crime scene detectives who worked the Landfill had their own stories to share. One of those was Frank Tegano, a retired New York City Police Department crime scene detective. I had known Frank for some time, and we had worked together in the late 80s at the 120th Precinct in Staten Island, New York.

Frank spent his years as a detective in the Crime Scene Unit and was temporarily assigned to the 9/11 Staten Island Landfill World Trade Center Recovery Site. His main assignment was to help with the identification and recovery of the body parts that were found at the sifting locations. He worked with a forensics team and highly trained anthropologists to identify human remains.

At one point in an interview about his recollections, Frank asked if I had ever heard about the Red Cross worker. As he asked that question, he turned the key to a vault of memories that I had completely put away. The memories all began to come back. "The Red Cross worker who would walk around and serve sandwiches and coffee by the sifting machines?" Before he could even finish his question, I responded yes. This was a memory that I had left dormant for years. Suddenly I was able to explain that one random day I was at the tent where the daily assignments were handed out and I overheard two police officers talking. One of them was asking the other if he saw the Red Cross worker walking with a tray of sandwiches. He explained that the woman headed toward him, and he didn't think anything of it. Then he had looked around to see if there were other Red Cross workers with her and when he looked back at her, she vanished. He kept repeating to his friend that she was gone, that she just vanished into thin air.

I told Frank that I had forgotten all about that woman wandering the site. I remembered that three other detectives from the Bronx reported seeing a woman with sandwiches over by the large sifter. They claimed in their recollection of the event that they would call to her but she would not respond, just walk away and disappear behind a pile of debris.

Frank described the woman as African-American dressed in an old 1950s style nursing uniform, which we later realized was the old traditional Red Cross uniform, similar to those worn during the time of World War II. He said that he saw her one time when he was exiting the crime scene trailer. Frank said that he happened to look in the direction of the sifters and noticed a nurse dressed in white walking around the debris field carrying something that looked like a tray of sandwiches. When he first saw this image, the person mixed in well with everyone else because of the white surgical scrubs the sifter workers wore. Initially I wasn't positive about what I had seen until later I was hearing that other people had witnessed the same thing. Many of us were unable to make sense of it, the nurse in white serving food at the sifting machines.

I expressed to Frank that I had seen her a few times and that every time, she would appear to be walking towards me from about fifty yards away. Then as I would take a second glance, trying to understand what I was looking at, she would be gone. The first time I saw her was a day that I was not feeling very well, so I decided to go to the medical trailer that was set up by the FBI. When I exited my vehicle and began to turn toward the front of the trailer, I saw in the distance a woman dressed like a nurse all in white walking around one of the sifter machines. At first, I turned away and continued to walk into the medical trailer. As I was being attended to, I suddenly couldn't get the sight out of my head.

From the first time I had experienced this phenomenon, I was confused, not that she might have been a spirit or a ghost because I can honestly say that was not my first thought. My job was centered on facts, not fiction, fantasy, or science fiction, so my initial response was confusion. It struck me very odd that someone was serving food at the sifters, even stranger that someone was around the sifting and debris piles without a breathing apparatus and white surgical-type scrubs, which were standard attire at the sifting locations. The dust that came off the sifting machines was always blowing in every direction and would have made serving food impossible in that area. The food would have been completely covered with dust before anyone could take a first bite. The thought of eating in that area would be physically nauseating between the smells of cement, twisted steel, possibly human flesh, everything else mixed into the mud, and methane gas from the decomposing garbage. I had seen workers every once in a while by the sifters catching a cigarette break but definitely not eating. It later hit me after the rumors started to spread about the "nurse" that this could possibly be paranormal. Frank and I agreed that whether or not the presence of that nurse was real, it was extremely strange and unexplainable. This was definitely something that no one was able to explain. When we thought about how much death we were surrounded by, it was hard not to think of something spiritual.

The Red Cross nurse wasn't the only unexplainable sighting that I had heard of or experienced at the Landfill. Late night sightings made their way around the dimly lit section. During the nighttime surveillance, seeing was difficult. The area was not only dimly lit but also windy with dirt and dust swirling in all different directions. Every hour we would have to do surveillance around the area to make sure the autos were secure. I can remember many times we would go in and out of the vehicles to inspect them for vandalism or to take a count that none was missing. The pound was close to the West Shore Expressway, providing easy access to the highway. That facilitated different types of crime in the auto pound. In early November, a sanitation worker was caught trying to remove tires and rims from a car. We once caught another sanitation worker siphoning gas from a truck, so the possibility of someone trying to steal an auto would not have surprised me.

There were many times my detectives or detectives from other units who were covering the pound on our days off reported that while conducting routine surveillance, they thought they saw what appeared to be shadows or large black masses moving around the autos. I really never questioned what anyone saw because we began to hear more and more stories just like these reports throughout the Landfill.

There were additional reports that images or figures were seen walking in restricted areas and non-restricted areas. Some reported trying to call out to these figures, but they would just walk away and disappear into the darkness. There were reports of figures and even a dog seen at what I refer to as "Fire Truck Row," where all the New York Fire Department fire trucks were stored along with other police cars, trucks, and ambulances that were removed from Ground Zero during the excavation process. These vehicles were devastated, some beyond recognition. These vehicles in many ways became the final resting place for many of the fallen firemen and first responders.

Over 4,500 human remains were recovered at the Staten Island Landfill. That adds up to many spirits that could be wandering, possibly looking for closure. A woman dressed in a Red Cross uniform handing out sandwiches, trying to feed the workers, maybe trying to provide comfort whether from this world or beyond; what appeared to be people seen walking in restricted areas and suddenly disappearing; or dark shadows/masses floating around the autos at the auto pound—why not? We may not be able to prove these stories; on many levels, they could be discredited by the workers' long hours, exhaustion, and the stress and tragedy that surrounded them on a daily basis. What made these stories believable was the number of the workers who experienced the same sightings and shared the same memories of what they saw.

This land should be considered "Hallowed Ground" just like Ground Zero. To me, it is sacred ground, the final resting places for so many who lost their lives that day and were transferred here. How many family members' loved ones are still there, whose remains haven't been found and identified? How many have had their ashes and remains uprooted and brought to this place? Why isn't their presence believable?

If someone had told me that two planes would intentionally be flown into the World Trade Center Towers, causing both Towers to collapse, taking the lives of thousands of people, I would not have believed it. So why not believe these stories and accounts from an unusual crime scene. Why can't we call them "Landfill Ghost Stories"?

7

Fire Truck Row

As we drove through the Landfill, starting at the beginning of "The Hill" past the auto pound approaching the sifters and the men in white suits behind the debris field, we could smell a different kind of death and sheer sadness.

There were quite a few different facets and sites to see and explore at this extensive crime scene at the Landfill. Every turn up and down the hill demonstrated another aspect of destruction that took place on that infamous day in September. Each area had its own story, and in many cases, we didn't need help understanding the story it told. In specific cases, no words were needed. One place in particular that clearly spoke for itself was "Fire Truck Row."

At the end of the hill, this particular extension to the crime scene resembled a junk yard. It looked just like a scrap yard where someone might go to get spare or scrap parts. But past the overall junk yard appearance, it was so hard to miss the familiar sight and colors of our city's first responder vehicles. There were fire trucks, police cars, unmarked police cars, ambulances, and other emergency vehicles all situated in rows by departments.

All of the vehicles were piled on top of one another, at least four to five high. First were the fire department vehicles. After the fire trucks and other fire department vehicles, the next pile of stacked autos was police cars, port authority vehicles, and additional police vehicles bearing no significant name or insignia, and ambulances. Fire Truck Row literally took our breath away and instantly filled us with a special sadness.

This part of the Landfill crime scene boldly stood out because of the significant and memorable red and white colors of the fire trucks. As we approached the vehicles, it became harder and harder to tell the difference between them. Those that were crushed and burned so badly were difficult to identify. Often we could not tell what type of vehicle each was. The police and the first responder vehicles resembled those of the fire department vehicles and vice versa. They looked like pieces of abstract art. From afar we were able to see clearly and identify what they were because of the significant symbols and colors, but as we got closer to them, the colors and the clarity faded. At that point, we were faced with the sheer destruction and trauma that these vehicles endured, and we couldn't help thinking about those first responders who were in them.

As we drove through the vehicles or walked around them, we could smell death, along with the mixture of the methane gas and the remaining debris flying around. Even after leaving the area, it took a while to rid ourselves of the odor that lingered there. It followed us.

In some instances, we could see coats and stuff left inside the vehicles. In others, we couldn't even identify or see the difference from one item to the next as a result of the destruction. Initially I asked myself why these autos were situated separately from the auto pound. Then I realized that not only were they New York City property, but they were also, as a result of sentimental value, not to be displayed as "trophies" but to memorialize them in their own separate section for our fallen heroes and first responders. Those vehicles represented the 343 fireman and 23 police officers who were killed that day. This area was a unique and revered extension of the crime scene.

Fire Truck Row was visited frequently. Firemen would come on their days off. Off-duty police officers and those working the Landfill would also head over there, all with the same intention: to pay their respects to their fallen comrades. Often while I was there, there were firemen and officers standing around talking, sharing stories, and at times, laughing while recalling funny memories of their colleagues who had passed. It was similar to being at a wake, a unique wake, under different circumstances. There was a time when I was there and a group of off-duty firemen brought a six pack or two of beers and just sat there, telling stories and talking aloud to their perished colleague as if he were there with them. Family members of fallen heroes brought their children there to honor them. Whoever came, whether they brought beers or kids, whether they sobbed uncontrollably or laughed, these people needed to have a place to mourn. We were all there for the same reason, to remember, to thank, to pray, and to pay our respect to so many who gave everything on that day.

Off-duty firemen and police were not the only ones who came to visit Fire Truck Row. Civil service personnel of all ranks, especially the higher ranks within the fire department and the police department, as well as politicians and journalists from different cities, made their way up there to see the destroyed vehicles.

Journalists from various places often came to take tours of the Landfill, and many of them were interested in seeing Fire Truck Row and all of the destroyed first responder vehicles. I encountered journalists from numerous cities, including Los Angeles, Baltimore, and Washington. When they arrived at the Landfill, I would visit briefly with them and explain where we would be headed and ask whether they had any specific questions. At some point in the conversation, they would make reference to Fire Truck Row and were always interested in seeing the first responder vehicles. My belief is that the vast scene and quantity of first responder vehicles retrieved from Ground Zero were what drew such a crowd. A majority of those responders who were in those vehicles died that day. The vehicles symbolized death and destruction.

One day I was asked to give a reporter from the *Washington Post* a tour of the Landfill. I picked him up at the temporary headquarters and drove him around in a red, white, and blue SUV. I offered him a tour and told him to let me know where and when he wanted to stop so that he could take pictures. We first toured the auto pound. He looked around and began asking where the fire trucks were. Then we continued up the hill to the debris field to see the sifting machines. I took him to the cafeteria area where we got something to eat. Then we proceeded to the area where the men in white suits got their supplies to do their tours. As we continued to the back end of the sifting machines to the larger debris area, he took more and more pictures. The reporter continuously asked me when we would get to the area with all the first responder vehicles.

We finally came to Fire Truck Row at the end of the hill. He wanted to get out, walk around, and take pictures. I studied the look on his face because I was always curious to observe people's reaction to this area. It could be over-whelming for many. The reporter stood there initially and didn't say a word. A few moments passed, and he replied slowly and quietly that he didn't realize how many there were. Soon he went into his professional mode and went to work. He spent at least forty-five minutes walking around the area, and I watched him as he thoroughly inspected each fire truck and vehicle, looking inside intensely as if he were searching for something. He did not give the same attention to the police vehicles that he did to the fire department vehicles.

The reporter was gone a long time. When he returned to the SUV, he began to explain his experience at the

Pentagon in Washington. He said they lost over 120 people in Washington but nothing compared to the losses in New York and that he had a hard time comprehending how many first responders perished that day. He said his friend was a fireman. We drove back to the temporary headquarters in silence.

On many occasions on my own time, after a shift ended or right before my shift began, I would be drawn to visit Fire Truck Row. It was a place for me to stop and remember, thank and pray, and continue to do the job I was sent there to do.

8

Men in White Suits

The first night I left there, I remember getting home. I stripped, literally stripped in the street, and hosed myself down and hosed my truck down. I then experienced the worst headache of my life for the next few days, and I thought I was going to die. I thought I was having a stroke." This is how Dr. Brian Mignola, NYPD Police Surgeon, described the aftermath of his first visit to the scene. "The next time I went to the Landfill, I made sure to wear a re-breather before I even got off the highway, and I kept it on while I was up there. . . . I was there during the day one time, and all the detectives were in white level A-suits and were sifting through all the debris. It looked like a scene from a science fiction movie, like something from *Armageddon*. Coupled with everything going on, the methane gas from the garbage was bubbling up from the ground. It was such a surreal experience."

Dr. Mignola, who spent time at the Landfill and continues to care for many first responders who worked there, said he was shocked at how little precaution was taken on the part of the first responders as well as those in charge at the Landfill: "I couldn't believe how strong the smell of methane gas mixed with all the debris was, and people were eating in the middle of this. They had a mess tent. I said, 'You guys have to be out of your minds,' and I was looking at the bottles of water the workers were drinking from, and they were just full of the dust that was swirling around the Landfill. I remember shouting at them that they were out of their minds and that they needed to clean the bottles off."

Working at the Landfill left a picture that is hard to forget. That first night it was hard not to notice all the dust around us everywhere. It was under and over us and at times circling around us in slow moving clouds. Worse than the dust was the smell, the potent and undeniable smell of methane gas that would bubble up from under the ground. This was normal for a landfill, but what made the situation worse was the mixture of the smell of the methane gas and all the debris.

So many first responders endured this type of working condition day after day. Some were able to walk away without any health issues to speak about, but there were many of those unfortunate first responders who were not that lucky. There were claims that the air was safe to breathe by the Environmental Protection Agency at both Ground Zero and the Landfill. Only later did the consequences of exposure to this toxic environment become clear. Their stories have been captured in their own words:

Retired Detective Michael Tegano worked at the Staten Island Landfill two or three times a week from November 2001 until May of 2002:

> I was working in the Organized Crime Control Bureau Narcotic Division during the time of 9/11. They [NYPD] basically took the Narcotics and Housing Detectives to cover clean up, trying to keep all the street cops where they are needed, most on the streets. At first, I was instructed to go through surrounding buildings around Ground Zero to assess what kind of damage there was and then act as security for various sites. Eventually I was reassigned to the Landfill.
>
> There I was working the conveyor belt, sifting through debris and rubble hoping to find the

remains of people who were killed along with any personal effects. I could remember some days we would find nothing. One day a Glock19 9mm handgun was found. We just knew it was a cop's service gun. There were days we would sift a foot in a shoe or find a wallet. As time went on, items became harder to identify. No matter what we found, I hoped it could bring closure for those who lost someone. The Landfill provided as much as it could for those who would work there, but the conditions seemed pretty unhealthy. There was dust and debris everywhere, floating through the air and sticking to our outer garments.

I know we played a large role in helping in the aid and recovery efforts and in turn helping to bring some kind of normalcy back to the city as well as some closure to those who lost someone, but honestly I don't need recognition for doing something I believed in my heart to be the right thing to do. It was my job. I would do it all over again if given the choice. I just wanted to be treated right by the NYPD. That's it. They offered us nothing at the time—no help, no assistance, no counseling—to help and make sense of everything that was happening. They sent us out there and never looked back. Everyone knew the air at Ground Zero and the Landfill could not have been good, but government and city officials would always be on television huddled together at press conferences telling us that the air was fine.

It was two years after I left the Landfill that cancer screenings were offered to us to check our health. So we went in, it was required, it was a day off. After we got screened, we were told that if you hear nothing in the next few weeks consider that a good sign. Sure enough I received a letter that I had to go for a follow-up. I was later diagnosed with non-Hodgkin's lymphoma.

Retired Detective Ernest Vallebuona and I worked together during my career. Mike and Ernie will be forever connected in a way that I can guarantee they wish they weren't:

I had just finished a late tour. I was on my way to Home Depot with my four-year-old son. At the time, I was a Staten Island resident. I witnessed the smoke billowing from the tower as I passed the Landfill on the highway. I was called to report to the 7th Precinct and assigned to the Organized Crime Control Bureau Vice Enforcement Division. After the first few days of trying to locate any survivors, my responsibilities would vary from day to day, from evidence collection to security to escorts. We would escort politicians who needed to see the destruction up close. I was assigned to the area at Ground Zero for about five months averaging three times a week. The smell was bad and never really improved. We would wear surgical masks at times and breathing apparatus despite the fact that we were told the air was fine to breathe. Around three years later, I was working a street fair in Harlem and started to exhibit symptoms of food poisoning, stomach pains and cramps, sweating, and diarrhea. Later that night when I got home, I went to the emergency room in Nyack, Long Island. After a battery of tests, I was informed that I could have cancer. I was officially diagnosed with non-Hodgkin's lymphoma as well as neuropathy in the arms and legs and renal failure. I have become diabetic due to the chemo treatments. My medical issues have been focused on curing my cancer. Any minor respiratory issues have been put on hold.

My life has changed for both better and worse. Living with cancer is very stressful because your world and your family's world is an uncertain place. But having lived through cancer opens your eyes to what is really important; it brings you in touch with your spiritual side. I try not to focus on all the 9/11 fanfare. The whole commercialization and politicizing sickens me. As a nation, we need to take care of our protectors, our warriors, and be better prepared to help the sick and wounded. God forbid this happens again.

Dr. Brian Mignola, NYPD Police Doctor and Surgeon, spoke on behalf of the many patients that he has treated over the past decade who were stationed at either Ground Zero or the Staten Island Landfill: "Set yourself aside for a minute, take yourself out of the emotional loop of what happened, and just observe and listen to the complaints. The majority of the first responders were complaining of chronic coughs and trouble catching their breath, and they all described a burning sensation in their lungs. Even those who did not know one another had the same kind of description of the burning in their lungs, both first responders from the Landfill and Ground Zero. I had one detective from upstate New York who never met this other detective from Long Island, New York, and they both had the same exact complaints. Other complaints were chronic stomach pain, sinus headaches, a lot of post-traumatic stress, and excessive fatigue. We then saw several cancers that started to pop up."

Mike Tegano and Ernie Vallebuona will always be connected, like many of the other first responders who have developed cancer over the years. Some have already sadly passed, probably as a direct result of the exposure to various toxic materials found at both the Landfill and Ground Zero. Both men developed non-Hodgkin's lymphoma, and both men worked with and around the same materials. The 1.45 million tons of twisted steel and cement from Ground Zero where Ernie worked was brought to the Landfill where Mike worked, and yet the powers that be, right after the September 11 attacks, continued to say that the air was safe to breathe.

Many of those who are sick will hopefully fight and beat their battle with cancer; many will not. They have succumbed to financial distress as a result of their medical bills and costs of treatments while not being able to continue working. In January of 2011, the government passed a new law, the James Zadroga 9/11 Health and Compensation Act, which claims to offer compensation and funding for those facing 9/11-related health problems and to continue to help provide those individuals with monitoring and treatment at least until 2015, but then what? We can only hope that our government will continue to aid and assist all those individuals who became ill as a result of their generous and brave assistance in the days and months following the worst tragedy ever to hit American soil.

9

Landfill to Hallowed Ground

The Staten Island Landfill, circa 1984, was a garbage dump, satisfying one main purpose: storing garbage and burning it. Infamously known as the "dump" by the residents of Staten Island, it was a place that I would go to with my dad when I was a kid whenever he had to throw out items that the local garbage men would not take. Who would've guessed all those years ago that many years later I would've been assigned there as part of a search and recovery site for a national tragedy? Who could've guessed that the "dump" would be considered the area containing the largest crime scene in American history?

The "Landfill" rose and was fully functional. The largest crime scene in American History opened in September of 2001 and closed in May of 2002. To me the memories and experiences there will never be gone. Even after over thirteen years, when I drive by the Landfill, I no longer see the "dump." I see a holy ground, a hallowed ground with bright lights that shine for miles, but all I can think about every time I pass is how many lives were affected there, mentally, physically, or both. I still think of it as a time that stood still. I think that I will begin to make the sign of the cross as I pass it, as I would if I were passing a Catholic church. I want to show my respect to those who gave so much of themselves on September 11, 2001, and to those whose final resting place is there, lost on "The Hill."

During the time I was assigned at the Landfill, along with my fellow detectives, we would venture out and just drive around. I was amazed to find the wildlife that is able to sustain there. There was a man-made lake that had to be ten acres wide where I saw people fishing. There were endless roads that went nowhere, 2,200 acres of landscape in all. This place was so big that it was once said that the Staten Island Landfill was the highest point on the eastern seaboard and that astronauts could see it from space. Now this Landfill will be known for so much more: a crime scene, a recovery site, a resting place, hallowed ground.

The facts are relatively clear. Approximately 4,512 body parts and pieces were recovered. Over 3,000 lives were lost that day. If we multiply the lives lost by how many bones there are in an adult body, the numbers are well over 600,000. To think only 4,512 bones or body parts were recovered from sifting through the debris of both Towers is staggering. These facts raise questions about where are the rest of the body parts and bones.

Sadly, with all the hard work put forth by our first responders and NYPD workers, we weren't able to recover nearly enough to help many families find closure. We knew it was going to be a tough task. There were so many families who lost loved ones on 9/11 and feel that their remains are still there at the Landfill. I have read that on occasion sifting still goes on at the site. According to the *Staten Island Advance*, the local Staten Island newspaper, in an article dated April 17, 2013, sixty-two fragments of bones had been recovered at the former Staten Island Landfill since sifting began again on April 1, 2013. Since 2010, some sixty truckloads of World Trade Center debris have been brought to the Landfill from Ground Zero as construction crews dig in new areas as they build the Freedom Tower.

A cemetery without tombstones and an untraditional crime scene, the Staten Island Landfill could be considered a final resting place. What rose from this "dump" is now hallowed ground. A memorial will one day stand at this Landfill, a place where family members can visit to reflect and pay their respects to their loved ones. A place that can be seen by all and maybe where tourists from all over the world will come to see where the two greatest buildings in the world came for their final resting place with those who were in the buildings on that infamous day. I realize that there is a memorial and museum built at Ground Zero, both places where people will go to mourn, reflect, and look. But there should also be something at the Landfill. I have heard in the past that a park will be built, and within this park, there will be some kind of memorial signifying how the Landfill was used during that moment in time. I hope there will be.

I remember being told that the elevation where the sifting was taking place rose almost two feet from the start of the sifting until the end. This was a time in my life I wish I could forget, a time I wish had never happened as the Landfill rose and became a complete working city. It is also important to keep in mind that there were many civilians that were assigned at the Landfill from privately owned construction companies who owned the sifting machines and worked countless hours away from their families. I am sure that they left something on the hill, and many memories were left with them.

I concluded from my time at the Landfill that it was an excellent choice to be utilized as the largest recovery site in the history of New York City. It was a small functioning city that became home to so many NYPD personnel who were assigned at the Landfill and those who visited on a daily or weekly basis to sift through rubble.

Remember this Landfill had an infrastructure that contained a temporary headquarters equal to City Hall, a mini-hospital, a cafeteria, a crime scene tent of all recovered remains, a junkyard for all first responder vehicles that were crushed, a harbor where debris was barged over from Ground Zero, sifting fields where the trucks unloaded their debris, and an auto pound set up at least one half mile from where debris was being sifted. The opinion of many has changed. The former Staten Island Landfill is now hallowed ground and should take its place in American history.

10

No Happy Ending

All gave some; some gave all. According to the New York Committee for Occupational Safety and Health, 30,000 people who either worked on the pile at Ground Zero, sifted through World Trade Center rubble looking for victims' remains at the Staten Island Landfill, or who lived in the area have gotten sick as a result of the toxins that emanated from the site.

As a retired New York Police Lieutenant, I became frustrated by the plight of the first responders and began to compile stories with the hopes of one day having a book published telling the world what I saw and heard, to tell of the people I knew who became sick, to be a voice, a platform for them, a behind-the-scenes look at the six months I spent at the Landfill, a time that always makes me wonder if I'm the next one to get sick.

No happy ending is something that I always ponder. Not only does it make me think of those who are currently sick and those who have passed on, but it also makes me think about the families who have never had closure. Those families said good-bye to their loved ones on the morning of September 11, 2001 and never got a chance to see or hear from them again. I think about the people who received calls telling them that "we have your son's shin bone" or "we found your daughter's index finger." How could that be closure? How is burying a piece of someone saying good-bye? Some received a follow-up call telling the family that "we found another piece of your husband." Was it better to feel as if you had something to bury? I couldn't possibly imagine what that must have been like for those families. Personally, I would've preferred to have received a call, hoping that they would've found something, than those families who never received a call. At least then a family could have something to bury and have a place to visit to just say a prayer or reflect. Numerous stories just like these scenarios were reported.

According to the Associated Press, on April 3, 2013, an article stated, "Possible human remains found in new 9/11 debris uncovered at World Trade Center site 12 years later. Jim Riches pulled his firefighter son's mangled body out of the rubble at the World Trade Center, but the phone calls still filtered in years afterward. The city kept finding more pieces of his son at Ground Zero and the Staten Island Landfill." That father was cited as saying, "They'll call you and they will tell you, 'we found a leg bone. We found an arm bone; we held them all together and then put them in the cemetery.'" The article continued:

> Those are the phone calls, both dreaded and hoped for among the families of September 11 victims. And as investigators began sifting through newly uncovered debris from the World Trade Center this week for the first time in three years, those anxieties were renewed more than a decade after the attacks. But there was also hope that more victims might yet be identified after tens of millions have been spent on the painstaking identification process. Two potential human remains were recovered recently, according to the Medical Examiner's Office. We would like to see the other 40 percent of the families who have never recovered anything to at least someday have at least a piece of their loved one, Riches said. "They can't go to the cemetery and pray."

The city's last sifting effort ended in 2010. This time, crews were able to dig up parts of the Trade Center site that were previously inaccessible to workers, the city said. Some 2,750 people died at the World Trade Center in the 2001 terrorist attacks, but only 1,634 people have been identified. "We have been monitoring the World Trade Center site over time and monitor the construction," said Ellen Borakove, a spokeswoman for the medical examiner's office. "And if they see any materials that could possibly contain human remains, we collect that material."

About 9,000 human remains recovered from the ruins of the World Trade Center remain unidentified because they are too degraded to match victims by DNA identification. The remains are stored at an undisclosed location monitored by the medical examiner's office and will eventually be transferred to a subterranean chamber at the National September 11 Memorial and Museum. Some victims' families expressed impatience that the city has only just uncovered more debris. "Quite frankly they should've excavated this and searched it 12 years ago," said Diane Horning, whose son Matthew died in the attacks. "Instead they built service roads and construction roads and were more worried about the new buildings and tourism than they were about the human remains." Feelings like this and many other mixed reviews and emotions about the new museum and Freedom Tower will likely continue to surface.

The city's efforts to identify September 11 victims have long been fraught with controversy. In April 2005, the city's chief medical examiner, Charles Hirsch, told families his office would be suspending identification efforts because it had exhausted the limits of DNA technology. Just a year later, the discovery of human remains on a bank tower roof and then in a manhole near Ground Zero outraged families who said the search for their loved ones had been rushed initially. The findings prompted a renewed search that cost the city tens of millions of dollars and uncovered 1,500 pieces of remains.

Meanwhile, some victims' relatives sued the city over its decision to move 1.6 million tons of material from the Trade Center site to the Staten Island Landfill, saying the material might contain victims' ashes and should have been given a proper burial. The lawsuit was dismissed and un-successfully appealed to the United States Supreme Court.

As it embarks on combing through debris again, the medical examiner's office says it will keep monitoring the site as long as new areas are being dug out and exposed. Charles G. Wolf was pleased to hear about the renewed search, though he believes that his wife Katherine was vaporized during the attacks. Investigators have never found her remains. Years ago it bothered him that he had no grave to visit. Wolf said the opening of the September 11 Memorial has filled a hole in his heart, but he will never have closure. "You heal. You carry on," he said. "It's not closure."

The real question for many is what happened to the 1,116 missing 9/11 victims. For those who have never received a call that a loved one was found or a piece of a loved one was found, they must be left with a sense of emptiness that I can't describe in words. I can only sympathize with those families, but I cannot empathize with them. I can only try to imagine or put myself in that position for just a few seconds, and still it does not come close to experiencing those raw feelings of emptiness and loss, the not knowing. No happy ending, no closure, absolutely.

Now more than thirteen years after the catastrophic destruction of the World Trade Center the question remains of what could have happened to those victims who are still missing. In every building collapse in history, usually the victims' bodies have been recovered more or less intact. Falling buildings crush human bodies; they do not shred them into tiny pieces or cause then to vanish into thin air. Yet on September 11, 2001, the most famous building collapse in American history, more than 1,000 victims disappeared. Not a trace, not even a shred of skin, a fragment of a nail, or a shard of a bone from any of these bodies was recovered, despite the meticulous sifting that took place at the Staten Island Landfill by the men in white suits. For the human remains recovered that help identify over 1,600 victims, most were not intact bodies but pieces of bone and flesh. It is unfortunate to say, but the victims who have yet to be found, even the smallest piece of their DNA, will be spoken about in the same conversations about where all the furniture, computers, telephones, and filing cabinets were. Most of those items were just pulverized or vaporized. I know how hard that has to be for someone to accept, but I feel that all these years later it is the best explanation. On assignment at the Landfill for the six months, I never personally observed any mounds of office furniture or computers or filing cabinets. I would think that two buildings, 110 stories each, would produce some of these items, but from what I remember maybe a sifter would find a telephone keypad. I don't recall more than that.

Some believe that the Towers were blown to bits by explosives in addition to the planes that struck them. Many families who have lost someone share this belief. Other attempts to explain the devastation have suggested controlled demolitions in addition to the planes. These explanations reflect the need to make some sense out of why so many are still missing and nothing of these victims has been recovered.

In 2006, human bone fragments were discovered scattered all over the roof of the neighboring Deutsche Bank building. Those who believe the Towers were blown up use this as their watermark that the Towers didn't collapse but were exploded, explaining why so many victims were never recovered. Why were so many victims vaporized into thin air? I don't agree with these statements, but if accepting this explanation makes it easier for the families who have never received as much as a piece of skin of their lost family member, then so be it.

Another article, "September 11th Anniversary: The Remains of 9/11 That Were Never Found" (*Huffington*

Post Latino Voices first posted 09/09/11), states on behalf of a woman who lost her son,

> Whenever she wants to feel close to her son Paul, who died in the Sept. 11 attacks, Sophie Ortiz pulls out her journal and writes to him, usually the latest news about his daughter and other family. Paul's body was never identified, so there is no grave to visit. The journal has become a means for a mother to connect with her son. The young computer technician was one of the 1,121 people killed on 9/11 whose remains have never been identified. "It's like [my son] just disappeared. It would be better to know [what happened to him]," said Ortiz, who explained that the failure to recover her son's body made it more difficult to accept his death. The day of the attacks, Paul—or Paulie, as he was affectionately called by his family—was working an extra shift and had gone to the Windows on the World restaurant at the World Trade Center to install equipment for a conference. Moments after the first plane hit the tower, Ortiz, who was 21 at the time, called his father to say he was fine. Paul Ortiz, Sr. remembers the

conversation. "He asked, 'Dad, did you hear what happened?' A plane hit the World Trade Center. And I said, 'how do you know?' 'Because I'm here,' he said." Ortiz Sr. said his son told him not to worry, that firefighters were on their way. That was the last time they spoke. "I was sure he had managed to get out. We waited, waited and waited, and we never saw him again. I now understand that he never had a chance," he said. The Ortiz family scoured the city's hospitals hoping to find him, but there was no trace of the cheerful Puerto Rican young man who loved salsa and had twice thrown himself into a lake to save someone's life.

The *Huffington Post* article continues to explain the need of many of the victims' families to be able to have something to bury in order to properly proceed through the grieving process. In many cultures, the grieving process begins with burial; it provides closure so that the loved ones can begin the process. So many of families of the 9/11 attacks, like the Ortiz family, haven't been able to retrieve any remains of their loved one and have had to find other methods of coping with the loss and the grieving process:

Luis H. Zayas, director of the Center for Latino Family Research at the University of Washington in St. Louis, said it is more difficult to say goodbye to a loved one when you don't know how he or she died, or how they spent their last moments. Among Latinos, Zayas explained, burials are of great importance within the concept of death and how it is processed. Ortiz said that her faith and belief that she would see her son in the next life have helped her cope with the pain of losing him. "At first, all I wanted was to find him, to see him one last time. But it did not happen that way, and I must accept that and be satisfied with how things turned out. I had to seek another way to find peace," she said. As much as she wanted so much to see her son's body, Ortiz said she doesn't need to visit a grave to be near him. To feel Paulie in her heart, she only has to remember his laugh, his enthusiasm and the great father he would have been if he were still alive.

There must be many thousands of stories out there just like these, stories that reach to areas of heartbreak that is unimaginable. We are thirteen years removed from that infamous day, and people who have lost loved ones are still trying to cope the best way they can, either by writing in a journal to a loved one or visiting a grave or dealing with the fact that there will be no call that some part of a missing family member was found. No matter what the scenario is, people are trying to deal with this event and will continue because it has nowhere to go. September 11, 2001 happened in our backyard; the reminders are so strong and are constantly around. I worked through the tragedy, and now that I am retired, the one thing that really still reminds me of that day and why things will never be the same is the "Fallen Skyline."

Growing up in Staten Island, I can clearly remember seeing the World Trade Center from my old house, 49 Livermore Avenue. My street was one block from the JC Penney shopping plaza, and I could see the top of both buildings from the front of my house. They would peak right over the roof of JC Penney's. The two Towers were always a sign of strength and power as I would look at them. Especially as a young boy, I took pride in telling people that I could see the "Twin Towers" from our block. On September 11, 2001, the New York City skyline changed dramatically, and the view from my block was never the same.

Both Towers were finally completed in 1975 after years of construction. What is now known as Battery Park City was built on the Landfill removed from the foundations of both Towers. The World Trade Center officially opened to the public on April 4, 1973. At the time, the two 110-story buildings became the world's tallest buildings.

What a lot of people don't know is the original construction project was proposed in 1946. Not until 1964 when then Governor Nelson Rockefeller looked at the model with the architect, Minoru Yamasaki, did the dream become a reality. Construction began in 1966, and the World Trade Center opened in 1973. It took roughly seven years to build and about eleven seconds to destroy.

I know that people in general endure and move on. I know that buildings will be rebuilt, and that is evident from the Freedom Tower, which is near completion and stands taller than the World Trade Center did. I wish those buildings were still there and no one had died and no one was sick, but that is not the reality of the situation. The reality is to deal with the tragedy and try to move on, for those families who lost loved ones and for all the first responders who gave so much of themselves. All must stay strong.

Epilogue

Staten Island Landfill, 2014

Almost thirteen years have passed since I was last at the Landfill. To be honest, I had a lot of anxiety about returning after all these years and all those memories. After many unsuccessful attempts at reaching out to various city officials and parks department employees, Maria and I headed out on our own to see the Staten Island Landfill. We were curious to see if there had been any changes or renovations made to "The Hill" since our time there so many years ago.

On our arrival, we were met with serious obstacles. Security at the Landfill is the tightest I had ever seen it. By memory and sheer instinct, I directed us to the entrance and exit from when I worked here. Our first stop was the auto pound. The Landfill, being as large as it is, 2,200 acres in all, was divided by the West Shore Expressway. There is a road used by only those working the Landfill that connects the two sides and travels under the Expressway, a road many don't realize exists.

As we approached the auto pound, despite the security guards who would let us in only so far, we were able to get a good glimpse at what it looks like now. We exited the vehicle, I took a deep breath, and I knew it was something I had to do, not just for the book, but for me. This book has forced me to remember so much about that time in my life, and as I approached the auto pound, it all just seemed surreal. I can't believe that so many years have passed.

The auto pound was gated, as I remembered, but this time it housed work trailers, not autos. We walked around, and I was hoping to see if there were any remnants of thirteen years ago, maybe a sign "WTC Auto Pound" or an auto or paperwork, but there was nothing. We walked for a good twenty minutes and then eventually returned to our car and proceeded to the next area.

We began to drive and search for the hill, the location where all the sifting took place, the bulk of the crime scene. There were many different entrances and exits to the Landfill. At this point, Maria and I were just trying to get as close a view as possible. We entered one area off the main service road and encountered tons of construction. We tried to get in closer.

We were stopped by a security guard who wouldn't let us any further. We were approximately a few hundred feet below the part of the hill where sifting took place. The security guard told us that no one is allowed beyond that point without proper credentials and that they are so strict about letting anyone near there, that a couple of weeks ago a family who lost someone in 9/11 with an employee from Homeland Security was turned away from going up there. He couldn't tell us why that group was turned away as well. We also asked him if he knew if a memorial had been set up or if there was going to be. He sadly shook his head and said that he knows that there isn't one there now and hasn't heard anything about there being one set up any time soon.

We left the security guard and tried another area where we had heard that new soccer fields had been built on the Landfill, which was part of the new renovation process for the new park that the NYC Parks Department is developing. This park should be, when it is completed, double the size of Central Park in New York City. As we drove around to all the different areas, we could see all the construction taking place to take this "dump" to transform it into a large park facility. Parts of the park will be done in phases, based on when a specific part of the Landfill had been capped and closed.

As we entered the entrance of Arthur Kill Road, we walked onto the soccer fields. It is a nice facility with turf and a track where people were running; however, Maria and I were both able to smell the distinct gas odor that surrounded us. From the soccer field, as we looked up, we could see the hill where sifting took place. We could see how vast it extended and how one part of it is still a mountain of dust and dirt and the other is all overgrown landscape.

We left the soccer field and tried one more entrance to get closer. We drove along a rocky road and continued to ascend, making our way up a makeshift path until we reached a point where we couldn't go any further. We exited the vehicle. I began to play tour guide, for my one customer, Maria. Just to see Maria's face, as I pointed and rambled on and on about where everything was and what took place at different locations, was worth the effort to get back to this location. I could tell by her expression that this has brought together everything I have told her since day one of our book project.

As we began our "tour," I walked with Maria and tried to explain as best as I could where each trailer or tent was, so she could envision "The City" as it was years ago. We spent about forty-five minutes there; the view was spectacular. As we walked back down to the car, I took one last look, remembering that small city that rose and accomplished so much. Now it is just flat ground, but to me it will always be much more. I can only hope that in the future, during all the renovating and developing, they provide a memorial for all those whose lives were lost.

Acknowledgments

Thank you to my wife, Laura, for always believing in me and for understanding that this book had to be written, not only to keep the memory of 9/11 alive, but to help me better understand that period in my life. To my sons Anthony, Dominic, and Frank, thank you for being my inspiration and my heroes. To my parents Anthony and Arlene Marra, thank you for always being supportive of my ideas. To my partner and dear friend Maria Abbate, thank you for helping me write my story and becoming one with these stories.

—Frank Marra

I am thankful for my wonderful family, my husband, Michael, and my three beautiful children, Alexa, Michael, and Delilah, for always supporting me in all my endeavors. A special thank you to Frank, who has been a great friend and partner as well as an inspiration for putting this book together. Through Frank, I was able to become a part of his experiences and learn so much more about a time period in our history that will live in infamy.

—Maria Bellia Abbate

We would extend a special thanks and acknowledgment to the following people: Brian Mignola, MD; Richard Levenson Jr., PsyD, CTS; Ernest Vallebuono; Michael Tegano; and Frank Tegano.

About the Authors

Frank Marra worked at the Staten Island Landfill World Trade Center Recovery Site from September 2001 until February 2002, an experience that served as inspiration for *From Landfill to Hallowed Ground: The Largest Crime Scene in America.* His law enforcement career included seventeen years with the New York Police Department and the rank of Detective and then Lieutenant. He was born in Staten Island, New York, and currently resides in Millstone, New Jersey, with his wife Laura and three sons, Anthony, Dominic, and Frank.

Maria Bellia Abbate, inspired by Frank's experiences at the Recovery Site, was eager to assist in helping to put all his stories and memories together to create *From Landfill to Hallowed Ground.* Currently she is a teacher in Staten Island. A native of Brooklyn, New York, Maria lives in Millstone, New Jersey, with her husband Michael and her three children, Alexa, Michael, and Delilah.

Photos

Debris from Ground Zero arrives by barge at the Landfill on Staten Island. Approximately ten tons of debris was being processed daily for evidence related to the attack.

October 16, 2001, Staten Island, NY. Piled together are various destroyed civil service vehicles that were barged over from Ground Zero, stored separately from the Auto Pound.

October 16, 2001, Staten Island, NY. Piled together are the fire trucks and other fire department vehicles that were brought over from Ground Zero. This is known as "Fire Truck Row" at the Landfill.

October 16, 2001, Staten Island, NY. Shown here are workers at the Landfill, "Men in White Suits," during the rake and shovel recovery process. Debris removal was a round-the-clock operation.

October 16, 2001, Staten Island, NY. Large sifters were brought in, early on, during the search and recovery process at the Landfill.

October 16, 2001, Staten Island, NY. Piece of one of the planes is recovered at the Landfill.

August 2014, Staten Island, NY. Photo depicts the construction currently going on during the Fresh Kills Landfill transformation into a NYC Park, not far from "The Hill" where the sifting took place post 9/11.

August 2014, Staten Island, NY. Overgrown landscape covers the other side of "The Hill" where sifting took place. Not much renovation or changes seemed to have taken place except natural transformation.

August 2014, Staten Island, NY. Photo shows newly constructed soccer fields created as part of the Fresh Kills Landfill park development. Above, back, and behind the soccer fields you can see part of "The Hill" where search and recovery took place.

August 2014, Staten Island, NY. Shown here is the Auto Pound and what it looks like today, where all the autos were taken after 9/11. This is under the West Shore Expressway, on the other side of the Landfill where sifting took place.

THE LIVING TRADITION
OF CATHOLIC MORAL THEOLOGY

Other Books by Charles E. Curran

Catholic Higher Education, Theology,
  and Academic Freedom
Tensions in Moral Theology
Toward an American Catholic Moral Theology
Directions in Fundamental Moral Theology
Directions in Catholic Social Ethics
American Catholic Social Ethics: Twentieth-Century
  Approaches
Moral Theology: A Continuing Journey
Transition and Tradition in Moral Theology
Issues in Sexual and Medical Ethics
Catholic Moral Theology in Dialogue
New Perspectives in Moral Theology

The Living Tradition
of Catholic Moral Theology

CHARLES E. CURRAN

UNIVERSITY OF NOTRE DAME PRESS
NOTRE DAME   LONDON

Library of Congress Cataloging-in-Publication Data

Curran, Charles E.
    The living tradition of Catholic moral theology / Charles E.
Curran.
        p.   cm.
    Includes bibliographical references and index.
    ISBN 0-268-01296-2
    1. Christian ethics — Catholic authors.   2. Sociology,
Christian (Catholic)   3. Sexual ethics.   4. Catholic church
— Doctrines.
    I. Title.
BJ1249.C8175   1992
241'.042 — dc20   91-51118
                                                          CIP

To
Matthew H. Clark
Bishop and Friend

Contents

vii

Introduction

The basic thesis of this volume is stated in the title —
Catholic moral theology is a living tradition. This contention rests on the traditionally accepted Catholic understanding
that each generation must understand, appropriate, and live
the Christian message in the light of its own history, culture,
and time.

The essays brought together here have been written for different particular occasions over the last three years. No
attempt has been made to impose an artificial unity upon
them. However, almost by definition in these changing and
challenging times in Catholic moral theology, the practitioner
of the discipline shows in whatever she or he writes that moral
theology involves a living tradition.

The first chapter deals with tensions in the Roman Catholic
church today and suggests why the tensions are more severe
than they should be. I believe that official Catholic social
teaching exemplifies well what to be a living tradition means,
and various chapters in this book discuss how hierarchical
social teaching has developed over the years. As in any living
tradition, tensions exist in official Catholic social teaching
(which are explicitly addressed in chapter 3).

Within Roman Catholicism today, especially in the United
States, many other Catholic theologians who share my general
perspective also agree that the hierarchical social teaching
constitutes the most adequate and helpful aspect of the work
of the hierarchical teaching office in the church in general.
The hierarchical teaching on sexual ethics and on ecclesiology
fails to employ the same historically conscious methodology

characteristic of official Catholic social teaching. Within Catholic eccesiology the primary area of difference between, on the one hand, many Catholic theologians who share with me the perspective that we might call a Second Vatican Council spirit and, on the other hand, the concerns of the hierarchical leadership involves especially the meaning, understanding, and exercise of the hierarchical magisterium, or teaching office, in the church. Three of the early chapters in this volume call for a change in official sexual teaching, ecclesiology, and the exercise of the hierarchical magisterium on the basis of the methodological approaches that are already found in contemporary official Catholic social teaching. The adjective *living* is often missing today in Catholic hierarchical sexual teaching and ecclesiological awareness. The best of the Catholic self-understanding now and throughout its history, however, calls for such a historically conscious and living tradition.

The fourth chapter examines the work of Richard A. McCormick, who has been at the forefront of many developments of contemporary moral theology. He has often taken positions that differ moderately from the positions taken by the hierarchical teaching office, especially in the areas of medical and sexual ethics. In my judgment McCormick employs in exemplary fashion the casuistic method that characterized an older sort of Catholic moral theology. McCormick's use of this method in coming to conclusions that seem more apt and suitable for the needs of the present thus illustrates the continuities and discontinuities of a living tradition.

The last four chapters discuss perennial issues in moral theology that come to the fore today in the changing realities of our contemporary existence. The relationship between Christian and human morality has been a continually recurring question, but chapter 7 focuses on this relationship in terms of the social moral order and official Catholic social teaching today. The eighth chapter frequently cites Thomas Aquinas on the relationship between divine providence and human responsibility, but the question has become much more existential today because of our increased technological prowess and because of the experience of the absence of God that has been felt in so many tragic events in human history which are symbolized, above all, by the Holocaust. Theology has claimed throughout its history a necessary freedom for its work; chapter 8 reflects more specifically on the theory and practice of the accepted American understanding of academic freedom when applied to the realm of Catholic theology. The Catholic tradition has maintained that nations cannot and should not be pacifist, and while the final chapter accepts that position it maintains that in the light of many present realities we resort too quickly and readily to the use of military force.

As the relationship between the present and the fullness of the reign of God, eschatology serves as an important basis for the fact that Catholic theology involves a living tradition. Eschatology justified the insistence of Vatican Council II that the church is a pilgrim church. And if the church is a pilgrim church and Catholic moral theology is a living tradition, then practitioners of moral theology will share in both characteristics. In the last five years I have experienced in a very personal way the pilgrim existence of a Catholic moral theologian in the American academy. Like all pilgrims I have been strengthened and supported by many people along the way. To name all who have helped me is impossible since there are so many, but I would be seriously remiss if I failed to render public thanks to all who have encouraged and supported me.

Some of these essays were first written while I was the Visiting Brooks and Firestone Professor of Religion at the University of Southern California. Many of the chapters were written during my year as the Goodwin-Philpott Eminent Scholar in Religion at Auburn University. Chapter 9 briefly recounts how the administration of Auburn violated the institution's academic freedom as well as my own. However, at Auburn I met many committed and dedicated colleagues who courageously stood up for academic principles and led the university senate to censure the president on this issue. I wish them well in their efforts to have all the constituents of Auburn University share their academic commitments and concerns. In many ways I spent a very enjoyable year in Auburn thanks to these colleagues and many others, especially my associates in the Department of Religion—James Dawsey and Richard Penaskovic, the department's head. I am grateful to Richard and his wife Nancy for their friendship. Elsie Reynolds has done more than anyone else at this time to facilitate my writing, having graciously and effectively spent many hours every week on my work without any added recompense.

My institutional peregrinations have now ended. I am grateful to my colleagues and the administration of Southern Methodist University for offering me a permanent academic home as the Elizabeth Scurlock University Professor of Human Values. Jack and Laura Lee Blanton made this appointment possible by their generous endowment of this chair. SMU has provided me a stimulating, friendly, and collegial environment.

I appreciatively acknowledge the permission of the following publishers and periodicals to republish materials that first appeared in their publications: D. Reidel Publishing Company, for "Sexual Ethics in the Roman Catholic Tradition," which first appeared in Ronald M. Green, ed., *Sex, Religion, Medicine, and Morality; Theology Today,* for "100 Years of Catholic Social Teaching: An Evaluation"; Paulist Press, for "Richard A. McCormick and the Living Tradition of Catholic Moral Theology" and "The Teaching Function of the Church in Morality," which originally were published in Charles E. Curran, ed., *Moral Theology: Challenges for the Future;* Crossroad-Continuum, for "What Catholic Ecclesiology Can Learn from Official Catholic Social Teaching," which was originally published in Rosemary Radford Ruether and Eugene Bianchi, eds., *Toward a Democratic Church;* Orbis Press, for "Catholic Social Teaching and Human Morality," which was first published in John A. Coleman, ed., *One Hundred Years of Catholic Social Thought: Celebration and Challenge; The Proceedings of the Catholic Theological Society of America,* for "Providence and Responsibility: The Divine and the Human in History"; Duquesne University Press, for

"Academic Freedom: My Experiences and Reflections," which was first published in George S. Worgul, ed., *Academic Freedom; New Theology Review,* for "Military Force and the New World Order."

1. Tensions in the Roman Catholic Church Today

The existence of tensions within the Roman Catholic church today is well known by all. Here I attempt to get behind the headlines and the sound-bites to discuss from a theological perspective the underlying causes of the tensions. But first, a few preliminary remarks are in order.

Not necessarily a word with negative connotations, *tension* is always a sign of life. Were there no tensions, there would be no life. Perhaps in the long run the tensions now experienced in Roman Catholicism will be creative. At the present, however, many of them are experienced as negative and destructive.

Tensions within the church are not the primary religious concerns facing humankind and the church today. The fundamental issue will always remain, explore, and center on the possibility of belief in a good, gracious, and saving God. This question each generation faces in the light of its own time and circumstances. For many people today the God question is raised in light of the question of evil. How can one believe in a good and gracious God in the midst of the suffering, injustice, and oppression that are so prevalent in our world?

Within the church itself some tensions will necessarily be a part of the life of the community. The members of the Christian community will always fall short in their adherence to the faith and to the gospel. How do faith and grace, on the

1

one hand, intersect with human finitude and weakness, on the other? How, then, can the community ensure that its faith will be handed on to the young? How should religious education be carried out?

To concentrate only on tensions is of course one-sided. Many good things are going on in the contemporary Roman Catholic church. Think, for example, of the greater consciousness and involvement of the church in the struggle for social justice, the increased interest in prayer and in reading the Bible on the part of all members of the community, and the emergence of new forms of community.

However, contemporary Catholicism is also well aware of the negative and destructive tensions which engender much anger and disillusionment within the church today. Disagreement with official hierarchical teaching, especially in the matter of sexuality, is widespread. Catholic women rightly resent the failure of the church to recognize their gifts and call them to positions of leadership and ministry. Pastoral ministers often feel caught between the official church and the conscience and beliefs of the community in which they live. Theologians are fearful that Roman authorities have reduced their role merely to explaining and defending hierarchical teachings. Minorities tend to feel helpless and unappreciated. Especially in the English-speaking world religious women and their communities have been disappointed by the Roman authorities' response to their attempts at renewal in the light of the charism of their community and the signs of the times. All people must recognize the existence of these destructive tensions in the Roman Catholic church today.

The purpose of this chapter is to explore in greater depth the ultimate reasons that lie behind the present negative tensions in the contemporary Roman Catholic church. The first section will discuss three significant sources of the major and perennial tensions that exist and that are necessarily endemic to any religious community that both believes in continuing revelation from God and claims universality. The second section will explore factors that aggravate these ecclesial tensions today.

Major and Perennial Tensions

Tension Between Past and Present

Christianity is often described as a religion of the book —
the Bible. According to Christian and Catholic belief, God
has revealed God's self and work in different times and places
but especially in Jesus and in the scriptures. However, the
scriptures were themselves written in a particular time and
a particular place. So the problem is this: How can we who
live in different times and places be faithful to the word and
work of Jesus and to the scriptures? As is evident, this question faces any religion of the book. Much of the discussion
on the topic is analogous to discussions about the proper
interpretation of any originating document, even the United
States' Constitution.

In general, the Catholic theological tradition has recognized that the contemporary Christian cannot merely repeat
what was said in biblical times. The Catholic tradition has
strongly resisted the insistence on scripture alone as the sole
authority. Rather, Catholic theology has emphasized scripture and tradition as well as faith and reason. Within such
a perspective a very significant role belongs to theology as
faith seeking understanding and understanding seeking faith.[1]

The Catholic approach recognizes that each age must
try to understand, appropriate, and live the word and work
of Jesus in the light of its own historical and cultural circumstances. One can never merely repeat the biblical word. The
biblical word, like Jesus, is both divine and human. This
word is limited by the times and places in which it was uttered.
Thus, Roman Catholicism strongly opposes any sort of biblical fundamentalism.

The danger in Catholicism has been to give too little
importance to scripture and to absolutize the second element
in each of its distinctive couplets of scripture and tradition,
faith and reason. Thus, tradition was absolutized and became
a separate source of revelation. Reason was absolutized so that
Catholics claimed that reason alone could prove the existence

of God and the credibility of the Catholic faith. Roman Catholicism has not always avoided the danger of overemphasis in its approach, but its basic perception has clearly recognized that the Christian community must try to understand and live the gospel message in the light of its own time.

The history of Catholicism bears out this theoretical understanding. Perhaps the most significant period in the development of the church's self-understanding occurred in the fourth, fifth, and sixth centuries, as the church tried to conceive and formulate some of its basic beliefs—Who is God? and Who is Jesus Christ? The position gradually emerged that in God are three persons and one nature whereas in Jesus is one person and two natures, one divine and the other human. To arrive at such a concept and articulation, the church adapted Greek Neoplatonic philosophical notions of *nature* and *person* that are obviously not found in the scriptures themselves. Nowhere do the scriptures explicitly make the trinitarian and christological affirmations that have characterized Christian belief since the sixth century.

Sacramentality, too, has been a very distinctive characteristic of Catholic teaching and life.[2] Since God is mediated in and through the human, the divine presence and action are known and experienced in and through the human. In a broad sacramental view, Jesus is the sign and symbol of God, the church is the sacrament of Jesus, and individual sacraments are truly sacraments of the church. The recognition of sacraments is truly characteristic of Catholic belief. Again, problems have arisen when individual sacraments have been absolutized and their essentially mediating role has been forgotten, too often as the result of an absolutizing and quantifying approach: the Catholic church claimed more grace and greater holiness because it had seven sacraments and other churches had fewer, or even did not count them at all. However, the acceptance of the sacramental system illustrates the characteristic Catholic insistence on mediation, analogy, and incarnation. For our present purposes the development of the sacramental system clearly stands out. Over time the church came to recognize *seven* sacraments. But in fact, for the greater part of its existence, the church has not acknowledged the existence of seven sacraments. Only in the twelfth century did the community recognize marriage as one of the sacraments. Here again the need for the church to understand, live, and appropriate the word and work of Jesus in the light of the changing situations of time and place is illustrated. Never merely repeating the words of the past, Catholicism has lived and grown in the face of development and ongoing tradition, and significant discussions about the meaning of both development and tradition will continue to be very important for the life of the church.

I am in basic agreement with the characteristic understanding of Roman Catholicism that is perhaps best referred to as *creative fidelity*. The Christian community must always be faithful to the word and work of Jesus, but such fidelity cannot be limited merely to repeating exactly what was said in the past. Creative fidelity calls, rather, for the church under the inspiration of the Spirit to make the message its own in the light of its different communal and historical understandings at different times. Pope John XXIII, at the beginning of the Second Vatican Council, called attention to the important difference between the truths of faith and how these truths are enunciated and formulated.[3] However, creative fidelity and the characteristic Catholic self-understanding go beyond such a distinction between truth and its formulation. For lack of a better word, *development* has occurred even in the truth and understandings themselves. I do not want to accept a theory of progressive development so that what comes later is always better than what came before. Rather, each generation must try to understand, live, and appropriate the message of the gospel as best it can. Tension between the past and the present will always exist. Fundamentalists do away with this tension by insisting only on repeating the words and concepts of the past. Modernists, in the strict sense of the label, avoid the tension by not giving enough importance to the revelation of God in the word and work of Jesus and in scripture.

Creative fidelity recognizes the need for the tension between the past and the present and provides a basic approach for dealing with such tension. Catholicism has never embraced a fundamentalist interpretation of scripture, but one might justly accuse Catholicism at times of a fundamentalism of hierarchical magisterial teaching. However, the basic Catholic understanding and tradition recognize that magisterial statements are themselves historically and culturally conditioned. In principle, I think the Catholic tradition in its acceptance of creative fidelity provides an adequate perspective for dealing with the perennial tension of trying to be Christian in circumstances different from the original revelation of God in Christ.

The Tension of the Universal and the Particular

The basic tension of the universal and the particular affects every aspect of the human from anthropology to epistemology so that its role in ecclesiology should not come as a surprise. The universality of the Christian message stands out in the gospel itself and in the life of the early church. Wherever the church is found, however, the community of the people of God exists in a particular place and time. With a growing acceptance of the facts of greater historical and cultural differences, the tension between the universal and the particular, or local, has become even more pronounced.

How has the Catholic tradition dealt with this tension? Historically, Roman Catholicism has emphasized the universal at the expense of the particular. For example, until twenty-five years ago the liturgy, at least for the Roman rite, was in the same language throughout the world. No Christian church or denomination so stresses its universality as the Catholic church. The very name Catholic underscores the importance of the universal. Universality is accented by stressing the role in the church of the bishop of Rome as a primacy not only of honor but also of jurisdiction. No other church has structures that lay so much weight on universality.

In a number of ways, however, the Second Vatican Council tried to give a greater role to the particular and local churches. The council introduced the vernacular into the liturgy even though the original wording of the council was much more restrictive than the subsequent practice.[4] The liturgical renewal was one important way of acknowledging formally that the church is primarily the local community of the disciples of Jesus as it celebrates its reality in the sacraments and primarily in the eucharist.

Especially in the treatment of bishops, the council tried to undo some of the overemphasis on universality that arose from a one-sided emphasis on the church's petrine office.[5] Bishops are not merely delegates and vicars of the pope: the individual bishop is the shepherd of a particular diocese and forms a part of the college of bishops that together with the bishop of Rome shares in the solicitude for all the churches. The rightful role of the individual bishops and of the college of bishops was spelled out at Vatican II, which helped to balance and overcome the exaggerated accent on universality that came from overstressing the papal office and which in a number of ways gave a greater recognition to local churches.

How should we deal with the tension between the universal and the particular or local aspects of the church? Clearly, the two extremes that try to do away with the tension must be avoided. In the last few years there has been much talk about the destructive tensions between the church in the United States and the Vatican. I readily acknowledge these tensions but also point out that the United States is not the only local church to experience problems with Rome. Think, for example, of Brazil or Nicaragua or the Philippines or Holland or Zaire.

In the midst of these problems some people have talked about the need for a United States Catholic church which is independent of Rome. I strongly oppose such a move, insist on the need for a universal church, and ask that the great temptation to use religion for one's own purposes be resisted. By belonging to a universal church community, one can and must be in critical dialogue with others and learn from others. A United States Catholic church would tend in an inordinate way to promote national interest and not necessarily the interests of the gospel or of the church catholic. We need a universal community of churches to prevent a nationalistic or local distortion of the gospel and of the community of the disciples of Jesus. Recall, for example, what happened to many churches in the United States at the time of the Civil War: those churches with a greater stress on local autonomy tended to split in two because of the members' political interests. The church universal is one important way for local churches to confront honestly their own pretentions, sinfulness, and arrogance.

On the other hand, throughout its history and perhaps even more so in the time immediately before the Second Vatican Council, Roman Catholicism tended to emphasize its universal character. The question is easily understood and formulated: How can the church properly weigh and balance both its universality and its particularity?

Catholic ecclesiology can and should learn from Catholic social ethics, which has made the principle of subsidiarity one of its characteristic positions. This principle was explicitly formulated by Pope Pius XI in *Quadragesimo Anno* (1931),[6] but its basic premises have traditionally formed a part of Catholic social ethics. The state or the most universal form of government exists as a help (*subsidium*) and should only be involved when individuals, voluntary groups, neighborhoods, and smaller governmental bodies are not able to do what needs to be done for the common good. Such an approach tries to avoid both individualism and totalitarian bureaucratism. Government at the highest level should encourage and enable all citizens to do their proper part and should intervene only in accomplishing those tasks that other, smaller groups or individuals cannot do. Such a principle is totally in keeping with the best of Catholic ecclesiology, with its recognition of church as the local eucharistic community, the parish, the diocese, the national and regional church, and the church universal. To be sure, however, for many years and even centuries before Vatican II, the tendency had been toward an ever greater centralization, with its concomitant emphasis on universality. However, the Catholic tradition can and should develop its ecclesiology in accord with a legitimate understanding of the principle of subsidiarity (chapter 6 will discuss in greater detail the application to ecclesiology of the principle of subsidiarity).

Authority and Freedom

A perennial ecclesiological question concerns the roles of authority and freedom in the church.[7] This issue will surface in a number of contexts in this book. The tension between authority and freedom is intimately connected with the more fundamental question of the relationship of the individual to the community. That historically Roman Catholicism has heavily accented authority and has tended to downplay freedom would seem to be a commonplace.

Catholic anthropology, social ethics, and ecclesiology have stressed the communitarian aspect of human existence and have reacted strongly against the dangers of individualism. An overemphasis on freedom, especially "freedom from," is characteristic of individualism. Catholic anthropology insists, on the other hand, that, more than just an individual, the person is a social being who is part of a web of significant social relationships beginning with the family, including many others, such as the neighborhood, and finally embracing political communities on the local, regional, and national levels.

Some people in the United States were surprised by the critical stance of the 1986 pastoral letter of the United States Catholic bishops on the economy.[8] However, anyone familiar with Catholic ethical and theological traditions would notice readily that the pastoral letter explains and builds on the traditional Catholic approach. In a nutshell, the primary deficiency in the economic structure of the United States is a narrow individualism. All the major criticisms made by the bishops call for a more communitarian understanding. So-called conservative Catholic theologians in the nineteenth and twentieth centuries were also highly critical of capitalism, for that system illustrated individualistic freedom run amok in the economic sphere; according to this view, the capitalist should not be free to pay workers the least possible wages while attempting to make as much profit as possible.

Roman Catholic ecclesiology has insisted that the church is a visible human community and not just an invisible reality that highlights only the individual's personal relationship to God. The individual finds a saving God in and through the ecclesial community; God has called us as a people. Catholic ecclesiology has traditionally strongly rejected the American Protestant notion of the church as a voluntary society. All people are called to the church and no one is free to reject the call of God.

Such an anthropological perspective can never absolutize freedom. Freedom must be seen as one among many other virtues such as love, justice, and truth. History records how both in social ethics and in ecclesiology Roman Catholicism has had a difficulty in perceiving a legitimate role for freedom. In civil society Catholics opposed the Enlightenment with its insistence on freedom. Recall how long Roman Catholicism took to finally accept religious freedom — just over twenty-five years ago! And even in accepting religious freedom, Catholic theology could not absolutize freedom's value. At the present, the American Catholic church is engaged in much discussion about academic freedom in Catholic higher education. Chapter 10 will show that I strongly defend academic freedom, but I also recognize a danger in absolutizing freedom. The rationale for academic freedom in Catholic higher education is based, rather, on a pragmatic argument that takes into consideration many other values in addition to freedom alone.[9]

Within the church Catholicism has consistently downplayed freedom. Long ago St. Augustine justified the use of force by the civil authorities against heretics. Despite its more moderate church variety, the Inquisition insisted that truth and the good of the community were much more important than the freedom of the believer. Today many frictions exist as church authorities discipline women religious, politicians, and theologians who are accused of misusing their freedom. The ethical and anthropological understanding of freedom in the Catholic tradition coheres with an ecclesiology that emphasizes the church as a visible human society with special authority given to the hierarchy, especially to the bishop of Rome as the holder of the petrine office. These human office-holders in the church have the authority to guide, direct, and, in canonical terminology, to govern the church. Catholic theology and canon law acknowledge formally the teaching and ruling function of the pope and bishops. In short, Catholicism gives an important role to human authority under divine guidance in the church; in practice, governance in the church has often been exercised in an authoritarian fashion.[10]

The Catholic tradition, however, also contains important emphases that argue against authoritarianism. Not a law unto itself, authority must be subordinate to, and guided by, truth, justice, and love. Just as freedom is limited and not absolute, so too authority, even in the church, is limited and not absolute.

Many of the practical tensions in the Catholic church today deal with the hierarchical teaching office on moral issues, especially in the area of sexuality. The very term *teaching authority* raises many questions as to how, or even if, its two words and realities can go together. However, there are strains in the Catholic tradition that strongly oppose any author-itarian understanding of either teaching or ruling.

Especially in the area of morality, the Catholic tradition has insisted on an intrinsic morality.[11] Long ago Thomas Aquinas posed the central question: Is something commanded because it is good or is it good because it is commanded? Aquinas insists that something is commanded because it is good, which coheres with the notion of intrinsic morality. Not something imposed by an outside authority, morality is what is required for the true good and fulfillment of the person and the human community. No outside authority can make something right or good if it is not good in itself. Thus the role of any authority in moral matters must conform itself to the morally good, to what is for the good and for the fulfill-ment of the individual person and of the human community.

The Dogmatic Constitution on Divine Revelation of Vati-can II insists that the teaching office in the church is not above the word of God but serves it.[12] The teaching authority in the church is not the last word but must always conform to God's word and to the truth.

The Catholic concept of governing and ruling has been guided by this same intrinsic perspective. Thomas Aquinas understood human law (civil and ecclesiastical) as an ordering of reason for the common good made by the person who has charge of the community;[13] law is not primarily the work of the will but of practical reason. Here again, a command is made because it is reasonable and good. Recall that in the Judeo-Christian tradition the people pray above all that rulers might have the gift of wisdom. Thus, true ruling and governing cannot be authoritarian or arbitrary, for the ruler does not make something right or wrong but must conform to the reasonable and the good. And so the dilemma: Roman Catholicism has insisted on an authoritative teaching and ruling office in the church, and historically many aberrations have existed; but the church's tradition has consistently rejected authoritarianism and extrinsicism in both teaching and governing.

In my judgment the Catholic tradition has the tools to avoid authoritarianism in all its forms. The problem is posed too simply when put in terms of freedom versus authority or the conscience of the individual versus the dictate of authority. The problem is better stated in terms of three realities—the true, the reasonable, and the good, with both authority and conscience striving to recognize the true and the good. Such an understanding of the perennial problem both avoids the either/or approach that often characterizes the debate today and is also in keeping with the best of the Catholic tradition.

Volumes have been and will be written about the question of freedom and authority in all dimensions of human existence and also in the church. I want to point out briefly the correct way to pose and think about the question and to offer one very concrete practical suggestion for overcoming some of the exaggerated tensions in the church today.

On the one hand, membership in the Catholic community has some boundaries and involves beliefs and ways of acting that should be accepted by its members. To be Catholic means that one stands for something. A Catholic is not free to believe and do as he or she pleases. Theologians and others must cooperate in trying to spell out what the limits are.

Most of the contemporary problems of authoritarianism come from a tendency on the part of church officials to claim boundaries and limits in too restrictive a sense. More specifically, they fail to recognize in practice the distinction between the elements that are core and central to the faith and those that are more remote and peripheral; not all teachings and pronouncements are of the same value and importance. The Second Vatican Council referred to this reality as the hierarchy of truths.[14] Much criticism of the draft proposed for a new universal Catholic catechism centers precisely on the failure of the document to recognize the hierarchy of truths.[15] In many moral teachings the hierarchical church officers have failed to indicate that noninfallible teaching might be wrong. From an authoritarian perspective every teaching is of the same importance because the obligation is extrinsic and based on the authority that proclaims it. An intrinsic approach, however, will have to distinguish the various levels of church teachings. The challenge for everyone in the church is to live in accord with the famous axiom: In necessary things, unity; in doubtful things, freedom; in all things, charity.

The first section of this chapter has identified three very important and perennial tensions that face Roman Catholicism. In some of these areas the Catholic tradition has occasionally gone astray and not dealt properly with the tension. The tradition itself has the understandings and the resources to balance these tensions in a creative way, but in my judgment Roman Catholicism is not dealing with them adequately.

Factors Aggravating Ecclesial Tensions Today

In trying to deal adequately with the tensions as described in a general way above, we shall need to explore why the problems exist today in the first place before we can reach more positive solutions. Three factors help to explain why the church is experiencing tensions in a destructive and negative way: the need for structural change; the resistance to change; and theological differences.

Need for Structural Change

There can be no doubt that in the period immediately preceding the Second Vatican Council (1962–1965) Roman Catholicism was more centralized, authoritarian, and defensive than it had ever been before in its history.[16] This defensiveness, centralization, and authoritarianism had developed gradually over the centuries. In the polemic with Protestantism, Catholicism stressed its distinctive aspects, including the papal office. The Counter-Reformation saw church authority and centralization as very legitimate ways for bringing about some needed reform in the church. The church reacted similarly, and also very defensively, to the Enlightenment. In the eighteenth and nineteenth centuries, the Catholic church also strongly opposed political movements toward revolution and democracy. The Syllabus of Errors in 1864 constitutes a strong statement against much that was happening in the modern world.

The Catholic church became even more defensive and inward-looking in the latter part of the nineteenth century. As the temporal power of the papacy was lost, greater stress was given to its spiritual powers: the First Vatican Council in 1870 proclaimed papal infallibility. The papacy assumed an ever more expansive role as teacher and ruler not only in infallible matters but in all matters. At the end of the nineteenth and the beginning of the twentieth century, Rome condemned Americanism, modernism, and critical-biblical scholarship. Historians have pointed out that such condemnations naturally prevented the growth of a vibrant theology in the Catholic church in general and especially in the United States, for there took place with the modern world no dialogue, only condemnations of the present and attempts to find truth in a seemingly safe past. A monolithic philosophy and theology came to be imposed on the whole church.[17]

Meanwhile, the papacy was exercising an ever increasing role in the life of the church. Pope Pius XII, for example, frequently spoke out on many issues in morality; as time went on greater weight was given in Catholic theology to papal pronouncements and teachings. In accord with the papal encyclical *Humani Generis* in 1950, whenever the pope goes out of his way to address a controversy, the issue is no longer a matter for free discussion among theologians.[18]

From the beginning of the nineteenth century onward the papacy also played a much more active role in the appointment of bishops throughout the world.[19] At present, for all practical purposes all bishops are directly appointed by the pope and the officials in the Roman curia. This process, however, has existed in this form only since the nineteenth century and flies in the face of earlier tradition, according to which local bishops were appointed in a number of different ways although it has always been necessary that the bishop of Rome receive bishops into full communion. Thus we see the Catholic church in the middle of the twentieth century as more defensive, authoritarian, and centralized than ever before.

Technology was also significant in the development toward greater centralization in Roman Catholicism. Faster communication and transportation enhanced Roman authority and lessened the role of local communities. Many American Catholics today are startled to hear that in 1780 English was often used in the liturgy in the United States.[20] Before instant global communication many more decisions had to be made on a local level; when Rome lay a perilous month's or even year's journey away, close communication was impossible, even were it desirable. On the other hand, one minor church official has recently boasted that with car telephones a local bishop is now able to call Rome from any place in his diocese. Such regular appeals to Rome have without doubt eaten away at the legitimate role and function of the local bishop and of smaller groupings of bishops.

According to contemporary historians, the Catholic church was, for whatever reasons, never more centralized and authoritarian than it was in the period immediately preceding

Vatican Council II. The defensiveness of the church vis-à-vis the modern world had been illustrated by a string of condemnations in the nineteenth and twentieth centuries. The council, however, set an entirely new tone. The emphasis now was on dialogue with other churches and even with the world. There were to be no condemnations at Vatican II.[21]

Vatican II brought about great changes in Catholic understanding, theology, life, and practice. Two cautions, however, are in order. First, the council did not occur in a vacuum; the prophets of the biblical, liturgical, catechetical, ecumenical, and pastoral movements had been preparing the way towards change for some time. Second, many of the documents of the council reveal its transitional nature as they reflect an older theological approach. A danger exists, especially in the bleak and difficult days of the present, to become too triumphalistic about what Vatican II accomplished. Yes, continuity exists between the pre- and the post–Vatican II church, but the changes in Catholic theology and life have been most significant.

The changes in ideas and approaches has not been paralleled by a change in structure, which is always more difficult to change than ideas. As an academic, I always have the privilege, the opportunity, and at times the obligation to change my mind. A change of mind, however, can occur much more rapidly than a change of institutions and of structures.

The Catholic church has insisted that the divine is mediated in and through the human. I believe that this idea explains what is often referred to as the sacramental, incarnational, or analogical approach that distinguishes Catholicism from some other Christian confessions. In Catholicism the church is a visible human community that has laws and structures. In Protestantism the stress is often placed on the invisible church and the direct or immediate relationship of the individual to God. Canon law, or as some of its practitioners refer to it today, practical ecclesiology, has always played a significant role in Catholicism and always will.

In 1959 Pope John XXIII called for three new and significant steps to be taken in the life of the church—a diocesan synod in Rome, an ecumenical council for the universal church, and a reform of church law. Today, no one even recalls the Roman synod, and rightly so; no real reform or change came about from this assembly. Likewise, the new revision of the code of canon law, which went into effect in 1983, has been a great disappointment. Unfortunately, this new law does not put into practice and effect the changed understandings of Vatican II. In many ways the code merely updates and does not really reform the older code of 1917.[22]

Great changes have occurred in Catholic biblical studies, theology, liturgy, and philosophy in the last twenty-five years. However, the new code of canon law reflects few of these new understandings, and one result is a structural gap within Roman Catholicism. Since the church gives so much of a role to the human and to institutional structures, the split between the new understandings associated with Vatican II and the existing law is very significant. Certainly structural changes will always lag behind changes in ideas, but trying to pour new wine into old wineskins remains an acute problem. For example, the new law fails to implement the collegiality of bishops and the rights of all the baptized, so the attempt by Roman authorities to deny any doctrinal authority to national conferences of bishops flows from resistance to real structural change.[23] The exacerbation of tensions experienced in contemporary Roman Catholicism will continue and even grow until more adequate structures and legal institutions are in place. At the present, no available opportunity or means to bring about the needed structural change seems to exist. Perhaps the most that can be done now is to point to the problem—the great changes that have occurred in Catholic understanding, life, theology, liturgy, and religious life as contrasted with the basic continuity of structures that have existed since the church had become more defensive, centralized, and authoritarian than ever before.

Resistance to Change

Many of the strains experienced in contemporary Catholicism come from the unwillingness of some people to accept change in the church. This strain is felt in such practices as priestly celibacy as well as in areas that are claimed to be more doctrinal than disciplinary. For example, the vast majority of Roman Catholics in theory and in practice rejects the hierarchical teaching condemning spouses' use of artificial contraception, despite the hierarchical teaching office's adamant reiteration of this teaching.[24]

I shall concentrate here on areas that touch on what the hierarchical teaching office considers to be matters of doctrine rather than discipline, such as the teachings on contraception, homosexuality, divorce, and the role of women. (Chapter 2 will discuss sexual ethics in greater detail.) Why is there so much resistance to change in these areas? Many factors influence the positions of people who reject the possibility of change in the church in these areas today. I am sure many sociological and psychological factors enter into supporting such an entrenched mind-set, and often the persons involved are not even aware of these influences. In discussions, the temptation always exists to point out the weakest parts of others' positions. However, I think it is fairer and more honest to deal with what appears to be the strongest argument of those with whom one disagrees. So why do people in the church resist the possibility of change on such doctrinal matters as contraception? I think the primary reason why Pope Paul VI after his study of contraception was unable to change this teaching stems from his understanding of the authority of the church. Such a defense by definition can be dismissed as simply authoritarian, but we must recognize strong personal, spiritual, and theological reasons behind this position.

My personal experience has helped me to see this. When I first came to The Catholic University of America to teach moral theology in 1965, I was already calling for a change in the official Catholic teaching on artificial contraception. The senior professor in moral theology was strongly identified with defending the official position, but everyone recognized him as a true Christian gentleperson. Early on, we got together and discussed this issue among others. After some exchange of reasons he suddenly shifted the focus of the discussion. The question for him was primarily a question of the role of Holy

Spirit in the church and in his own life in the church. Could the Holy Spirit ever allow the church to be in error on such a significant point that affects the lives of so many believers? What about his own life and ministry? His vocation as a priest, a religious, and a theologian was to serve God and human-kind. He had defended the hierarchical teaching on many different platforms in this country. Perhaps no other single person had been so public and prominent in defense of this teaching. As he neared retirement and looked back on his life, was it possible that instead of helping people all these years he had actually been hurting them? God would not allow him and all others to be so deceived in this important matter.

There are no easy answers to my older colleague's poignant experience. I and others who share my positions cannot, how-ever, ignore the theological, spiritual, and personal dimen-sions of the problem.

The Catholic perspective, in my judgment to its great credit, has always seen the divine working through the human. Thus, Catholicism emphasizes that the human person is related to God not directly and immediately but mediately and indirectly through belonging to the visible community of the church. I firmly support this reality of mediation, which is sometimes called the *sacramental* or *incarnational* principle that is so distinctive of Catholic thought and ethos. However, the danger of the Catholic ethos is that the human is abso-lutized and becomes totally identified with the divine. Thus the church becomes more important than Jesus, or the sacra-ments are no longer seen as an encounter with the community of the church and with Jesus but have a separate meaning all to themselves.

Specifically, in terms of the teaching authority of the church, one must recognize with the Second Vatican Council a hierarchy of truths. Not all truths are of the same nature, importance, or centrality. One must distinguish what is core and central to the faith from what is more remote and periph-eral. Even the pre-Vatican II manuals of theology discussed at length the concept of theological notes and tried to characterize the centrality of a particular thesis on the basis of these notes.[25] These notes ran all the way from what was a matter of divine and revealed faith to what was theologically certain, and down to the lowest category of what was offensive to pious ears. Since the First Vatican Council, greater attention has been paid to the categories of infallible and noninfallible church teaching.

In my judgment, problems have arisen precisely because in practice Catholics often forget to make these distinctions. We suffer from what has been called creeping infallibility: all teachings take on the same characteristics as infallible teaching. But noninfallible teaching by its very nature is fallible—it may be wrong. Not all teachings are of the same importance or centrality and different levels of certitude exist.

We can well understand and empathize with the problem of my older colleague at Catholic University or even with the problem of the pope in dealing with artificial contraception but still realize that we have created the problem by failing to be true to the best interpretation of our own tradition. In recent times in conjunction with the developments toward greater centralization and authoritarianism within the church, we have failed to take note of the differences that exist with regard to levels of importance, centrality, and certitude of church teachings. There is no better way to illustrate the fallible nature of certain types of hierarchical teaching than by admitting that some such teaching has been and is wrong. To make such an admission will be difficult; some persons will be hurt by it. But such a recognition is necessary for the good of the church today. Until the Catholic church can publicly and directly admit that some of its noninfallible teaching has been erroneous, the present tensions of the church will only become more destructive and harmful. Surely we who advocate such changes must acknowledge and point out the boundaries and pace of change, but the hierarchical teaching office must make sure that everyone in the church is aware of the limited binding force of noninfallible church teaching.

Anyone familiar with the Catholic tradition knows how hard it is for the official church to admit that any of its teachings has been wrong. For example, in accepting a new teaching on religious freedom at Vatican II, the council did not concede that the earlier teaching had been erroneous. A theory of development was proposed that tried to justify both the previous teaching and the present teaching.[26] However, honesty and true fidelity to the Catholic tradition call for the hierarchical church to recognize the limited character of a great number of its teachings and to face the fact that at times hierarchical church teaching has been wrong in the past and can be wrong in the present and in the future.[27]

Theological Differences

Tensions within Roman Catholicism today are also exacerbated because different theological approaches are involved. Much of the contemporary discussions centers on ecclesiology and questions of freedom, truth, and authority in the church. However, some deep theological differences are also present and are exerting a significant impact. Bringing these theological differences to light should help future dialogue and discussion.

I first experienced this theological difference in reading the famous interview with Cardinal Ratzinger that was published in the fall of 1984.[28] I realized then that my own case with the congregation headed by Ratzinger was in deep trouble because of the theological differences at work. In that interview Ratzinger drew a very sharp distinction between the values, style of life, and sexual ethos proposed by the church and the values, lifestyle, and sexual ethos found in the United States. Caught between the two opposing positions, Catholic moral theologians in the United States too often chose to dissent from the church and its teaching. Ratzinger's theological perspective sees culture as opposed to the gospel and to the church, and he insists that theologians and believers must choose between them.

Such an understanding is not the distinctive Catholic approach that is often described as an emphasis on mediation or sacramentality. Of course, God cannot be identified with the culture. Human limitation and sin are also present in the world, and the fullness of redemption has not yet been accomplished. Certainly at times the church must strongly disagree with the culture and criticize it, but also the church can and should at times learn from culture and society precisely because of the belief that God can be present in our human contexts. History indicates how much the church has borrowed and learned from culture: Canon law assimilated many of the ideas and institutions of Roman law; Thomas Aquinas used Aristotle's secular philosophy to better understand and explain the Christian faith. Many facets of American culture, such as its individualism and materialism, must be criticized, but Roman Catholicism has learned from American culture the dignity of the individual person and the importance of human rights.

A one-sided countercultural approach is often proposed as a defense of the teachings of the church on sexuality. During the 1987 visit of the pope to the United States, the president of the United States Bishops' Conference stated on national television that the church is countercultural as a way of defending its sexual teachings; many people do not accept the Catholic church's sexual teachings, but the church must stand up to and deny the prevailing cultural ethos. Immediately following that interview, the public television station I was watching showed a special on the Vatican museum. How can an institution have one of the best museums and one of the best libraries in the world and still call itself countercultural?

I have often recalled with some irony that the biggest difference between Cardinal Ratzinger and myself is that I am much more of a Thomist than he is. The assertion must be properly understood. I am a Thomist in the theological sense in thinking that God works in and through the human. A positive correlation exists between the divine and the human. The glory of God is the human person come alive and destined for fulfillment.

Beginning with his graduate studies Ratzinger's own theological work has concentrated on Augustine and the Franciscan tradition. In keeping with the Augustinian perspective, Ratzinger can more readily understand the church and the world as being opponents. The church is identified with the city of God which is opposed to the human city or the city of the world. Thus, the church is seen as opposed to the contemporary ethos and as standing over against it in the name of God and truth. Although different interpretations of Augustine abound, theologians generally agree that Augustine downplayed the human whereas Thomas Aquinas was much more positive about the human and human reason.

Others have publicly pointed out the broader significance of these different theologies.[29] Within Catholicism at the present time, discussion centers on the true meaning of the Second Vatican Council. Two different theological groups, both of which firmly supported the work of the council, can be identified. One group includes such scholars as Rahner, Congar, Chenu, Schillebeeckx, and Küng and has urged the need for continuing reform in the spirit of Vatican II. Another group of scholars such as Cardinals von Balthasar, de Lubac, and Ratzinger, as well as Bouyer and others, is fearful that the post–Vatican II church has at times gone too far and has expressed grave reservations about many recent developments and proposals. The fundamental difference between the two groups is theological: The scholars in the first group are all theological Thomists with a greater appreciation of the human, whereas the second group consists primarily of scholars of the early church who have an Augustinian appreciation of sin and the corruption of the human.

A strong argument to use in defending hierarchical teaching on sexuality, which is not accepted even by the majority of Catholics, is to show the countercultural nature of the church. But, ironically, the Catholic tradition and its hierarchical teaching have consistently insisted that the position on these matters is based on natural law and on human reason and thus is open to acceptance by all. The hierarchical church cannot have it both ways. Yes, at times the church must stand up to the limitations and sins of the culture, but the church cannot by definition oppose culture. Sects such as the classical Mennonites are opposed to the existing culture;

the Catholic church is not a sect. Roman Catholicism must have room for Augustinians, but the whole church can never adopt a model of Christ-against-culture.

The second part of this chapter has pointed out three significant factors that are preventing change in contemporary Catholicism. Until these factors—the need for structural change, resistance to change, and theological differences—are faced and dealt with adequately, negative and exacerbated tensions will continue to exist, strain, and disrupt Catholicism.

NOTES

1. George H. Tavard, "Tradition," in Joseph A. Komonchak *et al.*, eds., *The New Dictionary of Theology* (Wilmington, DE: Glazier, 1987), pp. 1037–1041.

2. Richard P. McBrien, *Catholicism,* study ed. (Minneapolis, MN: Winston, 1981), pp. 731–816.

3. Pope John XXIII, Opening Speech to the Council, in Walter M. Abbott, ed., *The Documents of Vatican II* (New York: Guild, 1966), p. 715.

4. Constitution on the Sacred Liturgy, n. 36, in Abbott, *Documents of Vatican II,* pp. 150, 151.

5. Decree on the Bishop's Pastoral Office in the Church, in Abbott, *Documents of Vatican II,* pp. 396–429.

6. Pope Pius XI, *Quadragesimo Anno,* n. 79, in Terence P. McLaughlin, ed., *The Social Encyclicals of Pope Pius XI* (Garden City, NY: Doubleday, 1975), p. 247.

7. Thomas P. Rausch, *Authority and Leadership in the Church: Past Directions and Future Possibilities* (Wilmington, DE: Glazier, 1989); Richard Penaskovic, ed., *Theology and Authority: Maintaining a Tradition of Tension* (Peabody, MA: Hendrickson, 1987).

8. Thomas M. Gannon, ed., *The Catholic Challenge to the American Economy* (New York: Macmillan, 1987).

9. Charles E. Curran, *Catholic Higher Education, Theology, and Academic Freedom* (Notre Dame, IN: University of Notre Dame Press, 1990).

10. Hans Küng and Leonard Swidler, eds., *The Church in Anguish: Has the Vatican Betrayed Vatican II?* (San Francisco: Harper, 1987).

11. John Mahoney, *The Making of Moral Theology: A Study of the Roman Catholic Tradition* (Oxford: Clarendon, 1987), pp. 77–82, 103–108.

12. Dogmatic Constitution on Divine Revelation, n. 10, in Abbott, *Documents of Vatican II,* pp. 117–118.

13. Mahoney, *Making of Moral Theology,* pp. 224–258.

14. Decree on Ecumenism, n. 11, in Abbott, *Documents of Vatican II,* p. 354.

15. Thomas J. Reese, ed., *The Universal Cathechism Reader: Reflections and Responses* (San Francisco: Harper, 1990).

16. For an overview of the history summarized in the text, see McBrien, *Catholicism,* pp. 635–661.

17. Michael V. Gannon, "Before and after Modernism: The Intellectual Isolation of the American Priest," in John Tracy Ellis, ed., *The Catholic Priest in the United States: Historical Investigations* (Collegeville, MN: St. John's University Press, 1971), pp. 293–383.

18. Henricus Denzinger *et al.,* eds., *Enchiridion Symbolorum Definitionum et Declarationum de Rebus Fidei et Morum,* 32nd ed. (Barcelona: Herder, 1963), n. 3885, pp. 775, 776.

19. William W. Bassett, ed., *The Choosing of Bishops: Historical and Theological Studies* (Hartford: Canon Law Society of America, 1971).

20. Jay P. Dolan, "American Catholicism and Modernity," *Cross Currents* 31 (1981–1982): 150–162. See also Jay P. Dolan, *The American Catholic Experience* (Garden City, NY: Doubleday, 1985), pp. 109–110.

21. Pope John XXIII, Opening Speech, in Abbott, *Documents of Vatican II,* pp. 715, 716. See also John W. O'Malley, *Tradition and Transition: Historical Perspectives on Vatican II* (Wilmington, DE: Glazier, 1989).

22. Knut Walf, "The New Canon Law — The Same Old System: Preconciliar Spirit in Postconciliar Formulation," in Küng and Swidler, *Church in Anguish,* pp. 91–105.

23. Thomas J. Reese, ed., *Episcopal Conferences: Historical, Canonical, and Theological Studies* (Washington, DC: Georgetown University Press, 1989).

24. Andrew M. Greeley, "The Lay Reaction," in Küng and Swidler, *Church in Anguish,* pp. 284–288; George Gallup, Jr., and Jim Castelli, *The American Catholic People: Their Beliefs, Practices, and Voices* (Garden City, NY: Doubleday, 1987), p. 183.

25. Sixtus Cartechini, *De Valore Notarum Theologicarum* (Rome: Pontifical Gregorian University, 1951).

26 *Tensions in the Church Today*

26. J. Robert Dionne, *The Papacy and the Church: A Study of Praxis and Reception in Ecumenical Perspective* (New York: Philosophical Library, 1987), pp. 170-194.

27. André Naud, *Le magistère incertain* (Montréal: Fides, 1987).

28. Vittorio Messori, Colloquio con il cardinale Josef Ratzinger, "Ecco Perchè la Fede é in Crisi," *Jesus* (November 1989): 67-81.

29. David Tracy, "The Uneasy Alliance Reconceived: Catholic Theological Method, Modernity, and Postmodernity," *Theological Studies* 50 (1989): 548-556.

2. Sexual Ethics in the Roman Catholic Tradition

The Roman Catholic tradition in sexual ethics and sexual understanding has had a long history and has exerted a great influence on people and their attitudes both within and outside the Roman Catholic church down to the present day. At the present time, however, the Catholic tradition and teaching are being questioned not only by non-Catholics but also by many Catholics themselves.

The general outlines of the official Catholic teaching on sexuality are well known. Genital sexuality can be fully expressed only within the context of an indissoluble and permanent marriage of male and female and every sexual act must be open to procreation and expressive of love union. The natural law theory that supports such an understanding results in an absolute prohibition of artificial contraception, artificial insemination even with the husband's seed, divorce, masturbation, homosexual genital relations, and all premarital and extramarital sexual relationships. Virginity and celibacy are looked upon as higher states of life than marriage. Women are not allowed to be priests or to exercise full jurisdiction within the church.

Dissatisfaction with official Catholic sexual teaching came to a boil when Pope Paul VI in his encyclical *Humanae Vitae* of 1968 condemned the use of artificial contraception for Catholic spouses. Before late 1963, no Catholic theologian had ever publicly disagreed with the Catholic teaching that banned artificial contraception. But events in the church (especially Vatican Council II, 1962-1965) and in the world at large very quickly created a climate in which many Catholic married couples and theologians called openly for change in the official teaching. Nevertheless, after much consultation and hesitation, Pope Paul VI in 1968 reiterated the condemnation. His encyclical occasioned widespread public theological dissent from the papal teaching.[1]

Many Catholic couples disagreed with the teaching in practice. According to the statistics of the National Opinion Research Center in 1963, 45 percent of American Catholics approved of the use of artificial contraception for married couples, whereas in 1974, 83 percent of American Catholics approved.[2] Archbishop John Quinn of San Francisco, at the 1980 synod of bishops in Rome, gave the statistics that 76.5 percent of American Catholic married women of childbearing age use some form of contraception and 94 percent of these women were employing means that had been condemned by the pope.[3] Andrew Greeley concluded that the issuing of *Humanae Vitae* "seems to have been the occasion for massive apostasy and for a notable decline in religious devotion and belief"; he attributes the great decline in Catholic practice in the United States during the decade 1963-1973 to the teaching of this encyclical.[4]

Dissatisfaction with official Catholic teaching on sexual meaning and morality has been raised both in theory and in practice with regard to masturbation, divorce, and homosexuality. And many Catholic women have become disenchanted with the Catholic church because of its attitudes and practices concerning the role of women in the church, whose patriarchal reality is quite evident. Abortion has recently become a very heated topic in Catholic circles; one important aspect of the discussion centers on law and public policy, but the moral issue of abortion has also been raised. Although most Catholic theologians and ethicists remain in general continuity with the traditional Catholic teaching on abortion, some have strongly objected to this teaching.

And so a widespread dissatisfaction with hierarchical Catholic sexual teaching exists within Roman Catholicism today.[5] In general, I share that dissatisfaction, but my position does not involve accepting the impersonal, individualistic, and relativistic understanding of sexuality that is too often proposed in our society today. The purpose of my study is not to deal with all of the specific issues mentioned above or with any one of them in particular or in depth. This chapter will try, rather, to explain the negative elements in the Catholic tradition that have influenced the existing teaching, and I shall then appeal to other, positive aspects of the tradition that help formulate what I would judge to be a more adequate sexual ethic and teaching.

Negative Elements in the Roman Catholic Tradition

This section will briefly discuss five aspects of the Roman Catholic tradition in sexual ethics which in my judgment have had a negative effect on the church's official teaching — negative dualisms in the tradition, patriarchal approaches, overriding legal considerations, authoritarian interventions by the teaching office, and the natural law method justification.

Negative Dualisms

The Catholic tradition in sexuality has suffered from negative philosophical and theological dualisms. Platonic and Neoplatonic philosophy, which helped to shape the thought of the early church, looked upon matter and corporeality in general and sexuality in particular as inferior to spirit and soul. Theological dualisms often associated the bodily and especially the sexual with evil and sin. A habit of thought in the early church these dualisms influenced the first stage of sexual teaching in the West.[6] Such spiritualistic tendencies, however, have always been present in the church. Many contemporary Catholic dualistic attitudes about sexuality and about all aspects of spirituality have been influenced by the rigoristic Jansenism that reached its zenith in the seventeenth and eighteenth centuries, but Jansenism's influence has continued especially on a popular level.

Blaming Augustine for most of the negativity about sexuality in western Christendom is a commonplace. Before him, however, Ambrose and Jerome were even more censorious. Ambrose's thinking emphasized a series of antitheses that should not be mixed — Christian and pagan; Catholic and heretic; church and world; soul and body. Ambrose was a person of action and so his dualism viewed the body as a perilous mudslick on which the firm tread of the soul's resolve might slip and tumble at any time. Through conversion and baptism the Christian was caught up in Christ whose sexless birth and unstained body mediated between the fallen state of the human body and its glorious transformation in the future. According to Ambrose Christ's body was unscarred by the double taint of sexual origin and sexual desires or impulses. In such a context, virginity was truly the ideal. For Christian married people to avoid adultery and to abstain from intercourse at certain liturgical times and under certain conditions (e.g., menstruation, lactation) was not enough; the couple must also strive to minimize the ever-present possibility of unchastity connected with all sexual pleasure itself. Peter Brown, whose analysis I follow closely here, points out the important relationship of the sexual understanding to the social context of the time. The church itself, like Mary the perpetual virgin and like other virgins, is to keep herself undefiled from the *saeculum* (world) around her. The sexual and the social were closely related for Ambrose.[7]

Jerome stands out as the authority most fearful of sexuality in the early Christian West. His castigation of Jovinian for having placed married couples on the same plane as virgins contains some of his most vituperative language on sexuality. Even first marriages were regrettable, if pardonable, capitulations to the flesh; second marriages led one step away from the brothel. Jerome also left us the unfortunate legacy of understanding St. Paul's concept of the flesh as equivalent with sexuality. The spirit-flesh dualism was thus understood as the struggle against sexuality by Jerome, the most militant of the writers of the early church in his emphasis on female virginity, clerical celibacy, and the temptations and dangers of sexuality.[8]

According to Peter Brown, Augustine avoided somewhat the antitheses and dichotomies of Ambrose and Jerome.[9] For Augustine, marriage and intercourse, on the one hand, and human authority and human society, on the other, were not to be equated with sin, for they existed even in paradise. Martyrdom, not virginity, was the pinnacle of the Christian life. Augustine understood the fall of our first parents as a matter of obedience and the will. Before the fall, Adam's and Eve's sexuality was in perfect accord and harmony with the divine will. Uncontrollable sexual urges, like death itself, came about through the fall. Augustine contrasted to Eve Mary, the exemplar of perfect obedience rather than the defender of a sacred inner space against the pollution of the world.

The fall brought about in all of the children of Adam and Eve concupiscence of the flesh, which originated in a lasting distortion of the soul. As a result of their active disobedience, Adam and Eve were estranged from God and from each other and from their own conscious selves. Concupiscence affected everything and embraced more than sexual feelings, but uncontrolled sexual feelings (based on the text of Genesis that Adam's and Eve's eyes were opened and they knew they were naked) illustrated the fact that the body could no longer be controlled by the will. The sharp ecstasy of orgasm was an abiding sign of the limits of the human will because of original sin; had there been no fall, intercourse would have taken place at the command of the will solely for the purpose of procreation, not pleasure. As shown in the disobedience of the genital organs to reason and the will, concupiscence was the punishment of original sin that all the descendants of Adam and Eve would carry with them until their death.

Augustine formulated his very influential teaching on marriage in the light of this understanding, and he built on what had already been developing in the early Christian church. In turn, early Christian teaching on sexuality borrowed heavily from Greek stoic philosophy's belief in the laws of nature and duty, and saw itself as a response to other ethical positions that were based in gnosticism, such as the claim that marriage was evil, or that sexual intercourse had such a high value that it must be freed from the burden of procreation.

In the face of these more extreme positions, the early church came to the conclusion that sexuality had to be reserved for marriage and used only for the purpose of procreation, which was nature's intention. The motive for sexual intercourse in marriage had to be procreation and could not be anything other, especially pleasure.[10]

Augustine developed his teaching on marriage in the light of his own experience and on the basis of his differences with the Manichaeans and the Pelagians. For Augustine intercourse can be without sin only in the context of marriage, and marital intercourse is sinless only if it is motivated by the desire of conceiving a child and if no consent is given to any pleasure other than that coming from the anticipation of conceiving a child. The realistic Augustine recognized that not even a devout Christian could consistently confine her or his motive for intercourse only to procreation. Thus venial sin is usually associated with sexual relations even within marriage.[11]

Our purpose here is not to summarize the whole historical tradition or even Augustine's total position. However, we should note that Augustine's description of the three goods of marriage—*proles* (offspring), *fides* (fidelity), and *sacramentum* (the permanence of marriage)—became very influential in the Catholic tradition; further, they could excuse sexual expression within marriage. Augustine found two additional meanings in marriage that were taken over by a later tradition and were part of Catholic canon law until very recently—the mutual help or support of the spouses and what was called the remedy of concupiscence. Marriage allows an outlet for passion that protects a person from fornication and adultery. For spouses, even sexual relations simply to satisfy libido constitutes only a venial sin, which thus helps partners in the struggle against concupiscence.[12]

The early church's teaching on sexuality was influenced by several different dualisms, all of which downplayed the corporeal and bodily aspects of sexuality and the pleasure connected with sexual expression. The impact of this early development on subsequent Catholic tradition and teaching cannot be denied. Until the Second Vatican Council, Catholic teaching proposed that procreation and the education of offspring were the primary ends of marriage. The secondary ends of marriage are the mutual help of the spouses and the remedy of concupiscence basically as they were discussed by Augustine.[13] In the 1930 encyclical, *Casti Connubii,* Pope Pius XI also recognized the secondary end of conjugal love and gave more importance to personalist values of marriage. The American moral theologians John C. Ford and Gerald Kelly, writing in 1963, acknowledged that some people want to speak of sexual fulfillment rather than a remedy of concupiscence, but they still opted for the older term.[14] A more adequate understanding came to the fore at the Second Vatican Council, but its relationship to the older approach is still debated.[15]

Patriarchal Approaches

Recent feminist writings have correctly pointed out the patriarchal underpinnings of Roman Catholic life and thought. The hierarchical magisterium continues to insist that God's will demands that only males be admitted to the ministry of priesthood, but in the judgment of many women and men such a refusal shows the continuing and deeply ingrained patriarchy at work. I believe without any doubt that the primary internal issue facing the Roman Catholic church in the United States now and in the immediate future concerns the role of women in the church. The existence and influence of patriarchy in Roman Catholicism has been amply discussed elsewhere;[16] here I shall develop a few aspects of patriarchy as it affects the Catholic approach to human sexuality.

The subordination of the female to the male in sexuality and marriage as well as in all aspects of life has been a part of the Catholic tradition and has in general gone unquestioned until recently. The negative dualism in Catholic sexual understanding has been used to support the subordination of the woman to the man. From earliest times, the woman was identified with what was considered inferior: the bodily,

the corporeal, the emotional, and the material. The male
was identified with what was considered superior: the spiritual
and the rational.[17]

Catholic emphasis on synthesis, unity, and the hierarchical
ordering necessary to bring about societal unity also reinforced
subordination of women. Catholic social theory has insisted
that human beings are by nature social and political. For
individuals to come together in a true society authority needs
to organize and bring cohesiveness and unity to the community. Until comparatively recent times hierarchical organization and authority were thought to be necessary for society.[18]

Now then, marriage and family form a very significant
social human community, and here too is need for cohesiveness and unity, which according to the Catholic tradition are
brought about by a hierarchical ordering of the community
of marriage and the family. Pope Pius XI in his 1930 encyclical, *Casti Connubii,* still used such a paradigm to understand marriage and the family. Different roles and functions
are assigned so that a unified whole results, the husband
having ultimate authority and power. According to Pope Pius
XI the husband has authority over his wife and children while
ready submissiveness and willing obedience must characterize
the wife in accord with the command of the Apostle Paul.
However, submission should not infringe on the freedom and
dignity of the wife or oblige her to yield to unreasonable or
incompatible desires of her husband; and the wife is not on
the same level as children. The pope made use of an analogy
that has frequently appeared in the more recent Catholic
tradition — the husband is the head of the domestic body while
the wife is its heart. The analogy of the human body with
its different parts serves to explain the different roles that
people play in marriage with final authority resting with the
husband as the head.[19]

Anthropological dualism and a hierarchical ordering com-
bined in the early church to distinguish various degrees of
women in the church. Virgins, widows, and wives constituted
in that sequence a hierarchical ordering of the roles of women.
Emphasis on the superiority of virginity is still to be found
in contemporary documents of the hierarchical church.[20] In

the early church virginity took over the preeminent role that
had been given earlier to martyrdom. Until recently Catholic
liturgical documents referred to women saints as martyrs,
virgins, or neither martyrs nor virgins; no positive desig-
nation was to be used or even found for those who were neither
martyrs nor virgins.

Patriarchy and its effect on sexual understanding were
immeasurably strengthened by the fact that men had the
authority and power in the church and were the canonists
and theologians who wrote about these matters. The perspective of the celibate male naturally colored the whole approach
to human sexuality.

From my perspective a caveat should be entered here. I
do not think that people who have never experienced something should be excluded from thinking and writing about
it. We who have not experienced hunger and homelessness
must think and write about these problems. The whole process
of education is an attempt to grow through the vicarious
experiences we learn from others. I find it somewhat ironic
that within Roman Catholicism today married male lay
theologians and philosophers in the United States are among
the staunchest defenders of existing hierarchical sexual
teaching. However, it must be acknowledged that celibate
males need to be very self-critical in order to avoid their own
narrow prejudices and perspectives. Without doubt, the exclusive role of male celibates in church power and teaching on
all levels has colored Catholic sexual ethics.

One example in the history of Catholic sexual teaching that
shows the male bias was the rationale for the condemnation of masturbation. The general rule was that sexuality
existed for the purpose of procreation within a permanent
and indissoluble marriage. Masturbation was condemned
because such sexual actuation frustrated the procreative purpose of sexuality and the male seed. However, the condemnation of masturbation based on the frustration of the
procreative purpose of the semen obviously applied only to
males. The whole perspective of the teaching was masculine.
Later ethicists had to adduce a different rationale to con-
demn both male and female masturbation. In fact, a proper

understanding of female physiology and the function of the clitoris would logically lead to a questioning of the exclusive emphasis on procreation.[21] In many ways a patriarchal approach has had very negative influences on the Catholic tradition in sexuality.

Legal Considerations

The theology, ethics, and understanding of sexuality in the Catholic tradition have been greatly affected by the church's legal concerns. Marriage and sexuality have always figured prominently in church law because the church has a significant interest in the ordering of sexuality and marriage. In fact, even the new code of canon law promulgated in 1983 devotes more canons to marriage than to any other subject.[22]

The golden era of church or canon law began with the monk Gratian who in 1140 compiled all the laws of the church. The twelfth and thirteenth centuries witnessed a remarkable growth and systematization of church law in all areas but especially with regard to sexuality and marriage. At this time marriage was understood primarily as a contract that was entered into through the free consent of the spouses but became fully indissoluble only when consummated through sexual intercourse. "By the mid-thirteenth century western churchmen had arrived at a fairly clear consensus about the goals of the church's sexual policy, and canon law had devised workable solutions to many of the commonest difficulties."[23] After that time not much innovation and development of the basic understanding of marriage occurred.

As time went on, customary, royal, and secular law grew in dimension and comprehensiveness and played an evermore active role in the ordering of sexuality and marriage. Nevertheless, canon law still governs the understanding and practice of marriage in the Roman Catholic church. Marriage is entered into in accord with that law and judges decide cases about the validity of marriages on the basis of these canons.

Ever since the fifteenth and sixteenth centuries Catholic ethics have been closely associated with canon law, and nowhere has the association been closer than in the area of marriage. In the manuals of Catholic moral theology that came into existence in incipient form in the sixteenth century and served as the textbooks of moral theology down to the Second Vatican Council (1962–1965) the ethics of marriage and sexuality were discussed within the parameters of the canonical understanding.

The canonical understanding of marriage was enshrined in the 1917 code of canon law, which has since been replaced by a new law promulgated in 1983. The law that was in effect through most of the twentieth century basically codified what had been in existence for some time. In this legal understanding marriage is a contract brought about by mutual consent which is an act of the will whereby each party grants and accepts a permanent and exclusive right over the body of the other regarding acts which are of themselves apt for the generation of offspring.[24]

From a legal perspective, such an understanding of marriage has great advantages. A contract is a very significant and important legal instrumentality. Established legal criteria can be used to determine if the contracting parties truly enter into such an agreement. The object of this particular contract, understood as acts that are apt for generation, can be verified on the basis of visible and external human acts. As in any legal system, deft distinctions were worked out to deal with particular problems. One such distinction concerned the difference between giving the right to these acts and the exercise of that right. In dealing with marriage, Catholic jurists had to make sure that their theories were in accord with the basic approaches of the Catholic tradition. This distinction both recognized as valid the marriage of Mary and Joseph and acknowledged that procreation is the primary end of marriage.[25] There are also other positive aspects about the legal understanding of marriage in Catholic law. For example, the understanding of marriage as a consensual contract in the Middle Ages was a great step forward. The freedom, and even in some ways the equality, of the marriage partners were strongly affirmed by such an understanding.[26]

However, from the viewpoint of theological ethics the canonical view of marriage in the Catholic understanding is inadequate. The sacrament of marriage cannot be reduced to a legal contract, for marriage is a life-giving covenant of love. In its legal understanding Roman Catholicism had a theology of only the first day of marriage! Once the contract is properly entered into nothing more remains to consider or discuss. However, marriage is a dynamic reality that calls for continual growth and development, not just a contract made once and for all time.

The canonical understanding of marriage does not even mention love. Love apparently is not part of the canonical essence of marriage. In this legal understanding marriage is the giving of the right to acts which are apt for generation. The canonical approach gives emphasis to what is external, visible, and legally verifiable, but from a theological and ethical perspective the union of two bodies is the sign, symbol, and incarnation of the union of two hearts and two persons. There can be no doubt that the centrality of legal concerns in the Catholic tradition has distorted the meaning and significance of Christian marriage.

The Pastoral Constitution on the Church in the Modern World of the Second Vatican Council proposed a more adequate understanding of marriage. Marriage is an indissoluble partnership for sharing marital life and love. The document drops the older terminology of procreation as the primary end of marriage and maintains that marriage as an institution and marital love have as a natural characteristic the orientation to procreation and nurture. Some saw the conciliar document, which never mentions the word *contract* in connection with marriage, as changing the understanding of marriage in Roman Catholicism, but others interpreted it as merely a pastoral perspective that does not change the older juridical understanding.[27]

The new code of canon law promulgated in 1983 does not break away entirely from the older juridical and legal approach, but some definite steps are taken. The first canon on marriage (canon 1055) says that the matrimonial covenant by which a man and a woman establish between themselves a partnership for the whole of life is by its nature ordered toward the good of the spouses and the procreation and education of offspring. This covenant between baptized persons has been raised by the Lord to the dignity of a sacrament. But the second part of the canon maintains that a matrimonial contract cannot validly exist between persons unless by that very fact it is also a sacrament.[28] Thus, the new canon law still does not get away from understanding marriage as a contract. Throughout the Catholic tradition these legal concerns and considerations have predominated and in the process distorted the theological and ethical understanding of marriage.

Authoritarian Interventions

The Roman Catholic Church has insisted that the church is a visible community with authoritative leaders. Catholic faith recognizes a distinct pastoral teaching function for the pope and bishops in the church. However, many Catholic theologians today insist on a distinction between true authority and the abuse of authoritarianism. The abuse has unfortunately too often been present in Catholic life. The last chapter pointed out that the Catholic church had never been more centralized, more defensive, and more authoritarian than it was in the period immediately preceding the Second Vatican Council. At this time the hierarchical teaching office intervened in all areas of faith and morals but especially in ethical questions. *Humani Generis,* the 1950 encyclical of Pope Pius XII, maintained that whenever the pope goes out of his way to speak on a controverted issue it is no longer a matter for free debate among theologians.[29] Vatican II fostered a changed understanding of the church, and many people in the church recognized the legitimacy at times of public theological dissent from some noninfallible teachings.[30] A recent Vatican instruction, however, explicitly recognizes as legitimate only private communication from the theologian to ecclesiastical superiors about the personal difficulties that one might have with a specific teaching of the hierarchical magisterium.[31]

The development of the Catholic tradition on sexuality has suffered from an authoritarianism that has tended to preserve the status quo and to prevent any necessary development and change. For over three centuries common teaching in Catholicism has held, as the Latin axiom has it, *in re sexuali non datur parvitas materiae,* "in sexual matters there is no parvity of matter." This expression means that any direct sexual sin — even imperfect sexual actuation or pleasure — involves grave matter. According to the Catholic understanding, three conditions were necessary for grave or mortal sin: grave matter, full or sufficient deliberation, and full or sufficient consent. In popular understanding the teaching was often thought to say that every sin against sexuality is a mortal sin. Only in sexuality did the axiom hold that there is no parvity of matter;[32] in no other area of human existence was this true so that such a teaching once again highlighted sexuality as more dangerous and more important than any other aspect of Christian life. Today theologians rightly no longer even discuss this question. Authoritarian interventions prevented any free discussion of this question until the time of the Second Vatican Council. For example, in 1612, Claudius Acquaviva, the general of the Society of Jesus, forbade all Jesuits to question the existence of parvity of matter in sexuality even with regard to directly willed imperfect sexual actuation or sexual pleasure.[33] Theologians could not and did not discuss this point that so distorted the ethical understanding of sexuality.

Pius XII (ruled from 1939 to 1958) spoke authoritatively on more subjects than any other pope. Many of his teachings were in the area of sexuality. Catholic theology at the time saw its function as heavily involving the explanation and defense not only of papal statements but also of the decisions of the various congregations of the Roman curia. Decrees from Roman congregations would put an end to all theological speculation. The 1963 book on sexual ethics by John C. Ford and Gerald Kelly exemplifies well such an approach to theology. The index lists twenty-seven different topics on which Pope Pius XII spoke in an official capacity.[34]

The Second Vatican Council opened up new thinking and new approaches within Catholicism. Nevertheless, the council

itself showed the negative effects of authoritarian intervention in the matter of sexuality. Pope Paul VI took the issue
of artificial contraception out of the hands of the council and
reserved the decision in this matter to himself.[35] Sexual ethics
is one area where contemporary Catholic hierarchical teaching
refers regularly to pre–Vatican II teaching. As a result of
authoritarian intervention, this important area is left unquestioned and undiscussed in circumstances in which such great
change has come about in other church understandings and
approaches.

In the last few years the hierarchical teaching office in the
Catholic church has often taken action against theologians
writing in the area of sexuality. In Europe the interventions
have dealt with the work of Ambroggio Valsecchi and Stephan
Pfürtner.[36] In the United States church authorities have inter-
posed themselves in a number of different cases. Jesuit John
McNeill, after his book on *The Church and the Homosexual,* was silenced by church authorities and later dismissed
from the Society of Jesus when he broke silence to criticize
the document on homosexuality that was issued in 1986 by
the Congregation for the Doctrine of the Faith. Rome forced
the archbishop of Seattle to take away the imprimatur that
he had issued in 1977 for Philip S. Keane's *Sexual Morality:
A Catholic Perspective.* In 1977 a committee of the Catholic
Theological Society of America published *Human Sexuality:
New Directions in Catholic Thought,* a book that proposed
a newer theory and somewhat different conclusions about sexuality; church authorities not only published observations
expressing their disagreements but also took disciplinary action
against Anthony Kosnik, the chair of the committee that had
produced the volume.[37]

In 1986, after seven years' investigation, the Congregation
for the Doctrine of the Faith concluded that I was neither
suitable nor eligible to teach Catholic theology. The reason
for this judgment was my nuanced dissent from hierarchical
teachings on a variety of sexual issues such as artificial contraception, sterilization, masturbation, divorce, and homosexuality.[38] In the present climate, Catholic ethicists often steer
clear of the area of sexuality because they fear that action

might be taken against them by church authorities if their work disagrees with hierarchical teaching. However, without sustained and disciplined theological dialogue which at times will take the form of dissent the credibility of the hierarchical teaching itself will suffer and the need to develop the teaching will not be recognized.

Natural Law Justification

Catholic neoscholastic theology and philosophy, which reigned supreme before the Second Vatican council, developed a natural law theory to explain and justify hierarchical sexual teachings.[39] The Catholic tradition has generally emphasized that moral teachings dealing with life in the world are based not primarily on scripture but on the natural law which is available to all humankind. In general, natural law theory insists that human reason reflecting on human nature can arrive at moral wisdom and knowledge. However, two characteristics of Catholic neoscholastic natural law theory strongly supported the hierarchical teaching but have recently been increasingly questioned by many Catholic theologians — classicism and physicalism.

Classicism refers to a perspective that sees reality in terms of the eternal, the immutable, and the unchanging. The universal essence of human nature is the same in all times, places, and cultures. Such an approach insists on immutable absolute norms that are always and everywhere true. This understanding of reality results in a heavily deductive methodology and tends to absolutize the position of a particular period and culture by making it into an unchanging, universal, metaphysical reality. A more historically conscious methodology gives greater importance to the particular, the contingent, and the changing, without, however, embracing sheer existentialism or relativism. Historical consciousness generally employs a more inductive methodology and does not claim to achieve the absolute certitude of the more deductive approaches. Historical consciousness corresponds better to the reality of how sexual norms developed and evolved over time than does the approach of classicism.

Physicalism refers to the identification of the human and the moral reality with the physical and the biological aspects of the human act. The anthropological basis of physicalism understands the human being as a rational animal. The noun is *animality* and the rational modifies or adds to it but does not change basic, given animal or biological structures. Thus, for example, sexuality is understood as what is common to human beings and to all animals. The primary end of marriage and sexuality is what is common to both—the procreation and education of offspring. The human being may never interfere with the physical act of sexual intercourse so that artificial contraception is always wrong. But likewise artificial insemination even with the husband's semen is wrong because the physical act of insemination is normative and must always be present.

Catholic neoscholastic thinkers thus developed a natural law theory to explain and defend coherently hierarchical teaching and they claimed that such a theory was based on human reason and human nature and thus open to all. Such a theory is not, however, as universal as its defenders claim precisely because of the particular way they have developed this theory with its classicism and its physicalism.

In my judgment all of these factors have influenced and supported the development of the Catholic tradition and the present hierarchical teaching. However, this is only one side of the story.

Positive Aspects of the Roman Catholic Tradition

There are positive aspects in the Roman Catholic tradition that can serve as a basis for developing a more adequate sexual ethic. The first part of this chapter should not be seen only in a negative light. To be self-critical is itself a significant aspect of the Catholic tradition that follows from many of the perspectives that I shall develop shortly. It is important to know the negative facets so that one can correct them and avoid them in the future. From my perspective the positive characteristics of the Catholic tradition that will be developed here are more fundamental so that they can correct and overcome the negative. Five positive features of the Catholic tradition will now be considered: a positive assessment of the human, the balance of faith and reason, the roles of scripture and tradition, a communitarian approach, and a renewed, nonauthoritarian understanding of the teaching role in the church.

A Positive Assessment of the Human

The Catholic tradition has insisted on a positive appreciation of the human. A fundamental question for all religions asks how the divine and the human relate to one another. Salvation in the Catholic tradition has been understood as bringing the human to its own perfection and not a denial or repression of the human. The treatment of human beings in the *Summa Theologiae* of Thomas Aquinas (I^a II^{ae}, q. 1–5) begins with a discussion of the ultimate end of human beings, which is happiness or the basic fulfillment of their nature. The two fundamental drives in the human being are the search for truth and the quest for the good. No created or finite reality can ever fully satisfy either of these basic drives. God alone is the ultimate end of human beings because in the beatific vision our intellect will know perfect truth and our will will love perfect good. Many Catholic thinkers today would disagree with some features of the Thomistic understanding, but the Catholic tradition insists that salvation involves the fulfillment and ultimate happiness of the human being.

In the same manner as salvation, grace in the Roman Catholic tradition was never seen as opposed to the human. An old scholastic and spiritual axiom recognized that grace does not destroy nature but builds on it. Too often in the recent past, the axiom was understood as endorsing a two-story anthropology and understanding of reality—the realm of the natural on the bottom with the realm of grace or the supernatural on the top. But for our purposes the axiom indicates the positive relationship between human nature and grace.

The history of theology shows frequent shifts from a more transcendent to a more immanent understanding of God. The problem at times seems to be that if one gives a greater role to God, then one must give a lesser role to the human; or else one gives a lesser role to God and a greater role to the human. At its best the Catholic tradition has avoided this pseudo-problem. An ancient patristic adage asserted that the glory of God is the human person come alive. God's glory and human fulfillment are not opposed. Traditional Catholic teaching accents and acknowledges mediation and participation which not only are very central in Catholic theology but also influence the whole understanding of the divine-human relationship. Mediation avoids the need to choose between either God or the human: the human shares and participates in the goodness and the power of God. By attributing more to the human one does not take away from the divine, for God and the human are not in competition. Thus, the Catholic understanding has traditionally seen the human as a good which through grace and salvation is brought to fulfillment and perfection.

In ethics or moral theology the Catholic tradition has insisted on the goodness of the human and of human reason in arriving at moral wisdom and knowledge. The natural law approach has been a distinctive characteristic of Catholic moral methodology and until the recent past distinguished Catholic ethics from many forms of Protestant ethics.[40] Natural law is a complex theory, but in the first place it responded to this question: Where do the Christian and systematic Christian ethical thinking find moral wisdom and knowledge? While some people maintain that only in revelation can the Christian find moral wisdom and knowledge, natural law theory recognizes that human reason on the basis of human nature can arrive at true moral wisdom and knowledge. A glance at any textbook of Catholic moral theology in the period before the Second Vatican Council indicates an almost exclusive emphasis on natural law. Appeals to scripture were usually only in the form of prooftexts used to corroborate what had already been determined and decided on the basis of natural law. Hierarchical Catholic teaching in all areas, including sexual and social ethics, emphasized a natural law methodology. Some facets of how human reason and human nature were understood were problematic, but the method itself gave great importance to the role of the human.

The theological basis for the natural law theory rested on the doctrine of creation. God created the world and saw that it was good. Human beings can discern through their reason the order that God puts into the world and how they as human beings should act in accord with God's plan. Unlike some other Christian approaches, the Catholic understanding does not see sin as totally destroying or doing away with the reality of creation.

Catholic moral theology can be criticized for not giving enough importance to the reality of sin and its effects on the human. The optimism of natural law theory has at times adversely affected the Catholic approach precisely because the theory did not stress enough the role of sin. I agree wholeheartedly that sin does not destroy the order and reality of creation but nevertheless has affected it. To overcome in the Catholic tradition the dangers of a one-sided emphasis on the goodness of creation and the human as well as the dangers of separating the order of nature from the order of the supernatural, I have proposed what I call the stance or basic perspective of moral theology. The Christian and Christian ethics understand the world and all in it in the light of the fivefold Christian mysteries of creation, sin, incarnation, redemption, and resurrection destiny—mysteries that touch all human reality. Whatever exists shows the goodness of creation, has been somewhat affected by sin, but is touched by the incarnation and redemption while always falling short of the fullness of resurrection destiny. I have criticized recent Catholic moral theology and hierarchical church teaching for at times overemphasizing the basic goodness of the human.[41]

The Catholic acceptance of the goodness of the human determined not only the methodology of moral theology but also the positions taken on many important questions. A very significant question in social ethics concerns the understanding of political authority and political structure. Some Christians

have seen political structure and the state as an order of preservation brought about by God to keep sinful human beings
from destroying one another. In such a view, the state exists
primarily to keep order and to prevent evil from getting out
of hand. In the Catholic tradition, political society or the state
is seen as natural and based on human nature. Human beings
are by nature social and are called to live in political society,
for only in such society can human beings begin to achieve
their fulfillment and perfection. The end of political society
in such an approach is the positive one of working for justice
and the common good.[42]

The Catholic tradition in all aspects and especially in ethics
has upheld the basic goodness of the human, an approach
that should logically also color the whole attitude to human
sexuality. Here, too, I would employ the same stance. Sexuality as created by God is good; sin can and does affect
human sexuality; through the incarnation and redemption
sexuality and the sexual relationship are touched by the saving
love of God, but sexuality like all human reality will be transformed in the new heaven and the new earth of the mystery
of resurrection destiny.

The Catholic emphasis on mediation forms the basis for
insistence on sacramentality.[43] Sacramentality can be understood in a very broad and general sense; here everything that
has been created comes forth from the hand of God and shows
forth and reveals the creator. Likewise, redemption is mediated and revealed in and through the human and human
history. Thus all the good that exists in the world is a sacrament or sign that reveals the presence and work of God. All
creation shows forth the glory of God.

The sacramental understanding of all reality serves as the
foundation for the role of the sacraments in Catholic life and
worship. The fundamental reality is that God is mediated in
and through the human, and the primary sacrament of God
is Jesus, for his humanity makes visible the saving power and
presence of God. The church or the community of disciples
of Jesus is the sign that makes present the reality of the risen
Jesus at work in the world. The seven sacraments are the privi-

leged signs by which this community celebrates the presence in our midst of the risen Jesus. Basic human realities such as a celebratory meal become the way in which the church celebrates the saving presence of God in our midst.

The human reality of marriage has been recognized as one of the seven specific sacraments. Thus, the marital and sexual union of husband and wife become the sign and symbol of the union and fruitful love of God for God's people. Such a sacramental understanding can never disparage the human in general and in this case, human sexuality in particular. Joan Timmerman has made sacramentality the primary basis for her theological ethic of sexuality.[44] Thus, the basic acceptance of the human is a very fundamental tenet of Catholicism and must influence how sexuality is understood. The negative dualisms of the tradition must be corrected in the light of this more basic and fundamental vision.

Faith and Reason

The Catholic emphasis on the goodness of the human is expressed in the epistemological order by the insistence that faith and reason cannot contradict one another. The tradition has warmly embraced this acknowledgment of reason and its fundamental compatibility with faith. Such an understanding in its own way is a great act of faith in the power of reason. History shows that Catholicism has not always lived up to this theoretical understanding, but the basic principle has been a cornerstone of Catholic theology.

Theology has played a significant and important role in Catholic life, for theology is necessary for the continued existence of the community of faith which must always try to understand, live, and appropriate in a self-critical way the word and work of Jesus. Theology has been understood as faith seeking understanding and understanding seeking faith—strong assertions that faith and reason are not enemies but allies.

The compatibility between faith and reason can be seen in many different ways. The first universities came into existence under the auspices of the church. The church fostered the search for truth and was not afraid of reason. The earliest empirical scientists were themselves theologians and philosophers who were committed to finding out the truth.

The history of Catholic theory and practice shows the fundamental compatibility between faith and reason. The early church borrowed heavily from Greek philosophy in its attempt to understand better the Christian faith and message. Thomas Aquinas ranks as the most outstanding theologian in the Catholic tradition; his genius was to use Aristotelian thought, which was just then coming back into the world of the European university, in order to interpret and explain better the Catholic faith. From a more practical perspective, Catholicism took over many characteristics of Roman law and employed it for the governance of the church.

History shows that there have been many tensions between faith and reason. Often the Catholic church has lost the nerve of its medieval theologians who boldly asserted that faith and reason cannot contradict one another. Aberrations have led the popular imagination to see an insuperable gulf between faith and empirical sciences. But in theory Catholicism has always been open to the insights of human reason and has found truth in and through the use of human reason.

Two points are most relevant for our concerns here. Catholic approaches must learn from whatever the human sciences can teach us about human sexuality. Faith does not supply for the defects of reason. Yes, every science is limited and no one empirical science can ever be totally identified with the human, but the sciences can furnish important knowledge about human sexuality.

Second, at times too supportive of human reason, Catholicism has tended to become overrational and has not given enough importance to nonconceptual knowledge and to human inclinations and feelings. However, the same basic theological understanding that supports reason also supports a positive role for nonconceptual knowledge and for human inclinations and feelings. All of these are important sources for a proper understanding of human sexuality. In theory, Roman Catholicism is thus open to search for and find the meaning of sexuality in and through all aspects of human experience. In theory, Catholic theological ethics has at its disposal everything that can contribute to a better understanding and appreciation of the meaning of human sexuality and the values and principles that should guide its expression.

Scripture and Tradition

The Catholic emphasis on scripture and tradition also equips Catholic thought with perspectives that are conducive to a more adequate understanding of human sexuality. I do not agree with all of the ways in which scripture and tradition have been understood in the Catholic approach, but the basic thrust of this understanding provides helpful perspectives for trying to develop an adequate theology and ethics of sexuality. The preceding chapter pointed out that the acceptance of scripture and tradition means that the word and work of Jesus must always be understood and appropriated in the light of the ongoing historical and cultural realities in which we live. Revelation has not been identified only with the words of scripture. And, ironically, the method of feminist biblical criticism shares a basic compatibility with the traditional Catholic approach; Catholicism has always been willing to bring other presuppositions to bear on how one interprets the Bible.

A proper understanding of tradition does not see it as something that has ceased but as an ongoing attempt to understand the word and work of God in changing circumstances.[45] The church must constantly be striving to know and live better the meaning of human sexuality in light of the changing conditions of time and place.

One possible drawback to the Catholic understanding of tradition involves identifying what has always been as a true divine tradition that reveals the will of God. Thus, for example, official Catholic hierarchical teaching claims that the historical reality of the church's never having ordained women is proof of the divine will.[46] But to the contrary, the Catholic recognition that God works in and through the human can provide strong support for saying that the tradition of not ordaining women has depended upon the sociological contexts of time, place, and culture and does not represent the eternal and immutable will of God.

By taking tradition seriously the Catholic church has also paid great attention to its own historical development, as the important place in Catholic tradition of historical studies bears out. The renewal of the Second Vatican Council was heavily influenced by a return to the sources. The realities of the twentieth century were criticized in the light of what had existed in earlier periods in the life of the church. Here too, lies a possible danger of merely absolutizing what is past or of not giving enough weight to the signs of the times, but traditions and history have always been studied and appreciated in Roman Catholicism.

Such an interest in historical development should be helpful in trying to determine how certain understandings were arrived at and how particular values and norms came to the fore. The critical study of history can also unmask some of the shortcomings and problems that have existed in the past and even continue today.

Recently, many significant monographs have been published that deal with historical developments with regard to matters of sexuality and gender. Some of these studies have triggered dangerous memories that have been forgotten or were purposely erased from the living consciousness of the church. But an interest in tradition and historical development is of great importance to our learning about these emerging realities. Perhaps most significant here are studies about the role of women in the church. For example, the role of women in the medieval church has been the subject of much recent scholarship.[47]

In trying to discern the present it has helped to know how the past came about. John T. Noonan, for example, has published an exhaustive history of the Catholic teaching on contraception; on the basis of historical research, he concluded that

52 *Sexual Ethics in the Catholic Tradition*

Roman Catholicism could and should change its teaching that condemns artificial contraception for spouses.[48] Earlier Noonan had studied a change of the teaching on usury in Catholicism and saw parallels for a similar change in the teaching on contraception.[49] Other important recent historical studies include Peter Brown's work on sexuality and the body in the early church; James Brundage's *Law, Sex, and Christian Society in Medieval Europe;*[50] and John Boswell's study of homosexuality in western Europe from the beginning of the Christian era to the fourteenth century.[51] In addition, much historical research has been carried out concerning Christian marriage.[52] These historical studies and others like them help to form a more critical appreciation of the tradition and how its has developed. The critical understanding and appreciation of the past can in turn assist in developing a more adequate sexual ethic for today.

A Communitarian Approach

In America the danger of individualism continues to be present, which affects our approach to many questions including sexuality. In my judgment the primary source of the criticisms made by the United States Catholic bishops in their recent pastoral letter about the country's economy stems from the individualism so prevalent in American life.[53] A similar danger exists that sexuality will also be seen in too narrow and too individualistic a perspective. The Catholic tradition in general and in its understanding of sexuality in particular has always avoided such a narrowly individualistic perspective.[54] The communitarian approach of Catholicism emphasizes that sexual relations involve both a committed relationship between two people and a concern for the broader society. The Catholic tradition has insisted that sexuality must always be connected not only to the individuals involved but also to the good of the species. Ironically, one can, and at times should, use the relationship to the species to argue for limits on the number of children to be had in certain situations. Historical studies such as Brown's and contemporary feminist concerns also insist on the social dimension of sexual ethics.[55] To be sure, important questions remain about how the communitarian and social aspects of sexuality influence our judgments and our governing values and norms, but especially in contemporary America one must be wary of too individualistic an approach.

A Renewed Understanding of the Hierarchical Teaching Role

At the present time in Roman Catholicism the issue of sexuality has become predominantly a question of ecclesiology. The primary and central concern is how the hierarchical teaching office carries out its function. This teaching office has been unwilling to change any of its positions and also has been unwilling to affirm the legitimacy of public theological dissent as well as dissent in practice from existing norms. This is not the place to develop an ecclesiology that would call for a less authoritarian understanding of the function of the hierarchical teaching office and recognize the legitimacy of some dissent on these issues within the church. Many of the existing controversies in Catholicism center on questions of authority and frequently include sexual issues. The last chapter developed the thesis that authority does not make something true or good; nonauthoritarian approaches to the hierarchical teaching office have been proposed, but in practice the pope and bishops have rejected such alternatives.[56] In chapter 5 I shall propose my understanding of how the hierarchical magisterium should function. I am not going out very far on a limb to assert that contemporary Catholicism will continue to experience tensions on these questions in the immediate future.

Roman Catholicism, like many other individuals and communities today, is struggling to generate a better understanding of human sexuality and the morality that should govern it. The struggle will not be easy and will never be fully achieved. A reflective and self-critical analysis showed many of the negative aspects in the Catholic tradition's attempt to

deal with sexuality in the past; however, this chapter also
pointed out some fundamental perspectives in the Catholic
tradition that should help it to correct the problems and to
develop a more adequate sexual ethic.

NOTES

1. Robert Blair Kaiser, *The Politics of Sex and Religion: A Case
History in the Development of Doctrine, 1963-84* (Kansas City, MO:
Sheed and Ward, 1985).

2. Andrew M. Greeley *et al.*, *Catholic Schools in a Declining
Church* (Kansas City, MO: Sheed and Ward, 1976), p. 35.

3. John R. Quinn, "New Context for Contraception Teaching,"
Origins 10 (1980): 263-267.

4. Greeley *et al.*, *Catholic Schools in a Declining Church*, pp.
152-154.

5. George Gallup, Jr., and Jim Castelli, *The American Catholic
People: Their Beliefs, Practices, and Voices* (Garden City, NY:
Doubleday, 1987), p. 183; Andrew M. Greeley, "The Lay Reac-
tion," in Hans Küng and Leonard Swidler, eds., *The Church in
Anguish: Has the Vatican Betrayed Vatican II?* (San Francisco:
Harper and Row, 1987), p. 283.

6. James A. Brundage, *Law, Sex, and Christian Society in
Medieval Europe* (Chicago: University of Chicago Press, 1987), pp.
57-76.

7. Peter Brown, *The Body and Society: Men, Women, and
Sexual Renunciation in Early Christianity* (New York: Columbia
University Press, 1988), pp. 341-365.

8. Ibid., pp. 366-386.

9. Ibid., pp. 387-427.

10. Theodore Mackin, *What Is Marriage?* (New York: Paulist
Press, 1982), pp. 80-126.

11. Ibid., pp. 137-138.

12. Ibid., pp. 138-142.

13. Ibid., pp. 192-204.

14. John C. Ford and Gerald Kelly, *Contemporary Moral
Theology II: Marriage Questions* (Westminster, MD: Newman,
1963), pp. 16-165, especially pp. 97-98.

15. Mackin, *What Is Marriage?* pp. 192-224.

16. See, for example, Rosemary Radford Ruether, *Contemporary Roman Catholicism: Crises and Challenges* (Kansas City, MO: Sheed and Ward, 1987), pp. 24-45.

17. Rosemary Radford Ruether, ed., *Religion and Sexism: Images of Women in the Jewish and Christian Traditions* (New York: Simon and Schuster, 1974).

18. Heinrich Rommen, *The State in Catholic Thought* (St. Louis: B. Herder, 1945).

19. Pope Pius XI, *Casti Connubii*, in Terence P. McLaughlin, ed., *The Church and the Reconstruction of the Modern World: The Social Encyclicals of Pope Pius XI* (Garden City, NY: Doubleday/Image, 1957), pp. 118-170.

20. Pope John Paul II, *Familiaris Consortio: The Role of the Christian Family in the Modern World* (Boston: St. Paul Editions, 1981), n. 16, pp. 29-30.

21. Joan H. Timmerman, *The Mardi Gras Syndrome: Rethinking Christian Sexuality* (New York: Crossroad, 1986), p. 17.

22. Thomas P. Doyle, "Marriage," in James A. Coriden *et al.*, eds., *The Code of Canon Law: A Text and Commentary* (New York: Paulist Press, 1985), p. 740.

23. Brundage, *Law, Sex, and Christian Society*, p. 485.

24. Mackin, *What Is Marriage?* p. 12.

25. Ibid., pp. 10-15.

26. Ibid., pp. 146-172.

27. Ibid., pp. 248-327.

28. Doyle, in Coriden *et al.*, *Code of Canon Law*, p. 730.

29. Francis A. Sullivan, *Magisterium: Teaching Authority in the Catholic Church* (New York: Paulist Press, 1983), p. 209.

30. Ibid. See also Charles E. Curran and Richard A. McCormick, eds., *Readings in Moral Theology No. 6: Dissent in the Church* (New York: Paulist Press, 1988).

31. Congregation for the Doctrine of the Faith, "Instruction on the Ecclesial Vocation of the Theologian," *Origins* 20 (1990): 117-126.

32. H. Kleber, *De Parvitate Materiae in Sexto* (Regensburg: Pustet, 1971).

33. José M. Diaz Moreno, "La doctrina moral sobre la parvedad de materia 'in re venerea' desde Cayetano hasta s. Alfonso," *Archivo teológico granadino* 23 (1960): 42-47.

34. Ford and Kelly, *Contemporary Moral Theology II*.

35. Kaiser, *Politics of Sex and Religion*, p. 63.

36. Ludwig Kaufmann, *Ein ungeloster Kirchenkonflikt: Der Fall Pfürtner* (Freiburg, Switzerland: Exodus, 1987).

37. Leslie Griffin, "American Catholic Sexual Ethics," in S. Vicchio and V. Geiger, eds., *Perspectives in the American Catholic Church 1789-1989* (Westminster, MD: Christian Classics, 1990), pp. 247-250.

38. Bernard Häring, "The Curran Case: Conflict between Rome and the Moral Theologian," in Küng and Swidler, *Church in Anguish*, pp. 235-250.

39. Charles E. Curran and Richard A. McCormick, eds., *Readings in Moral Theology No. 7: Natural Law and Theology* (New York: Paulist Press, 1991).

40. John Mahoney, *The Making of Moral Theology: A Study of the Roman Catholic Tradition* (Oxford: Clarendon, 1987), especially pp. 72-115 and 224-258.

41. Charles E. Curran, *Directions in Fundamental Moral Theology* (Notre Dame, IN: University of Notre Dame Press, 1985), pp. 29-62.

42. Rommen, *The State in Catholic Thought.*

43. Kevin W. Irwin, "Sacrament," in Joseph A. Komonchak *et al.*, eds., *The New Dictionary of Theology* (Wilmington, DE: Glazier, 1987), pp. 910-922.

44. Timmerman, *Mardi Gras Syndrome*, pp. 1-9.

45. John W. O'Malley, *Tradition and Transition: Historical Perspectives on Vatican II* (Wilmington, DE: Glazier, 1989).

46. Congregation for the Doctrine of the Faith, *Declaration on the Question of the Admission of Women to the Ministerial Priesthood* (Washington, DC: United States Catholic Conference, 1977).

47. E.g., Elizabeth A. Petroff, ed., *Medieval Women's Visionary Literature* (New York: Oxford, 1986).

48. John T. Noonan, Jr., *Contraception: A History of Its Treatment by the Catholic Theologians and Canonists,* text ed. (Cambridge: Harvard University Press, 1986).

49. John T. Noonan, Jr., *The Scholastic Analysis of Usury* (Cambridge: Harvard University Press, 1957).

50. See above, footnotes 6 and 7.

51. John Boswell, *Christianity, Social Tolerance, and Homosexuality* (Chicago: University of Chicago Press, 1980).

52. E.g., Mackin, *What Is Marriage?*

53. National Conference of Catholic Bishops, *Economic Justice for All: Pastoral Letter on Catholic Social Teaching and the U.S.*

Economy (Washington, DC: United States Catholic Conference, 1986).

54. Lisa Sowle Cahill, *Between the Sexes: Foundations for a Christian Ethics of Sexuality* (New York: Paulist Press, 1985), pp. 139–143.

55. Timmerman, *Mardi Gras Syndrome,* pp. 50–68.

56. See, for example, Francis A. Sullivan, *Magisterium: Teaching Authority in the Catholic Church* (New York: Paulist Press, 1983); William W. May, ed., *Vatican Authority and American Catholic Dissent* (New York: Crossroad, 1987); Richard Penaskovic, ed., *Theology and Authority* (Peabody, MA: Hendrickson, 1987); Curran and McCormick, *Readings in Moral Theology No. 6.*

3. One Hundred Years of Catholic Social Teaching

On 15 May 1891, Pope Leo XXIII issued his encyclical *Rerum Novarum* on the condition of workers.[1] This letter marked the beginning of a series of documents of the hierarchical Roman Catholic church that have now come to be known as modern Catholic social teaching.[2] In general, the approach of these documents can be described as moderately reforming. Official Catholic social teaching usually does not take a radical position in terms of proposing completely new and different structures; rather, the church's reforming mode coheres with many other emphases in the Catholic theological tradition.

My evaluation of one hundred years of official Catholic social teaching will concentrate on the future, but I claim no ability to know what the future holds; my analysis will be much more modest than attempting to predict what will happen. This chapter will discuss some unresolved tensions in official Catholic social teaching at the present that will have a bearing on the direction of the teaching in the future. The material will be treated under three aspects: theology, ecclesiology, and methodology.

Theology

Eschatology and Anthropology

Eschatological and anthropological approaches result in differing perspectives on what might be called a more optimistic or a more pessimistic view of the world. A more fully realized eschatology and a Christian anthropology that recognizes a true goodness in creation and the presence of redemption even now overcoming the power of sin will tend to come down on the more optimistic side. An eschatology that contrasts the present and the future and an anthropology that gives more significance to sin will be more pessimistic about human life in this world and the possibility of justice and reform.

Almost by definition, the natural law methodology that served as the basis for official social teaching through the early 1960s tends to have a more optimistic view. On the basis of human reason and by examining human nature and the world, human beings are able to discover what is just and right. The papal encyclical *Pacem in Terris,* the last document (1963) to take this tack exclusively, can be criticized for what has been called a natural law optimism. The method is based on the order that the creator has imprinted on the human heart and that conscience reveals and calls for acceptance.[3] But in the human heart and in human society there also exist disorder, sin, pride, and other evils, and therefore human societies are not able to live in peace and harmony with one another. The very title of the encyclical indicates its optimism — and the limitation of its method. Then and even now one could perhaps just as easily write an encyclical entitled *War in the World.* Although no worldwide conflicts have occurred, wars have frequently broken out in all parts of our world (chapter 10 will discuss the use of military force today).[4]

The Pastoral Constitution on the Church in the Modern World integrated natural law into a more theological approach but still came out on the optimistic side.[5] The eschatology definitely is realized with the emphasis being on Christ who has come now as the new human being. The future dimension of the reign of God does not receive enough attention in the theoretical part of this document.[6] The generally optimistic evolutionary and developmental tones of the document flow from its perspective.

Later documents have recognized in theory a greater presence of sin and have been strong in pointing out many of the problems and difficulties in the world. The survey of the contemporary world in Pope John Paul II's, *Sollicitudo Rei Socialis* (1987) spends twelve paragraphs dealing with negative characteristics of the contemporary world, especially the widening gap between the northern and the southern hemispheres that shows in so many different ways.[7] Only one long paragraph is devoted to the positive aspects of the contemporary scene.[8] However, in this context of a mainly negative picture of the present, John Paul II insists that the church must strongly affirm the *possibility* of overcoming obstacles which by excess or by defect stand in the way of development and true liberation. Grounded in an anthropology that has confidence in human beings despite the presence and power of sin, the document affirms the necessary qualities and energies that exist in human persons who are created in the image of God, placed under the empowering influence of Christ, and aided by the efficacious action of the Holy Spirit.[9] We can accurately describe these later documents as exhibiting a cautious or realistic optimism about human beings and human possibilities in the social order.

In the future, official Catholic social teaching must be willing to recognize the growing diversity within Roman Catholicism on the questions of anthropology and eschatology. For example a comparatively small but very significant Catholic social movement in the United States, the Catholic Worker movement, originally founded by Dorothy Day and Peter Maurin, emphasizes voluntary poverty, witness, and pacifism and at the same time has taken a more negative view of the world and has accented the future dimension of eschatology.[10] And in the area of war, Catholic social teaching has now come to accept the more radical position of nonviolence as a legitimate option for individuals in some circumstances.[11] Similar recognition of more radical approaches must also come in the areas of social and economic teaching.

Christology

Christology has assumed a larger place in Catholic social teaching since the Second Vatican Council introduced in this sphere a more explicitly theological approach. Recent church documents, especially those of John Paul II, employ a Christology from above, or a descending Christology. With its roots in the Johannine understanding and in the formulations of the Council of Chalcedon (451 C.E.), this Christology from above has been traditional in Roman Catholicism. Christ is the preexisting Logos who took on a human nature and saved us by the paschal mystery. Individual human beings, through the church, share in the salvation brought by Jesus and in the satisfaction wrought by Jesus on the cross. Such a soteriology abstracts from concrete historical and social realities; salvation is the gift communicated through the incarnation and redemption to all humankind.

John Paul II's very first encyclical as pope was entitled *Redemptor Hominis, The Redeemer of Humankind.* Christ the redeemer of the world penetrated in a unique and unrepeatable way the mystery of human beings and entered into the human heart. The pope then cites the Second Vatican Council to indicate that only in the mystery of the incarnate word does the mystery of the human being take on light. As the new Adam in the revelation of the mystery of God and of God's love, Christ fully reveals the human person to each human's self and brings to light the high human calling. By the incarnation the Son of God is in a certain way united with every human being.[12]

Such a Christology has different emphases and different ramifications from the method of a Christology from below. A Christology from below begins with the historical Jesus and his life, ministry, death, and resurrection. This second sort of Christology is exemplified well in the work of Edward Schillebeeckx; greater importance is given to the humanity of Jesus, and Christology depends more heavily on the scriptures and their understanding today. This perspective carries with it a very concrete and social soteriology.[13] Liberation theology similarly illustrates the emphasis of a Christology from below. Jesus is identified with the poor, the oppressed, the victims, and the outcast: those who opposed Jesus were the powerful in society, but Jesus always sided with the victims; discipleship calls the Christian to follow Jesus and to carry on his work. Here soteriology is also very concrete and social, and such a Christology calls for an ever-closer link between faith and daily life, between theory and practice. Jesus as a sign of contradiction provokes opposition and division. Thus, the abstract and ahistorical character of salvation gives way to very concrete, particular, personal, and historical approaches.[14] In the future, Catholic social teaching must more deeply, broadly, and heavily stress a Christology from below with all its ramifications.

Ecclesiology

The ecclesiology of Catholic social teaching will also call for some attention in the future. Here I shall consider five facets of ecclesiology—the church-sect typology, the universal and the particular dimensions of the church, the process of formulating official church teaching, the tension between the church as mission and as institution, and justice in the church.

The Church-Sect Typology

In the view of Ernst Troeltsch and Max Weber the sect is understood as a small, exclusive, religious group that emphasizes rigorous ethical standards, sees itself in opposition to the world and to the culture, and is determined not to compromise its pure ideals. On the other hand, the church is a universal community, open to embrace all, that calls its members to live in the world and to try to transform it. Such an institution promotes a social teaching to guide life in this world where the members of the church work together with all humankind for a more just human society. By this typological definition, a church is less rigorous and less radical than a sect. Troeltsch rightly saw in Roman Catholicism the best illustration of the church type. The official Catholic social teaching of the last one hundred years exemplifies the type, for the teaching is proposed both for members of the Catholic church and for all other people of good will in an attempt to create and work for a more just society.[15] Chapter 7 will defend the thesis that there is one social moral order that is the same for all people whether they are Christian or not.

However, in the last few decades, some developments within Catholicism resemble the approaches more closely associated with the typology of the sect. Nonviolence and pacifism have definitely become more influential in Catholic contemporary life although traditionally they have been more closely associated with the sects. For the first time in the modern Catholic tradition, the Pastoral Constitution on the Church in the Modern World recognized that according to the Catholic interpretation, individuals, but not nations, might opt for nonviolence. This document immediately adds, however, a condition to its acceptance of nonviolence that clearly shows its unwillingness to embrace a sectarian understanding: nonviolence is praiseworthy "provided that this can be done without injury to the rights and duties of others or of the community itself."[16] The American Catholic bishops in their 1983 letter on peace and war went even further, for they put no conditions on the acceptance of nonviolence by individuals.[17] Catholic life and experience in the United States have witnessed a greater accent on pacifism and have also seen other approaches that have some similarities to traditional sectarian options. The Catholic Worker movement provides a good illustration of this emphasis with its voluntary poverty, pacifism, and personalism.

In the future, Catholic social teaching will have to recognize a greater pluralism in this area. In a sense, the church must be big enough to incorporate some options that have traditionally been associated with the sect. Does this mean that Catholicism will become both a church and a sect at one and the same time? How can these diverse aspects within Roman Catholicism be best understood and explained?

The Troeltschean church–sect typology, like most typologies, has often blurred in practice. Perhaps a typology is not the most useful way to understand how Roman Catholicism can incorporate within itself some approaches that seem to have affinities with traditional sectarian attitudes. In my judgment, Catholicism can never withdraw from the world and consider its own existence as a community apart from the world and life in the world. Catholicism by its very nature emphasizes the universal and involvement in the world.

Perhaps these developments now and even more so in the future can be understood in somewhat different categories from the church–sect typology. Some writers have thought that Roman Catholic monasticism illustrates a sectarian approach. H. Richard Niebuhr in his classical study of *Christ and Culture* put monasticism into the type of Christ against culture.[18] However, I do not think that monasticism really fits into that category. To understand monasticism as a total flight from the world is not accurate. I have often mused that some of the best liqueurs and wines in the world have been named after monks and monasteries! Monks believed in celebrations and recognized that good wine and good food should be appropriate elements of their celebrations. Medieval monks were devoted to scholarship and preserved in art and manuscript much of the culture of the western world. Contemporary monks such as Thomas Merton have not seen the cloister as a flight from the world.[19] I do not believe that monasticism should be seen as a sect. Rather, I understand monasticism to lay weight on and bear witness to important attributes that will also have a bearing and an influence on the world. The traditional religious vows of poverty, chastity, and obedience involve a commitment to three very significant attitudes or values in Christianity; a person attests to these values because of their inherent importance and significance for the world. So too some are called to bear witness to peace through a commitment to pacifism. Such an emphasis would not necessarily involve the typological category of Christ against culture or a flight from the world. In fact, such a witness tries to speak to the world and to be recognized.

Now and increasingly so in the future, Catholicism will embrace attitudes and approaches that have often been associated with sects. However, I do not think Catholicism should become sectarian in terms of seeing itself as an isolated community over against the world. Nonviolence, voluntary poverty, and other similar, chosen ways of life can be understood in a way that sees the church as relating to the world and as trying to bring about greater justice.

The Church: Universal and Particular

Another important aspect of ecclesiology involves the universal and the particular or local dimensions of the church. As the first chapter pointed out, Catholicism has traditionally stressed the church universal, as Catholic social teaching in documents that have been issued from the highest authority in the universal church illustrate well. However, since the Second Vatican Council more attention has been paid to local churches and to regional and national groups of churches, even while overemphasis on the role of the papacy in the church has continued to be perceived. Roman Catholicism will always have a petrine office, but that office must be considered together with the bishops of individual dioceses and with the whole college of bishops in union with the bishop of Rome. The hierarchs in turn must serve the entire people of God, for the church is primarily and above all the people of God. At the present time, Roman authorities are insisting on a very centralized understanding of the church, but I hope that in the future greater acceptance will be extended to local and national church bodies.[20]

The great importance of local, national, and regional churches has already been very evident in Catholic social teaching. The bishops of Latin America have issued many significant statements on liberation theology beginning with the documents of the Medellin conference in 1968. These writings have set the tone for the pastoral and social involvement of the church in Latin America in the last few decades.[21] Similar pastoral documents have been offered by other groups of bishops throughout the world. In the United States, the American Catholic bishops have issued documents on social questions for most of this century; however, the process, timeliness, and content of their recent pastoral letters on peace and on the economy have given great public attention to these documents.²² On the issue of peace and war, many other bishops' conferences also put forth pastoral letters at about the same time as the one proposed by the United States bishops.²³

The ecclesiological emphasis on local, national, and regional churches coheres both with the ethical recognition of growing diversity throughout the world and with the difficulty of making statements that apply all over the world. Here too one can note a growing acknowledgment of this problem in the documents themselves. In 1931, Pope Pius XI proposed a plan for the reconstruction of the social order that he thought could be implemented throughout the world. The plan, which was often called moderate corporatism or solidarism, was seen as a model that would avoid the problems of both socialism and capitalism.²⁴ Within thirty years, however, his successors admitted that the plan was not workable and they no longer mentioned it.²⁵ Contemporary Catholic social teaching has not attempted to produce a plan or a blueprint to be followed throughout the world but has proposed, rather, a set of criteria based on human dignity and human rights that are to be used to evaluate and reform existing systems.²⁶

Historicity and the recognition of diversity have already strongly influenced Catholic social teaching. In his apostolic letter *Octogesima Adveniens,* Paul VI was very forthright: "In the face of such widely varying situations, it is difficult for us to utter a unified message and to put forward a solution which has universal validity. Such is not our ambition nor is it our mission. It is up to the Christian communities to analyze with objectivity the situation which is proper to their own country, to shed on it the light of the gospel's unalterable word, and to draw principles of reflection, norms of judgment, and directives for action from the social teaching of the church."²⁷ Thus in the future, a greater role must be given to local communities without, however, denying some place for more universal documents and statements.

Both contemporary Catholic ecclesiology, despite some reservations in Rome, and the diversity existing in our world point toward an approach that has long been associated with Catholic social teaching about the political order, namely, the principle of subsidiarity. According to the principle of subsidiarity, the higher and more universal level should intervene only when the smaller and more local level cannot manage the task. The principle when applied in social morality tries to give a proper place to the role of individuals, of voluntary societies, and of local, state, and federal governments.[28] Chapter 1 maintained that a similar approach should exist in Catholic ecclesiology. Now this chapter will explore the application of the principle of subsidiarity to social teaching.

A place for more universal statements will always exist, but they will be more general by their very nature. The universal church and local churches today are well served by the approach of John Paul II who frequently reminds the first world of the problems of the third world and of the complicity of both east and west in the problems of the south.

A greater recognition of the role of local and national churches will inevitably bring about a greater diversity within Catholic social teachings. The example of what occurred when a number of different conferences of bishops were addressing questions of peace, war, and deterrence illustrates what will be a more common occurrence in the future. In January 1983 the Vatican called for a consultation in Rome with Vatican officials and bishops from France, West Germany, Great Britain, Belgium, Italy, and the Netherlands to meet with United States bishops who had already issued drafts of their proposed pastoral letter. The United States bishops had shown that their document was going to extend universal teaching in the sense of making specific judgments, such as no first use of any nuclear weapons. Many of the other hierarchies (e.g., the French and the West Germans) opposed such a position. Roman officials wanted to avoid any kind of contradiction about Catholic social teaching and to ensure a legitimate freedom with regard to particular judgments about social issues.[29] At that meeting and later, the bishops of the United States clearly delineated different levels of their teaching—

universally binding moral principles (e.g., noncombatant immunity and proportionality), the teaching of popes and of the Second Vatican Council, and the application of these principles and teachings to particular cases. Their prudential judgments on complex and specific cases, which are applications of these more general principles and teachings, are not official church teaching in the sense of being binding in conscience but, rather, are to be given serious attention by Catholics.[30]

As a matter of fact, the United States bishops' position on no first use of even small nuclear weapons was not accepted by some other bishops' conferences. Such diversity is legitimate within the Catholic community, however, since prudential judgments on complex social issues cannot claim to have a certitude that excludes the possibility of error and that calls for universal agreement within the church.

According to the United States letter, there could be no diversity on the level of universal principles and of official teaching of the popes and of the recent Vatican Council. However, a comparison of the different pastoral letters on peace indicates that a variety of interpretations does exist on the level of universal principles. The United States pastoral letter insists very strongly on the principle of discrimination or noncombatant immunity and makes this principle a central part of its teaching. The West German bishops do not explicitly employ the principle of discrimination and strongly indicate that they do not accept an independent principle of discrimination but only the principle of proportionality in determining what is legitimate in the course of fighting a just war.[31]

In the future, with probably more statements from regional and national groups of bishops, the diversity within Catholic social teaching will be more evident. In my judgment more concrete principles are definitely open to question. Diversity on specific principles can and should exist within the church. In an ideal future, I would also see the possibility that at times statements of regional or national churches might question and disagree with official Catholic teaching on the universal level. The collegiality of bishops will not be a reality in the Catholic church until groups of bishops or individual bishops can publicly disagree with official church teaching that is not core and central to the faith.

Formulating Official Church Teaching

Who speaks for the church and how does one speak for the church? Official Catholic social teaching has always seen itself as speaking *for* the church and thus is distinguished from the social teaching of the World Council of Churches which sees itself as speaking *to* the church.[32] The Catholic approach claims to teach in a binding manner for the whole church. I think it is fair to say that the World Council of Churches' documents have often been more prophetic and more specific than official Vatican documents precisely because the council does not see itself as speaking for the church. *Prophetic* is a word that is frequently used and abused, but official teachers in the Catholic church must be circumspect in what they say precisely because they are speaking for, not to, the church. The need for the other function — speaking *to* the church — always remains, but that is not the primary pastoral teaching ministry of pope and bishops as it has been employed in Catholic social teaching.

In speaking for the church, one must respect the legitimate freedom of the church's believers. The general nature of Catholic social teaching, which does not enter into specifics, attests to this respect. Recall that when the United States bishops wanted to be more specific, they pointed out that their specific judgments are not teaching that binds all Catholics. I am basically in accord with the position taken by the United States bishops on these questions, but legitimate diversity can also exist on the level of more specific principles and of hierarchical teaching that is not core and central to the Catholic faith.

More attention must be given in the future to how the universal teaching is composed especially if it is meant to speak for the whole church. Up to now papal documents have usually been written in secret by only one or a few advisers. A few years ago, Oswald von Nell-Breuning, the German Jesuit, told how he was commissioned to write what became Pope Pius XI's 1931 encyclical *Quadragesimo Anno.* Von Nell-Breuning was not permitted to enlist any other collaborators in his work.[33] The United States bishops in their pastoral letters on peace and the economy offered an excellent example of a participative, open, and public way of composing church documents that better coheres with an understanding of official teaching as serving the entire people of God. An ecclesiology that emphasizes the church as the people of God can be seen in the composition of these pastoral letters. The committees that drafted the letters consulted widely with all interested parties and then made the drafts public so that the whole world would comment on them. The process itself has turned out to be an excellent instrumentality, perhaps even more important than the final documents themselves.[34]

In recent years, after meetings of the international synod of bishops, the synod has made some recommendations to the pope, who then issues a document.[35] In my judgment, such synods should issue public documents in their own name as a synod and should not just be advisers to the pope. But at least more and broader consultation has gone into these papal documents than into most documents in official Catholic social teaching. The documents of the Second Vatican Council, of course, were the result of a much more collegial and participative process, but then again it was limited to the bishops alone.

In the future, documents from the universal teaching office need to be written and developed with a greater participation of and collaboration with the whole people of God. An ecclesiology that emphasizes the whole people of God and the collegiality of bishops calls for such a process.

If these documents speak for the church, they must be owned by the whole church. Consequently, the church must truly educate its own members about the church's teachings. The question of handing on the tradition of the Catholic faith to all the people of God and especially to the young has become a very significant issue in the life of the contemporary church. Most Catholics, even in the past, have not been that aware of the social teachings of the church; more important than the issuing of statements is the need for education.

The Church as Mission and as Institution

A fourth ecclesiological problem for the future of official Catholic social teaching on the universal level concerns the tension that pulls, like many times in the past, between the church as mission and the church as institution. To protect the institution of the church measures are sometimes taken that appear to oppose the mission of the church. Perhaps the most celebrated example of this tension was the failure of church officials and others to speak out against the Holocaust. Church statements, if they speak for the gospel and out of the gospel, will at times criticize existing power structures and perpetrators of injustice and oppression. Such statements will not be well received by those who are so challenged. From my perspective, the church as institution is not something necessarily bad or negative; Catholic theology insists on the church as a visible human community. However, at times the institution's urge for survival as institution can and does interfere with the true mission of the church.

A somewhat analogous question is the relationship between the church as a church with its social mision and the church as a temporal society that is part of the diplomatic world of sovereign states. The dual role of the papacy both as the center of the universal church's unity and as a temporal ruling office creates a tension that can readily cause conflicts of interest. As a temporal ruler, for example, the pope must receive other heads of states and have diplomatic relations with them, even if strong disagreements with the policies of a particular person or government exist.

This particular tension would be resolved if the Vatican ceased stressing its double identity. I think that the Catholic church would be better off if it retained only its unique religious identity and did not also insist that it was a sovereign state. The tensions between being a church and being a state are obvious and at times can easily distract from the religious mission of the church. On the other hand, realism indicates that the Roman Catholic church in the immediate future will not shed its role as a sovereign state and a participant with other states in international diplomatic activity. However, the dual identity will continued to be a source of tension for the social mission of the church in the future.

Justice in the Church

Only in 1971 did official Catholic social teaching acknowledge explicitly the connection between justice in the world and justice in the church. The synod of bishops in 1971 recognized "that anyone who ventures to speak to people about justice must first be just in their eyes." This document goes on to specify such subjects as the protection of the rights of all in the church, the right to fair wages and working conditions for church employees, the right of women to participate in the life of the community, the right to suitable freedom of expression and thought, and the right to justice that is speedy and gives the accused the right to know his or her accusers.[36] The ethical reasons that underpin the synod's statements are obvious. One cannot preach to others what one does not practice. However, a pre–Vatican II ecclesiology did not and could not take such an approach. If the church is a perfect society, as it has claimed to be for centuries, then there is no need for self-criticism. Vatican II emphasized the pilgrim nature of the church and to some extent even the sinful nature of the church. The human and sinful aspects of the church constantly call for criticism and conversion. Chapter 6 will explore this issue in greater detail.

The need for the church to be critical about its own witness to peace, poverty, and justice will become even more prominent in the future. Many Catholics today do not think that the church itself lives up to what the synod of bishops said in 1971. At the present and even more so in the future, the role of women in the church will be seen as an issue of justice, despite official denials to the contrary.

Social-Ethical Methodologies

Four areas of concern will have to be dealt with in the future approach of the hierarchical teaching office to the social teaching of the church in the area of social-ethical methodologies: an explicitly Christian approach as contrasted with an inclusively human approach, an emphasis on an organic and ordered society as distinguished from a more conflictual model, a multiplicity of different methodologies, and the discrepancies between the ethical methodologies currently employed in Catholic social teachings and the methodologies used in hierarchical teachings on sexual issues. Chapter 7 will develop my approach to the issue of an explicitly Christian or an inclusively human methodology. The other three issues will briefly be treated here.

Cooperation and Conflict

The tradition of Catholic social ethics insisted long before 1891 on an organic understanding of society. Catholic ethics emphasized that the state is a natural society insofar as human beings are called by nature to enter into social and political society in order to achieve their own good and fulfillment. This view understands society as an organism with all the different parts working together for the good of the whole. Such an understanding of society runs contrary to all philosophical and societal positions that consider political society as an evil that restricts the freedom of the individual. The Catholic organic view of society has often appealed to the metaphor of the body, with the hierarchical ordering of all parts that then work together for the good of the whole,[37] as moderate corporatism or solidarism that Pope Pius XI proposed for the economic order reflects. Capital and labor should not oppose one another but, rather, labor, capital, consumers, and all interested persons should work together harmoniously for the common good.

The traditional Catholic stress on an organic, hierarchically structured civil society explains the reluctance of Roman Catholic thought to accept democracy and basic human freedoms and rights. Catholics felt that democracy and human freedoms and rights were too individualistic and would result in corrosive and negative effects on the community. Pope Pius XII was the first Catholic pope to prefer democracy over all other forms of government.[38] Only in 1965 did the Declaration of Religious Freedom of the Second Vatican Council accept religious freedom.[39] In 1963 in *Pacem in Terris* Pope John XXIII proposed the first detailed explanation of human rights in official Catholic social teaching. To its credit, *Pacem in Terris* also included social and economic rights such as rights to food, clothing, and shelter as well as the political and civil rights that had been central to Enlightenment thinking.[40] Finally, Catholic social teaching came to accept that freedom, equality, and participation are important aspects of the common good of society.[41] However, even here, the Catholic tradition insists not only on "freedom from" but also on "freedom for." Likewise, rights exist together with corresponding duties.

In the Catholic organic view of society the heavy emphasis was on order, cooperation, and working together for the common good, but conflict was not totally denied. The broader Catholic ethical tradition accepted killing in self-defense, the just war theory, and even tyrannicide. Official Catholic social teaching from its very beginning with *Rerum Novarum* in 1891 sanctioned the right of workers to organize and to work for their own betterment. The accent of Catholic social ethics and of the official Catholic social teaching on order and harmony and the downplaying of conflict all cohere with Catholic ecclesiology. The church is universal and is called to embrace all; all should be able to find a home in the church where they can live together in mutual love and respect. In theory, the church has never ceased to point out that in Christ Jesus there is neither rich nor poor, male nor female, Jew nor gentile.

In recent times, more conflictual approaches have come to the fore. In the United States perhaps the most distinctive expression of Catholic social action has been the sort of community organization developed by Saul Alinsky and now heavily supported by the Catholic Campaign for Human Development. Conflictual tactics have been a primary method employed by such groups. Catholic social ethics has paid scant attention to what has probably been the most distinctive Catholic social action taking place in the United States today. In the 1950s, when Alinsky was actually working primarily with Catholic organizations in Chicago, some Protestant clerics and theologians strongly criticized his controversial tactics. However, then and even more so later, many Protestant thinkers and activists strongly supported the Alinsky method.[42] The best illustration of a conflictual method in contemporary Catholic social ethics is the liberation theology that has emerged in Latin America.

The future will probably bring a greater emphasis on more conflictual approaches on the part of many. How can such an emphasis coexist with the more organic view of society? First of all, the organic society approach has been modified somewhat over the years as is evident in the greater recognition given to democracy, freedom, and human rights in the contemporary Catholic tradition. However, the emphasis on people called to live in a community that seeks the common good that flows back to the good of the individuals has continued to be a fundamental position in official Catholic social teaching. I do not see how the Catholic tradition could ever adopt a totally conflictual view of civil society; there could be more emphasis on conflict as a tactic but not as an ultimate reality, for some conflict can be good and necessary as a means to a more just and fair social order. Gregory Baum, for example, has proposed a theory of partial solidarity that avoids the problems created by theories of class conflict.[43] The organic model of society will continue to be modified, but the basic emphasis on a communitarian understanding of human beings and society will remain.

Pluralism of Social-Ethical Methodologies

Until the 1960s Catholic social teaching insisted on a rather monolithic neoscholastic natural law methodology. Since then, however, Roman Catholic theology in general no longer claims to operate out of a perennial philosophy. From a theological perspective official Catholic social teaching no longer employs a natural law theory alone but has brought in appeals to scrip-

tural and theological warrants. From a philosophical perspective the more recent documents employ a greater personalism,
as illustrated in John Paul II's many writings. *Laborem Exercens,* for example, emphasizes the person and the subjective
aspect of work over the objective aspect of work done.[44] A
greater historical consciousness with its use of a more inductive
methodology became more apparent in the tradition culminating in *Octogesima Adveniens* of Pope Paul VI, which also
employed the philosophical concept of utopia.[45] However,
John Paul II does not seem to be as open to historical consciousness as was Paul VI.

The method of liberation theology is quite different from
the method employed in the social encyclicals. Liberation
theologians lay weight on praxis, commitment, and a theo-
logical-liberative hermeneutics. In a recent book with a more
conciliatory tone, Leonardo and Clodovis Boff insist on a very
complementary relationship between official Catholic social
teaching and liberation theology. The two sets of discourse
operate on different levels and have different objectives: "But
to the extent that the social teaching of the church provides
broad guidelines for Christian social activity, liberation theology tries, on the one hand, to integrate these guidelines into
its own synthesis, and, on the other, to clarify them in a
creative manner for the specific context of the third world."[46]
I think such an understanding too readily passes over the
glaring differences in the two methodologies.

The greater pluralism of methodologies in Catholic social
ethics will in the future cause more strains for official Catholic
social teachings on a universal level. Catholic social teaching
obviously must choose one or another methodology. In the
world of a growing diversity of methodologies it will be more
difficult to propose official Catholic social teaching for the
whole church.

Discrepancies between Methodologies
in Catholic Social and Sexual Teaching

As noted earlier, official Catholic social teaching and the
documents that express it endorse a moderate or realistic
optimism about society, and such an approach has a basis

in anthropology, eschatology, and ecclesiology. However, the official documents proposing Catholic sexual teaching have a very different tone. Here the teaching of the church is often proposed as countercultural and a sign of contradiction; the church says "yes" to the "no" of the world. Catholic teaching is also described as being prophetic, which means to show that it stands out from, and is opposed to, the teaching that is often found in the world. Pope John Paul II employs such an approach in his defense of Catholic opposition to artificial contraception and of other Catholic positions in the area of sexuality.[47] The irony is that such teachings also claimed to be based on the natural law that is available to all humankind. One can readily see that a good way to defend church teaching that is not accepted by most people is to claim that the gospel which is the basis for such a teaching is countercultural and will often be seen in opposition with the mores of the time. However, such a practical defense and shoring up of the teaching raises questions of consistency both with the natural law basis for such teaching and with the attitude to the world that is found in official Catholic social teaching.

The more philosophical aspects of the methodologies of the two different types of documents also differ significantly. The documents proposing social teaching have gradually adopted a more personalistic, historically conscious, and relationality-responsibility approach to ethics. Chapter 6 will explain in greater detail the development of a historically conscious methodology in official Catholic social teaching. The official sexual teachings rely on a methodology that is more naturalistic, classicist, and legalistic. The differences in the methodological approaches are glaring.[48] To be sure, differences exist between personal and social ethics, but these methodological differences cannot be explained away that easily. In the future, Catholic teaching will have to come to grips with the reality of these contrasts.

However, a tension between the methodology of personal or sexual ethics on the one hand and of social ethics on the other hand also exists in the world of Catholic moral theology in general as distinguished from official hierarchical teaching. For example, a recent book of readings in fundamental moral theology uses many different articles from different authors, but for the most part there is unanimity in proposing a more transcendental methodological approach with its emphasis on the subject.[49] However, such an approach is not very well suited to social ethics and is ordinarily not employed in social ethics. Social ethics by it very nature deals with the subject matter of the structures of society and the ways to try to bring about structural change. Thus Catholic moral theology and not just Catholic official teachings must face the problem of discrepancies and clear differences of approach in the methodologies used in the personal sphere and in the social sphere.

In conclusion, the major problem that will face official Catholic social teaching is a growing pluralism. It is not enough, however, just to say that this pluralism is a good thing and should be encouraged. Some methods seem contrary to the Catholic tradition and others cannot be dismissed easily as only complementary. This chapter has tried to discuss some of the more important issues that are unresolved at the present and that will continue to face official Catholic social teaching in the future.

NOTES

1. Pope Leo XIII, *Rerum Novarum,* in David M. Byers, ed., *Justice in the Marketplace: Collected Statements of the Vatican and the United States Catholic Bishops on Economic Policy, 1891-1984* (Washington, DC: United States Catholic Conference, 1985), pp. 9-41.

2. There is no official canon of these documents. Reception by the whole church has played an important role in choosing the documents to be included in this list. The following documents are usually included: Pope Leo XIII, *Rerum Novarum* (1891); Pope Pius XI, *Quadragesimo Anno* (1931); Pope John XXIII, *Mater et Magistra* (1961); Pope John XXIII, *Pacem in Terris* (1963); Second Vatican Council, *Gaudium et Spes* (1965); Pope Paul VI, *Populorum Progressio* (1967); Pope Paul VI, *Octogesima Adveniens* (1971); Synod of Bishops, *Justitia in Mundo* (1971); Pope Paul VI, *Evangelii Nuntiandi* (1975); Pope John Paul II, *Redemptor Hominis* (1979); Pope John Paul II, *Laborem Exercens* (1981); Pope John Paul II, *Sollicitudo Rei Socialis* (1987); Pope John Paul II, *Centesimus Annus* (1991). There are different collections of these

documents, but problems exist with most collections. Some omit the earlier encyclicals; some contain other materials; some include only selections from certain documents; many have become out of date and do not include later documents. I will usually cite Byers, *Justice in the Marketplace,* because it contains all the documents mentioned above with the exception of the last two, but the complete documents are not always given. Other collections include: Joseph Gremillion, ed., *The Gospel of Peace and Justice: Catholic Social Teaching since Pope John* (Maryknoll, NY: Orbis, 1976); David J. O'Brien and Thomas A. Shannon, eds., *Renewing the Face of the Earth: Catholic Documents on Peace, Justice, and Liberation* (Garden City, NY: Doubleday Image, 1977); Michael Walsh and Brian Davies, eds., *Proclaiming Justice and Peace: Documents from John XXIII–John Paul II* (Mystic, CT: Twenty-third, 1984).

3. *Pacem in Terris,* nn. 5–7, in Byers, *Justice in the Marketplace,* p. 151.

4. This very point was made in a fascinating Vatican document of lesser importance that points out many changes that occurred in the ten years since the publication of *Pacem in Terris.* See Cardinal Maurice Roy, "Reflections on the Occasion of the Tenth Anniversary of the Encyclical *Pacem in Terris* of Pope John XXIII," (11 April 1973), nn. 91, 92, in Gremillion, *Gospel of Peace and Justice,* p. 548.

5. For a fuller development of this point, see my *Directions in Catholic Social Ethics* (Notre Dame, IN: University of Notre Dame Press, 1985), pp. 43–69.

6. The future aspect of eschatology and the reign of God is absent from chapters 1 and 2 of part 1 of *Gaudium et Spes* (nn. 22 and 32), but the future aspect is recognized in chapter 3 (n. 39). See Gremillion, *Gospel of Peace and Justice,* pp. 260–261, 268, and 273–274.

7. John Paul II, *Sollicitudo Rei Socialis* (Vatican City: Vaticana, 1987), nn. 14–25, pp. 21–43.

8. Ibid., n. 26, pp. 43–46.

9. Ibid., n. 47, pp. 94–95.

10. See William D. Miller, *A Harsh and Dreadful Love: Dorothy Day and the Catholic Worker Movement* (Garden City, NY: Doubleday Image, 1974): William D. Miller, *Dorothy Day: A Biography* (New York: Harper and Row, 1982).

11. *Gaudium et Spes,* n. 78, in Gremillion, *Gospel of Peace and Justice,* p. 315.

12. John Paul II, *Redemptor Hominis,* n. 8, in Walsh and Davies, *Proclaiming Justice and Peace,* p. 246.

80   *Catholic Social Teaching*

13. Edward Schillebeeckx, *Jesus: An Experiment in Christology* (New York: Crossroad, 1981).

14. Jon Sobrino, *Christology at the Crossroads* (Maryknoll, NY: Orbis, 1978); Matthew Lamb, *Solidarity with Victims* (New York: Crossroad, 1982).

15. Ernst Troeltsch, *The Social Teaching of the Christian Churches*, 2 vols. (New York: Harper, 1960). Troeltsch distinguishes three main sociological types—the church, the sect, and mysticism.

16. *Gaudium et Spes*, n. 78, in Gremillion, *Gospel of Peace and Justice*, p. 315.

17. National Conference of Catholic Bishops, "The Pastoral Letter on War and Peace: The Challenge of Peace: God's Promise and Our Response," n. 118, *Origins* 13 (1983): 12.

18. H. Richard Niebuhr, *Christ and Culture* (New York: Harper, 1975), pp. 56ff.

19. Michael Mott, *The Seven Mountains of Thomas Merton* (Boston: Houghton Mifflin, 1984).

20. For the contemporary debate about the role of national conferences of bishops, see Thomas J. Reese, ed., *Episcopal Conferences: Historical, Canonical, and Theological Studies* (Washington: Georgetown University Press, 1989).

21. Second General Conference of Latin American Bishops, *The Church in the Present-Day Transformation of Latin America in the Light of the Council*, vol. 2: *Conclusions* (Washington, DC: United States Catholic Conference, 1973); John Eagleson and Philip Scharper, eds., *Puebla and Beyond* (Maryknoll, NY: Orbis, 1979); Edward L. Cleary, ed., *Born of the Poor: The Latin American Church since Medellín* (Notre Dame, IN: University of Notre Dame Press, 1990).

22. For a collection of earlier statements by the Roman Catholic bishops of the United States, see J. Brian Benestad and Francis J. Butler, eds., *Quest for Justice: A Compendium of Statements of the United States Catholic Bishops on the Political and Social Order 1966-1980* (Washington, DC: United States Catholic Conference, 1981); "The Pastoral Letter on War and Peace," *Origins* 13 (1983): 1-32; National Conference of Catholic Bishops, *Economic Justice for All: Pastoral Letter on Catholic Social Teaching and the U.S. Economy* (Washington, DC: United States Catholic Conference, 1986).

23. For the text and commentaries on the letters by the West German and French bishops, see James V. Schall, ed., *Out of Justice, Peace: Winning the Peace* (San Francisco: Ignatius, 1984).

24. *Quadragesimo Anno*, nn. 76-98, in Byers, *Justice in the Marketplace*, pp. 67-73.

25. Richard L. Camp, *The Papal Ideology of Social Reform: A Study in Historical Development, 1878-1967* (Leiden: E. J. Brill, 1969), pp. 128-135.

26. David Hollenbach, *Justice, Peace, and Human Rights: American Catholic Social Ethics in a Pluralistic World* (New York: Crossroad, 1988), especially pp. 87-100.

27. *Octogesima Adveniens*, n. 4, in Byers, *Justice in the Marketplace*, p. 225.

28. *Quadragesimo Anno*, n. 79, in Byers, *Justice in the Marketplace*, p. 68; *Mater et Magistra*, nn. 53-58, in Byers, *Justice in the Marketplace*, pp. 114-115. Note that *Mater et Magistra* recognizes a need for a greater state intervention in the light of growing complexities and problems.

29. Jan Schotte, "Rome Consultation on Peace and Disarmament: A Vatican Synthesis," *Origins* 12 (1983): 691-695.

30. "The Challenge of Peace," nn. 9-12, in *Origins* 13 (1983): 2, 3.

31. Charles E. Curran, *Tensions in Moral Theology* (Notre Dame, IN: University of Notre Dame Press, 1988), pp. 140-141.

32. For a comparison of official Catholic social teachings and the statements of the World Council of Churches, see Thomas Sieger Derr, *Barriers to Ecumenism: The Holy See and the World Council of Churches on Social Questions* (Maryknoll, NY: Orbis, 1983).

33. Oswald von Nell-Breuning, "The Drafting of *Quadragesimo Anno*," in Charles E. Curran and Richard A. McCormick, eds., *Readings in Moral Theology No. 5: Official Catholic Social Teaching* (New York: Paulist Press, 1986), pp. 60-68.

34. For a description of the process and the debates involved in the drafting of the pastoral letter on peace and war, see Jim Castelli, *The Bishops and the Bomb: Waging Peace in a Nuclear Age* (Garden City, NY: Doubleday Image, 1983).

35. E.g., Pope John Paul II, *Familiaris Consortio: The Role of the Christian Family in the Modern World* (Boston: Daughters of St. Paul, 1981).

36. *Justitia in Mundo*, in Byers, *Justice in the Marketplace*, p. 257.

37. For a classical understanding of the state in Catholic tradition, see Heinrich Rommen, *The State in Catholic Thought* (St. Louis: B. Herder, 1945).

38. Donal Dorr, *Option for the Poor: A Hundred Years of Vatican Social Teaching* (Maryknoll, NY: Orbis, 1983), pp. 76-79.

39. Abbott, pp. 675–696.

40. *Pacem in Terris,* nn. 9–45, in Byers, *Justice in the Marketplace,* pp. 151–159.

41. *Octogesima Adveniens,* n. 22, in Byers, *Justice in the Marketplace,* pp. 234–235.

42. David Finks, *The Radical Vision of Saul Alinsky* (New York: Paulist Press, 1984); and Sanford D. Horwitt, *Let Them Call Me Rebel: Saul Alinsky—His Life and Legacy* (New York: Alfred A. Knopf, 1989).

43. Gregory Baum, *Theology and Society* (New York: Paulist Press, 1987), pp. 32–47.

44. *Laborem Exercens,* n. 35, in Byers, *Justice in the Marketplace,* pp. 315–316.

45. *Octogesima Adveniens,* n. 35, in Byers, *Justice in the Marketplace,* pp. 239–240.

46. Leonardo Boff and Clodovis Boff, *Introducing Liberation Theology* (Maryknoll, NY: Orbis, 1988), p. 37.

47. Pope John Paul II, *Familiaris Consortio,* nn. 29–30, pp. 47–49.

48. Charles E. Curran, "Catholic Social and Sexual Teaching: A Methodological Comparison," *Theology Today* 44 (1987–1988): 425–440.

49. Ronald P. Hamel and Kenneth R. Himes, eds., *An Introduction to Christian Ethics: A Reader* (New York: Paulist Press, 1989), pp. 49–307.

4. Richard A. McCormick and the Living Tradition of Catholic Moral Theology

The Decree on Priestly Formation of the Second Vatican Council called for the renewal of moral theology.[1] No one can doubt that tremendous changes have occurred since those days. The theme of this book maintains that moral theology is a living tradition based on the creative fidelity that should mark the pilgrim existence of the community of the disciples of Jesus; and I also pointed out in the first chapter that the Catholic church in the period immediately preceding the Second Vatican Council was more centralized, authoritarian, and defensive than it had ever been before in its history. In the eyes of some people the changes that have taken place in Catholic moral theology since the Second Vatican Council make the discipline unrecognizable to one who knew it only in its pre-Vatican II form. However, despite these significant developments, a great deal of continuity in contemporary Catholic moral theology is to be found with what existed in the past.

The purpose of this chapter is to explore the living tradition of moral theology by looking at what has occurred in Catholic moral theology since the Second Vatican Council and then by focusing in a particular way on the moral theology of Richard A. McCormick, a Jesuit priest who is acknowledged to be one of the most significant international voices in Catholic moral theology during this period.

Catholic Moral Theology since Vatican II

Like so many other realities in the Catholic church, moral theology has undergone significant and widespread changes in the period since the close of the Second Vatican Council in 1965. Before the council, the manuals of moral theology that were the textbooks of the discipline had originated in the *Institutiones Theologiae Moralis* which came into existence in response to the reforms proposed in the sixteenth century by the Council of Trent.[2] Today's moral theology differs from moral-theological manuals in scope, method, and context, but significant continuities remain.

Scope

The primary purpose of the manuals of moral theology was to train confessors to perform their function as judges in the sacrament of penance. Confessors had to know which acts were sinful and whether the sin was mortal or venial. Within this narrow scope the manuals were individualistic, act centered, and minimalistic.

The scope of contemporary moral theology is life centered and emphasizes not just the acts or the doing of the person but the being of the person — anthropology and the basic orientations, attitudes, values, and virtues that should characterize the follower of Jesus. The Christian is called to the fullness of discipleship, not just to the minimum of avoiding sin. The roles of groups, associations, and nations must also receive great attention in discussing contemporary moral realities.

The moral-theological manuals came into existence after the Council of Trent to fulfill a very important pastoral need in reforming the life of the church. However, problems arise from equating such practical handbooks with all of moral theology. Even before the Council of Trent a casuistic strand in Catholic moral theology had existed that was connected especially with various formats of the sacrament of penance. As elaborated in the *Summa theologiae* of Thomas Aquinas, however, Catholic moral theology had a much broader purpose than the later manuals. Catholic moral theologians in the post-Vatican II era recognize that both the modern needs of moral theology and the historical tradition of the field are much broader in scope than the handbooks that had become identified with the entire discipline before the Second Vatican Council.

Method

The manuals employed a legal model of the Christian life. The objective norm of morality was the law which embraced the eternal law, divine positive law, natural law, and human law both in the church and in civil society. Conscience was the subjective norm of morality and conscience had to conform itself to the various laws comprising the objective norm of morality. An extrinsic and voluntaristic approach supported the legal model: the source of obligation came not from the moral reality itself but from outside it, from the will of the legislator; something is good because it is commanded. Ironically, such an approach deviated dramatically from the position of Thomas Aquinas, who insisted on an intrinsic and rational approach to morality—for him, something is commanded because it is good. The official Catholic teaching of the hierarchical magisterium was nevertheless interpreted according to the legal, juridical, and voluntaristic approach. The teaching authority of the church required submission and obedience on the part of Catholics.[3]

The manuals of moral theology did not in fact give much importance to the theological aspects of the discipline. For all practical purposes the natural law, understood as human reason reflecting on human nature, was the method employed. Appeals were made to the scriptures but as prooftexts often taken out of context to support a conclusion which had already been reached on the basis of a natural law approach. Aspects of Christology, grace, eschatology, and other theological disciplines did not enter into the arena of moral theology.

From a philosophical perspective the handbooks were wedded to a neoscholasticism that had frequently wandered away from the best of Thomas Aquinas. This neoscholasticism

was looked upon as the perennial philosophy; behind such
an understanding lay a classicist mentality with its emphasis
on eternal truths and immutable essences. A deductive methodology cohered with these particular philosophical underpinnings. Such a philosophy had not made the turn to the
subject, so the emphasis was all on the object.

Contemporary moral theology has been moving away from
the manuals of moral theology in all these areas.[4] The inade-
quacies of a legal model are readily and generally apparent.
Always having a place in the moral life, law cannot be the
primary model to be used to understand the God–human relationship. Teleological, deontological (but not juridically deontological), and responsibility models have been proposed in
place of the older legal model of the manuals. Thus the role
of official church teaching that comes from the hierarchical
magisterium is to be seen according to the new models
primarily under the category of teaching and not of juridical
authority imposing rules.

From a theological perspective attempts have been made
to understand moral theology as a theological discipline in
dialogue with systematic theology, spiritual theology, and
sacramental theology. Christology, pneumatology, anthropology, and eschatology all have important bearing on moral
theology (the preceding chapter has discussed some of these
theological perspectives in Catholic social teaching). However,
significant questions are faced in the attempt to make moral
theology more theological. How can one integrate all these
aspects of so many different disciplines? How does Christian
morality relate to human morality (a question to be discussed
in chapter 7)?

From a philosophical perspective, Catholic moral theology
is no longer wedded to neoscholasticism, for a variety of
philosophical partners in dialogue exists today as we must
recognize a legitimate pluralism of philosophical approaches.
The demise of the perennial philosophy followed from the
rejection of classicism and the acceptance of historical consciousness. Greater emphasis is now given to the particular,
the individual, the contingent, and the developing. Such an
approach does not believe in eternal essences and embraces

a more inductive methodology. The turn to the subject has characterized much of contemporary Catholic theology, as seen in the work of Karl Rahner and Bernard Lonergan. The person is both subject and agent who expresses and molds his- or herself as a person in the act of doing something. Moral theology's emphasis on the role of the fundamental option and of conversion illustrates the role of the subject in contemporary thought.[5]

Context

Three changing contexts have greatly affected the discipline of moral theology—the church, the world, and the academy. The moral theology of the manuals existed in a church that accentuated the institutional, hierarchical, and juridical approach to its own life and existence. The church itself was often living in its own ghetto, withdrawn from the world. Fear of contemporary developments in the world erected barricades to keep the church pure from any outside defilement. Truth was sought and said to be found totally within the Catholic tradition that claimed to have a perennial philosophy and theology that could withstand the changing tides of any and all modern philosophies. Theology and moral theology found their natural home in seminaries and theologates; with their high walls and rustic settings, these institutions embodied separation from the world.

The Second Vatican Council emphasized the church as the people of God on pilgrimage. Many biblical metaphors were employed to move away from a single institutional model.[6] The hierarchical office exists as a service within the church and for the church but is not identical with the church. The role and gifts of all the people of God also become more important for the moral life of the church and for systematic reflection on that life. Whereas non-Catholic Christians had been treated in theological manuals only as adversaries, now true dialogue was opening up with other Christians and even with non-Christians, thanks to Vatican II's Decree on Ecumenism. And today Catholic moral theology maintains close contact with Protestant ethicians.

Moral theology is always done in and for the church. The most significant ecclesial aspect of moral theology in the post-Vatican II period has been the dissent on the part of many moral theologians, including Richard A. McCormick, from authoritative, noninfallible church teaching on moral matters. The question came to the fore especially in response to Pope Paul VI's 1968 encyclical, *Humanae Vitae,* which condemned artificial contraception for spouses. McCormick and others justify the legitimacy of such dissent on the fact that specific moral issues are removed from the core of faith and involve so much specificity and complexity that one cannot claim a certitude that excludes the possibility of error in dealing with them. The hierarchical magisterium has been reluctant to accept the legitimacy of such dissent (the next chapter will analyze McCormick's position on the magisterium and on dissent). Tensions between moral theologians like Richard A. McCormick and the hierarchical magisterium have been especially pronounced in the issues of sexual and medical ethics.

The whole approach of Vatican II stressed the need, not for isolation, but for dialogue with the modern world; the ghetto walls were torn down. Catholic Christians could learn from the world and from many others in the world. Dialogue does not mean acceptance of everything in the world but, rather, a critical and open encounter. Dialogue with the world is in keeping with the traditional Catholic emphasis on faith and reason.

Deep and significant changes have occurred in the world in the years since Vatican II. Throughout the world people are striving to live in a more just, participative, peaceful, and sustainable society. The hierarchical magisterium in the documents of popes and bishops deserves much credit for considering many of these issues.[7] Although seen all over the world, the quest for justice has impelled the development of particularly distinctive approaches to theology in the Third World. Liberation theology, which came to the fore in Latin America, maintains that the gospel's message aims to free humankind from oppression in all its forms—spiritual, historical, political, and economic; the preferential option for the poor has become an important part of Catholic social ethics due to the work of liberation theologians. In all parts of the world marginalized and oppressed people are struggling to participate ever more fully in the life of their society and to shape their own destinies. The other side of the coin requires society to enable all its members to enjoy and to participate fully in the life of that society. Also in the context of the struggle for justice and participation, issues about the role of women have begun to move into a position of prominence. Reflecting on this experience, feminist theology has been developed as a criticism of, and challenge to, much of what has gone before. Further, the intensity of the cold war, with our fear of nuclear annihilation, has subsided, but all around the globe incursions across the boundaries of other nations occur and revolutions for justice and independence within countries continue (chapter 10 will discuss the issue of military force and arms). Similarly, the modern world is much more conscious than ever before of ecology and of the threat to our environment from much of our contemporary technology. All of these developments have raised important issues and concerns for moral theology.

Before the Second Vatican Council Catholic moral theologians were practically the only theologians who were interested in medical ethics. However, burgeoning technological developments in biomedicine have occasioned many ethical dilemmas for our society. Today there exists the new discipline of bioethics, and Catholic moral theology now has many new issues and problems as well as new dialogue partners trying to deal with the concerns. Relationships among human beings have changed in many ways, and Catholic moral theology must also deal with these. Many tensions have become evident in dealing with the so-called sexual revolution. Yes, Catholic moral theology is concerned with many new issues and is developing itself and its own methodologies in the process. However, such changes and developments are in keeping with its fundamental and traditional stances of emphasizing the role of human reason and attempting to discover what the truly human is in the changing circumstances of time and place.

The context or space in which theology is done has also changed within Roman Catholicism. The isolated seminary was the primary locus for theology before Vatican II. Richard McCormick's personal history illustrates this change well. He studied theology at the Jesuit theologate in West Baden, Indiana. Later, he taught there and at its subsequent relocations to more urban centers so that the theologate would not be isolated. In 1974 he became the Rose F. Kennedy Professor of Christian Ethics at the Kennedy Institute of Ethics that had been established at Georgetown University. In 1986 he became the John A O'Brien Professor of Christian Ethics at the University of Notre Dame. No longer examined only in the seminary for those studying for the ministry, moral theology is also an academic discipline housed in the university. The discipline's academic nature has had significant ramifications. The new home of moral theology has helped to widen the scope of the older manuals, and moral theology in the college and university is in dialogue with all other subjects in the academy. Before Vatican II all the practitioners of moral theology were male clerics: Today the professoriate in moral theology includes women and many laypeople. The academic aspect of moral theology emphasizes the need for greater theoretical rigor and coherence in developing the discipline. Catholic theologians in the academy, especially in the United States, have insisted on the same academic freedom for their work that is part and parcel of American higher education in general. The hierarchical church has not accepted that freedom and problems continue to exist in this area (the ninth chapter will discuss some aspects of academic freedom and theology in Catholic institutions of higher learning).

Continuities

Despite so many changes, however, there are also significant continuities of post-Vatican II moral theology with the earlier Catholic tradition. Mediation has always characterized the Catholic theological approach so that in the area of morality the divine is seen as working in and through the

human. In the Catholic tradition grace does not destroy or
do away with the human. The primary emphasis on faith does
not do away with the human response of works.

In the light of this emphasis on mediation the Catholic
tradition has given great importance to the life and actions
of Christians in this world. The Christian and the Church
are not called to withdraw from the world but to transform
it. Life and action in the world have always been emphasized
in the Catholic tradition. The church works with all people
of good will to bring about greater justice and peace in the
world. Modern Catholic social teaching has been associated
with the papal social encyclicals beginning with Pope Leo
XIII's in 1891, but recently this social mission is seen as a
constitutive dimension of the preaching of the gospel and of
the church's mission for the redemption of the human race.[8]

Many moral theologians today question some aspects of
the philosophical understanding of the natural law methodology but agree with its basic theological insight that human
reason can arrive at true ethical wisdom and knowledge. Emphasis on the role of human reason in the epistemological
sphere illustrates the Catholic accent on mediation. Detailed
rational analysis of human action is necessary for the moral
theologian in order to arrive at moral truth.[9]

The Catholic tradition in morality, with its recognition of
the importance of human actions and the role of reason, has
employed casuistry as a means of arriving at the ethical evaluation of particular actions. Casuistry has been abused in the
past, but the discussion and comparison of specific cases con-
tributes to the forming of apt moral judgments about particular human actions.[10]

Moral theology continues to be a discipline in the service
of the church and especially in the formation of the consciences of members of the church and of the church community. As noted above, the development of moral theology
has been greatly affected by the church's penitential discipline.
Such a narrow understanding of the role of moral theology
has contributed to the need for its renewal at the present time,
but moral theology will always be important for the total life
of the church.

Richard A. McCormick's Contribution
to Moral Theology

The vision of moral theology depicted above is shared by many, but not by all, in the Catholic church today. Richard A. McCormick has made a great contribution to this understanding of moral theology, for he wants contemporary moral theology to be open, ecumenical, insight oriented, collegial, honest, centered on Christ, scientifically informed, adult, realistic, Catholic, and catholic.[11]

McCormick was born in 1922, entered the Society of Jesus in 1940, received his B.A. in 1945 from Loyola University in Chicago and his M.A. in 1950 from the same institution, did his theological studies at the Jesuit theologate at West Baden, and was ordained a priest in 1953. He received his S.T.D. (doctorate in sacred theology) from the Pontifical Gregorian University in Rome in 1957 with a thesis on the removal of a probably dead fetus to save the mother's life.[12] McCormick began his career as a moral theologian in 1957 at the theologate of the Jesuits which was then still at West Baden; he moved on after seventeen years to a chair at Georgetown University and then, in 1986, to his current chair at Notre Dame.

Our author's greatest contribution to moral theology are his "Notes on Moral Theology," which he published for twenty consecutive years from 1965 to 1984 in the journal *Theological Studies*. The custom for *Theological Studies* was to have two different authors review the literature in moral theology every six months. Such a policy was followed with McCormick until the first issue of 1977, when he reviewed all the literature from the previous year. McCormick was such a master bibliographic annotator and essayist that no other scholars could be found to match his gifts and abilities. His yearly "Notes" have been subsequently collected in two volumes: *Notes on Moral Theology 1965 through 1980* and *Notes on Moral Theology 1981 through 1984*.[13]

A word must be said about the literary genre of the "Notes." Its purpose is to review, analyze, and criticize current periodical literature dealing with moral theology. The task is daunting, and selectivity is necessary amid a field with such a large output. Objectivity calls for a brief but accurate description of each author's thesis. Analysis and criticism require perceptive and penetrating comments and responses. The material covers the whole area of moral theology and thus requires a breadth and depth that few people have, but brevity calls for all this to be done in a comparatively short space. McCormick became the acknowledged master of this genre, which is so much more than a simple bibliographical survey. Since he resigned in 1984 the editor of *Theological Studies* has had to divide his work up among a number of different scholars while McCormick still makes some occasional contributions.

As author of the "Notes" from 1965 to 1984 McCormick chronicled and gave direction to the tremendous changes that were taking place in Catholic moral theology. In both selecting the most important aspects of the current literature and responding to it he helped set and record the agenda for Catholic moral theology in one of the most tumultuous periods of its development. Authors of outstanding books can at times make very original and pace-setting contributions to a particular field, but such works by definition cannot touch the whole field. McCormick's "Notes" and his mastery of their genre, however, gave direction to the entire field of moral theology.

The author of the "Notes on Moral Theology" thus gave a perfect example of how one works with a living tradition, which the church and its theology also strive to do. A knowledge of the rich tradition of Catholic theology is important but one must also recognize that such a tradition must be continually developed, changed, and reappropriated in the light of ongoing historical, social, and cultural changes. One must avoid both the rigidity of an inflexible traditionalism and the itch for novelty that refuses to acknowledge the importance of a tradition. The moral theologian truly serves and conserves the tradition by recognizing it as a living tradition responding to the contemporary developments that have been momentous within both the world and the church.

The twenty years of McCormick's "Notes" illustrate well the characteristics necessary for one who deals with a living tradition—respectful, dialogical, open, critical, objective, serene, and never without a sense of humor. Our author frequently changed his mind in the course of this ongoing dialogue, for he was always open to be convinced by other, better arguments and reasons even though in the beginning he had often raised critical problems against some positions that he later embraced.

McCormick's mastery of this genre owes much to his own character traits and his writing skills. A moral theologian should be a judicious, objective, calm, well-balanced observer who needs to be convinced but is not unduly hesitant to decide and has the courage of his convictions. McCormick abounds in all these virtues. He does not have an enlarged ego or a need to dominate or control. Humility, honesty, and forthrightness characterize his person and his professional life. The author of "Notes" obviously has a penchant for the practical rather than the speculative, and he combines a rigorous, rational analysis with a pastor's concern for the dilemmas faced by many people in the church.

His literary style fits the genre of "Notes" perfectly. His writing is clear, crisp, succinct, respectful, and always to the point. His lucid and accurate summaries and his penetrating analysis show the work of a marvelous crafter of sentences and paragraphs. The approach and style of the "Notes" has become so much of a part of the Jesuit moralist that he approaches almost all his writing through dialogue with other authors. Thus in his "Notes on Moral Theology" McCormick has made a significant and singular contribution to moral theology.

However, there are limits to the literary genre that consumed so much of our author's time and energy. By definition such a genre does not and cannot provide opportunity for a systematic development of the field of moral theology in general or of any one topic. The material treated will necessarily be somewhat limited. Methodological issues such as Christology and eschatology are missing; questions dealing with orientation, character, and the virtues receive less attention. Broader social issues, such as ecology and the very concept of social responsibility, are not fully developed.

Quandary ethics and particular problems receive the most discussion.

The fault or, perhaps better, the limitation is not only McCormick's, however. Yes, he selected the materials to be discussed; but the genre itself, the traditional role of the Catholic moral theologian, and the issues facing society have contributed to the agenda for the "Notes." The genre of the "Notes" first involves a review of the recent periodical literature, so books and monographs are not explicitly treated. Because longer monographs usually deal with the more theoretical and methodological issues while periodical literature is better adapted to discuss particular problems and issues that arise in any given year, a survey of periodical literature does not give one the opportunity to stand back and analyze deeper issues and trends. Catholic moral theology has consistently dealt with the particular problems facing the church community in its life in the world and in the church itself, and a pastoral dimension has always formed an important part of Catholic moral theology. This strong practical orientation is evident in the "Notes." The call for ethical considerations in society today deals primarily with the pressing problems facing our world. Thus it is in the area of medical ethics that McCormick has responded to many of the dilemmas facing individuals and society today.

In his attempt as a moral theologian in the Catholic church to make this tradition a living reality our author has been more reactive than proactive. He has responded to the work of others in the "Notes" and thereby pushed forward his understanding and agenda. This is one very important way of dealing with a tradition and keeping it alive. Others will adopt more creative and even more radical approaches in their dealing with the tradition and trying to move it forward. The genre of the "Notes" makes it most expert practitioner an incrementalist reformer.

The generalists in moral theology might well be a dying breed, and one can understand why. However, in the "Notes" McCormick has shown how one can combine the breadth of the generalist with the depth of perceptive criticism of the specialist in all these issues. In general, social ethics has received less attention from McCormick than any other part of the discipline of moral theology. The area of his greatest interest has been bioethics, which was the area of his own doctoral dissertation and was perhaps influenced by the fact that his father was a well-known physician in Toledo, Ohio, and a president of the American Medical Association. Especially at the Kennedy Institute of Ethics at Georgetown, McCormick devoted much time to bioethics. His books in this area, which often follow the approach and the style of the "Notes," are *How Brave a New World?* and *Health and Medicine in the Catholic Tradition.*[14]

The American Jesuit's most significant contribution to fundamental moral theology has been his work on proportionalism, or the grounding of moral norms. This question arises in the light of the discussion in Catholic moral theology about many of the norms that are being questioned in sexual morality and of the broader considerations about situation ethics, utilitarianism, and the role of absolute norms in contemporary Christian ethics and moral philosophy. He has addressed this question frequently in the "Notes" as well as in his Père Marquette Lecture at Marquette University (*Ambiguity in Moral Choice*) and in a volume edited with Paul Ramsey (*Doing Evil to Achieve Good*).

In 1989 Georgetown University Press published *The Critical Calling,* which updates and expands essays that had appeared in the last few years and had dealt with some of the problematic issues facing Catholic moral theology. I have had the privilege of working with McCormick in coediting what is now a seven-volume series of *Readings in Moral Theology,* which treats significant topics in fundamental moral theology.[15]

McCormick has advocated positions in the last thirty years that differ from the positions previously held in the Catholic church. In the 1960s in dialogue with other Catholic moral theologians, McCormick gradually changed his position and accepted the morality of responsible contraception. He has proposed positions on sterilization, divorce and remarriage, homosexuality, artificial insemination, and the principle of double effect that also differ from the accepted teaching. Above all, he has insisted on the legitimacy of theological dissent from authoritative, noninfallible hierarchical teaching. However, our author has also relied heavily on the Catholic tradition to shape his approach to what should be done with the terminally ill and the dying. McCormick's readers see a scholar working out of a tradition that has shaped him but that he himself shapes in turn into a living tradition.[16]

I believe that McCormick's *traditionalism,* in the best sense of that term, is illustrated above all in his method. The full title of his latest book, a collection of previously published studies, gives convincing evidence about his approach and method — *The Critical Calling: Reflections on Moral Dilemmas since Vatican II.* In this book McCormick addresses some of the more important moral dilemmas that face Christians in our changing times. His concern is not primarily theory or method in the abstract but the concrete and particular dilemmas that Christians face in a changing world. The critical calling describes the function and challenge of the moral theologian in the church who is trying to study these problems in the light of the living tradition of Catholic moral theology. McCormick is primarily a casuist, that is, he studies the morality of a particular case in light of relevant norms and similar cases.

This approach of McCormick's most recent book is the same perspective that has consistently stood out in his works, especially "The Notes on Moral Theology." McCormick's most significant theoretical contribution is his development of proportionalism. Here too, however, the theory developed in the light of his dealing with particular questions. Our author began with his dissatisfaction with the principle of the double effect and with the practical consequences of its distinction between a direct and an indirect act. The theory of proportionalism developed as a better explanation of the ambiguity of moral decision making. Even his approach to elucidating the theory of proportionality relies very heavily on its application to particular cases. McCormick does not develop a metaphysics of human acts.[17]

McCormick's perspective and method of casuistry — a very venerable tradition in Catholic moral reasoning — have been associated historically with the work of the Society of Jesus.

The key to understanding McCormick is to realize that he has been shaped and formed by traditional Catholic and Jesuit casuistry.

The Catholic moral tradition has always placed a great importance on how Christians act. The gospel calls Christians to a new way of life and is not just something to be believed but also something to do. Traditionally, the Catholic emphasis has seen faith as mediated through works. At times Catholicism has not avoided the dangers of Pelagianism and semi-Pelagianism, with their insistence that we are saved by works and not by faith. The penitential discipline in the Catholic church has always emphasized the importance of particular actions and how one acts and lives in this world.

In this context, casuistry has played an important role in the Catholic church's approach to morality. Think about the early church which dealt with questions of Christian participation in the theater or in the military. However, the high point of casuistry was marked in the seventeenth and eighteenth centuries. Then and since in the Catholic church, casuistry has been intimately associated with the Society of Jesus. In fact the common enemies of casuistry and the Jesuits made both *casuistical* and *Jesuitical* into pejorative terms that were almost synonymous.[18]

The Jesuits' commitment to casuistry was intimately connected with their own self-understanding.[19] They were the first "worldly" religious community to be both bound by traditional vows and to work with and among people in the world. They were involved in the world and were active rather than being withdrawn and contemplative. They were counselors to rulers and to the elite. They provided guidance about how people should live their daily lives.

The Society of Jesus tried to carry out the reforms of the Council of Trent, one of which involved an increased and more fruitful celebration of the sacrament of penance. The training of Jesuit priests was geared to help them carry out their function as judges in this sacrament. The *ratio studiorum* or "plan of studies" of the Society of Jesus put heavy emphasis on casuistry.

The handbooks of moral theology that I mentioned earlier really began as the notes of professors who taught in the Jesuit seminary in Rome. The two-year course provided by the *ratio studiorum* was heavily oriented toward the practical issues and problems that people would face in the world. Every week in the Society of Jesus the members in each house all participated in the discussion of a particular case of conscience. Many books of cases of conscience were written by Jesuit theologians who first proposed the cases in the weekly conference with other Jesuits.

There were abuses of casuistry as there are abuses of all earthly realities. Casuistry is usually abused in a laxist manner by ingeniously finding ways to get around one's responsibilities and obligations. In the scriptures Jesus condemned some of his contemporaries for this abuse. In the seventeenth century the Holy Office condemned a number of laxist positions that had been proposed. Examples include the following: we are able to satisfy the precept of loving our neighbor by only external acts; one can as a rule kill a thief even to protect one gold piece; it is permitted for a gentleman to kill an aggressor who attempts to calumniate him, if the shame cannot otherwise be avoided; similarly, he may kill one who slaps or beats him, and then flees.[20] John Caramuel, a Cistercian monk and bishop, was called the "prince of laxists" while another moralist was known as the "lamb of God" because he took away so many sins.[21]

In the seventeenth century Blaise Pascal spearheaded a campaign against casuistry and Jesuits alike. Both were accused of laxism and of having diluted the moral obligations of the Christian life. Later on the Jesuits were suppressed by the pope.[22] In my judgment Pascal was wrong on both counts. Casuistry by its very nature is not laxist and the vast majority of Jesuit theologians were not laxists. However, through the efforts of Pascal and others casuistry often took on pejorative connotations.

The renewal of moral theology at the time of Vatican II reacted negatively to the casuistry of the manuals of moral theology. In my judgment the problem of the manuals was

not their casuistry as such but their reduction of all moral
theology to casuistry in order to determine the existence and
gravity of sinful behavior. The problem was the substitution
of casuistry for the whole of moral theology.

An old Latin axiom reminds us that "the abuse does not
take away the use." Albert R. Jonsen and Stephen Toulmin
have taken the title of their book *The Abuse of Casuistry* from
the statement of the Anglican casuist Kenneth Kirk: "The
abuse of casuistry is properly directed, not against all casuistry
but only against its abuse."[23] Casuistry is a very helpful and
necessary method of judging what should be done in quandary
situations. The use of the case method in law as well as in
business, medical, and personal ethics illustrates the important role of casuistry. It must always be one important aspect
or method in moral theology, but moral theology's approach
and method includes more; an important component of moral
theology casuistry is not the whole discipline.

Richard McCormick continues the best of the casuistic tradition. Deeply schooled and trained in the pre-Vatican II
casuistry of Jesuit education, our American Jesuit has brought
the skillful use of this approach to the problems facing the
church and the world in the post-Vatican II era. As a true
and good casuist, McCormick uses common sense, perceptive analysis, a critical intelligence, and an ability to cut
through the debate to the salient features of a problem. His
acute casuistic perspective explains why McCormick has been
so respected a contributor to Catholic moral theology in the
post-Vatican II era and at the same time indicates the areas
and concerns that lie outside his professional interests. McCormick in his person and in his work illustrates well the fact
that moral theology is a living tradition, which with its continuities and discontinuities always strives for creative fidelity
to the word and work of Jesus.

NOTES

1. Decree on Priestly Formation, n. 16, in Walter M. Abbott,
ed., *The Documents of Vatican II* (New York: Guild Press, 1966),
p. 452.

2. For the formation of the *Institutiones Theologiae Moralis,* see Louis Vereecke, "Preface a l'historie de la théologie morale moderne," *Studia Moralia* 1 (1963): 87–120. There is no definitive published history of moral theology, but the best available source is a mimeographed publication for students at the Accademia Alfonsiana in Rome — Louis Vereecke, *Storia della teologia morale moderna,* 4 vols. (Rome: Accademia Alfonsiana, 1979–1980).

3. The best available book in English on the development of moral theology which does not claim to be a thorough history is John Mahoney, *The Making of Moral Theology: A Study of the Roman Catholic Tradition* (Oxford: Clarendon, 1987). For his discussion of the developing issues of law and the teaching authority of the church, see pp. 116–174 and 224–258. For an overview of the history of moral theology and an evaluation of the recent moral theology in the United States, see my *Toward an American Catholic Moral Theology* (Notre Dame, IN: University of Notre Dame Press, 1987), pp. 3–51.

4. For my own methodological approach to moral theology, see *Directions in Fundamental Moral Theology* (Notre Dame, IN: University of Notre Dame Press, 1985), especially pp. 3–27.

5. For the turn to the subject in contemporary moral theology, see Mahoney, *Making of Moral Theology,* pp. 175–223.

6. Avery Dulles, *Models of the Church* (New York: Doubleday, 1974).

7. See, for example, John A. Coleman, ed., *One Hundred Years of Catholic Social Thought: Celebration and Challenge* (Maryknoll, NY: Orbis, 1991). See also above, chapter 4, where I discuss some of the methodological aspects of Catholic social teaching.

8. *Justitia in Mundo,* in David M. Byers, ed., *Justice in the Marketplace: Catholic Statements of the Vatican and United States Catholic Bishops on Economic Policy, 1891–1984* (Washington, DC: United States Catholic Conference, 1985), p. 250.

9. See Charles E. Curran and Richard A. McCormick, eds., *Readings in Moral Theology No. 7: Natural Law and Theology* (New York: Paulist Press, 1991).

10. For a significant and important work on casuistry that I will use in subsequent pages but with which I have some reservations, see Albert R. Jonsen and Stephen Toulmin, *The Abuse of Casuistry: A History of Moral Reasoning* (Berkeley: University of California Press, 1988).

11. Richard A. McCormick, *The Critical Calling: Reflections on Moral Dilemmas since Vatican II* (Washington, DC: Georgetown University Press, 1989), p. xii.

102   *Richard A. McCormick*

12.   Richard A. McCormick, "The Removal of a Fetus Probably Dead to Save the Life of the Mother" (S.T.D. dissertation, Rome, Pontificia Universitas Gregoriana, 1957).

13.   Richard A. McCormick, *Notes on Moral Theology 1965 through 1980* (Washington, DC: University Press of America, 1981); *Notes on Moral Theology 1981–1984* (Lanham, MD: University Press of America, 1984).

14.   Richard A. McCormick, *How Brave a New World? Dilemmas in Bioethics* (Garden City, NY: Doubleday, 1981); *Health and Medicine in the Catholic Tradition* (New York: Crossroad, 1984).

15.   Richard A. McCormick and I have edited the following volumes, all of them published by Paulist Press in New York: *Readings in Moral Theology No. 1: Moral Norms in Catholic Tradition* (1979); *Readings in Moral Theology No. 2: The Distinctiveness of Christian Ethics* (1980); *Readings in Moral Theology No. 3: The Magisterium and Morality* (1982); *Readings in Moral Theology No. 4: The Use of Scripture in Moral Theology* (1984); *Readings in Moral Theology No. 5: Official Catholic Social Teaching* (1986); *Readings in Moral Theology No. 6: Dissent in the Church* (1988); *Readings in Moral Theology No. 7: Natural Law and Theology* (1991).

16.   For an appreciation and evaluation of McCormick's work, see Charles E. Curran, ed., *Moral Theology: Challenges for the Future: Essays in Honor of Richard A. McCormick* (New York: Paulist Press, 1990).

17.   Richard A. McCormick, *Ambiguity in Moral Choice* (Milwaukee: Marquette University Press, 1973); Richard A. McCormick and Paul Ramsey, eds., *Doing Evil to Achieve Good: Moral Choice in Conflict Situations* (Chicago: Loyola University Press, 1978).

18.   Jonsen and Toulmin, *Abuse of Casuistry*, pp. 12–16.

19.   Ibid., pp. 139–152.

20.   Henricus Denzinger et al., eds., *Enchiridion Symbolorum Definitionum et Declarationum de Rebus Fidei et Morum*, 32d ed. (Barcelona: Herder, 1963), n. 2110, n. 2131, n. 2130.

21.   Mahoney, *Making of Moral Theology*, p. 138.

22.   Jonsen and Toulmin, *Abuse of Casuistry*, pp. 231–249.

23.   Ibid., p. 16.

5. The Teaching Function of the Church in Morality

The Christian community has always seen its belief in Jesus as entailing a way of life and as influencing how the individual Christian and the Christian community should live in this world. The distinctive aspect of the Roman church involves a hierarchical teaching office. Pope and bishops have a special teaching office in the church that is often said to have as its object both faith and morals. An important question for moral theology as the scientific and thematic reflection on the Christian moral life in the Catholic tradition concerns exactly how the hierarchical teaching office functions in the teaching of morality and its relationship to the consciences of believers and to other roles and functions in the church.

In the last few decades the role of the hierarchical teaching office in moral questions has become the most significant moral issue that the church has faced. Moral theologians have often had to delve deeply into the related theological discipline of ecclesiology to address the question adequately. Many practical implications of ecclesiology have surfaced in the contemporary discussions and disputes which often center on the possibility and legitimacy of dissent from authoritative, noninfallible hierarchical teaching in moral matters.

This perennial question came to the front and hottest burner in contemporary Catholic life and theology in reaction to *Humanae Vitae,* the 1968 encyclical of Pope Paul VI that condemned any use of artificial contraception for spouses.[1] Since then both in theory and in practice the question of dissent has been central in Catholicism. Is dissent from authoritative church teaching on moral matters legitimate? Do Catholics have a right to dissent? How frequently can dissent occur? What are the limits of dissent? How does the hierarchical teaching office in the church work? How should it work? What is the proper response of Roman Catholic believers to this teaching office?

Richard A. McCormick, whose general approach to moral theology was discussed in the last chapter, has not only lived through this stormy period in the life of the Catholic church, but he has been one of the most significant voices in interpreting what has been happening and why. By the nature of their vocation moral theologians deal with the practical day-to-day issues that face the life of the church and the world. McCormick's particular talents and gifts have emphasized scholarly involvement in such practical moral issues. As the last chapter pointed out, he stands tall in the long tradition of Catholic and Jesuit casuistry. For twenty years beginning in 1965 McCormick wrote the "Notes on Moral Theology" for the Jesuit publication *Theological Studies.*[2] These "Notes" reviewed the most important periodical literature in the Western world dealing with moral theology and won McCormick worldwide recognition for the perceptiveness of his analysis and criticism. He has not written a systematic treatise on moral theology; in addition to the "Notes" he has often addressed the burning issues of the day in short articles in *America,* the Jesuit weekly. Our author's discussion of the hierarchical teaching office in moral matters has been developed in this same context.

This chapter will document the development that took place in McCormick's own positions with regard to the teaching office in the church as he studied the practical and theological issues raised by the official Catholic teaching in artificial contraception in the 1960s. A second section will develop in the light of McCormick's approach and other contributions a more systematic understanding of how the teaching–learning process should function in the church in moral matters. A final section will criticize how the hierarchical teaching office has been operating in practice in the life of the church.

McCormick's Development

In recent years McCormick has often pointed out two different understandings of the hierarchical magisterium and how a change from one to the other took place in the light of developments within the church, especially Vatican Council II (1962-1965).[3] The older juridical model of the church, which was supported by a neoscholastic theology, heavily stressed the authority of the teaching office. Authoritative decrees required the submission and obedience of all Catholics. Theologians had the primary function of explaining and defending the teachings. In a more systematic discussion from 1969, the Jesuit moral theologian pointed out three characteristics of this overly juridical and neoscholastic understanding of the hierarchical teaching office in the church. Such an approach unduly separated the functions of teaching and of learning, with one consequence being a heavy emphasis on the right to teach but little attention to the duty incumbent on the teacher to learn. The total teaching function of the church was one-sidedly identified with the hierarchy and not enough importance was given to the role of everyone involved in the teaching office as seen especially in both the *sensus fidelium* and the scholarly work of theologians. Such an understanding highlighted and isolated a single aspect of the teaching function — the judgmental.

Theological changes brought about by Vatican II produced an understanding of the church as a communion and as the people of God and did away with the pyramid model with the hierarchy at the top as the real church. Likewise authority was reconceived as decentralized and as calling for dialogue and participation. In an ecumenical environment we must be more willing to be open to learning from other Christians and all human beings. Clergy and laity are now much better educated and informed. Laypeople have their own areas of competence. As a society we are more conscious that teaching involves an openness to learn through dialogue and entry into the learning and teaching process which is ongoing. As a result of these and other influences a new understanding of teaching has emerged in the church. This renewed approach has three characteristics: the learning process forms an integral part of the teaching process; teaching must be a multidimensional function with the judgmental being only one of its aspects; the teaching function involves the charism of many people, not just of the hierarchy.[4] Thus by 1970 McCormick recognized a new understanding of the teaching role of the church in moral matters. The new understanding did not dawn on him as a result of armchair theologizing but was the product of his own scholarly and personal involvement in the tumultuous period of the late 1960s. McCormick himself had begun teaching moral theology in 1957 with a very juridical notion of the church and of the teaching authority in the church. The development of his work came through his struggles with the question of authoritative church teaching in the late 1960s, especially as seen in the official condemnation of artificial contraception for married couples.

In his writings as late as 1964 the American Jesuit strongly defended the official teaching of the Catholic church condemning artificial contraception for married couples.[5] In this context dissent from official church teaching was not a burning issue for him. The historical context is necessary for understanding and interpreting what was taking place. No Catholic theologian had publicly questioned the official teaching of the church on artificial contraception before 1963.[6] Dissent was not really talked about as a significant theological issue. In retrospect, one is amazed by the rapidity of the changes that took place in Catholic self-understanding. The spirit of Vatican II certainly influenced much of this change, but cultural and societal influences also entered in. Five years after his strong defense of Catholic teaching on contraception, McCormick publicly questioned such teaching and upheld the right to dissent. Ironically, some statements made by Pope Paul VI actually contributed to McCormick's own change.

The historical record shows that McCormick has always been a moderate, and often his own position opens a middle ground between two extremes. On both the substantive question of contraception and the ecclesiological question of dissent McCormick clearly had to be convinced before he changed his earlier positions. But with his own honesty and dedication to the truth he had to express clearly his positions once he was convinced of them.

As late as 1965 McCormick maintained that the church can infallibly teach with regard to matters of the natural law, since such teaching is essential to the protection and proposal of Christian morality itself. According to the accepted understanding Catholic teaching could be either infallible or noninfallible. At that time our author also addressed the question of the relationship between authoritative, noninfallible church teaching on the natural law and the arguments proposed for such a teaching. Here again McCormick sought a middle way between, on the one hand, a new rationalism that would not accept a church teaching unless the reasons were clear and convincing and, on the other hand, an abdication of reason that would see no connection between the authoritative teaching and the reasons to support it. The magisterium makes sense precisely because arguments are not clear or at least not universally persuasive. We should not always expect to have clear answers and arguments *now*.[7]

McCormick at this time was still not convinced about the arguments for a change in the church teaching on artificial contraception, but the practical aspects of the question surfaced in the light of a June 1964 papal statement. Pope Paul VI admitted that the question of artificial contraception, especially in terms of the pill, was under study by a special commission. At that time the pope could not find sufficient reason for changing the norms that had been reaffirmed by Pope Pius XII. In the meantime Catholics should wish to follow a single law that the church authoritatively proposes. No one for the present should presume to speak in terms divergent from the prevailing norm. The problem for moral theologians concerned the status of this teaching. Was it now in doubt? Could Catholics in accord with the accepted theory of probabilism claim that the teaching was in doubt and be free to disagree with it in good conscience? According to McCormick, the pope had reserved this matter to himself, knew the practical urgency of the decision, was well informed on the literature, and had promised to speak soon and authoritatively. If the pope failed to speak soon on the issue, then one could only conclude that a state of practical doubt existed in the church.[8] Notice the juridical way in which the question was solved. Practical doubt will exist because the pope has not spoken on a matter of great importance that he is studying. The possibility of doubt arises from an omission by the pope and not from the intrinsic arguments or evidence.

A year later McCormick moved away from this juridical approach to the question itself. He interpreted Pope Paul VI as saying that as of 1964 the arguments against the norms proposed by Pius XII were not persuasive. As long as these arguments are not persuasive, the existing norms must be regarded as obligatory. The pope is the ultimate judge as to whether these counterarguments are persuasive and conclusive. However, the statement of Pope Paul VI could not mean that only if and when the pope speaks will it become clear that the counterarguments are sound and persuasive. For the pope to make such a statement, the arguments would have to be clear and sound before he speaks! The papal utterance does not make the arguments clear and persuasive. Notice the move within one year from an omission by authority to the intrinsic evidence of the arguments. But despite this change the author of the "Notes" could not bring himself to say that the arguments against the church's teaching on contraception were now convincing.[9]

Contraception continued to be the number one topic in Catholic moral theology in 1966. The majority report of the papal commission arguing for a change in the official teaching was leaked to the press. McCormick, writing in 1967, cautiously leaned toward the reasoning of the majority report, maintaining that not every act of contraceptive intercourse is morally wrong. But again, McCormick as a Catholic theologian had to deal with the practical aspects of the question. What was to be the proper attitude of spouses, priests, and other counselors in practice? Paul VI had brought up the problem again in an address in October 1966. The norm against artificial contraception could not be considered not binding. The magisterium of the church was not in a state of doubt but in a moment of study and reflection. McCormick now firmly rejected a legal and juridical understanding of the obligation resulting from the teaching of the hierarchical magisterium. The obligation of the faithful to obey church teaching comes from the teaching or doctrinal statement itself. If there were good and probable intrinsic reasons why the church may change her teaching on contraception, then the foundation for a certain obligation to follow that teaching had ceased to exist. This new papal address had not changed the practical aspects of the question. The teaching of the church was in practical doubt, and in good conscience church members could act against the existing teaching on the basis of a probable opinion to the contrary.[10] It could very well be that the pope was appealing to a legal and juridical obligation to continue to uphold the older teaching, but the author of the "Notes" could not accept such an understanding of the response due to the teaching office in the church.

Our Jesuit theologian later (1968) appealed to another papal address to justify his position. Speaking in 1966 while the birth control commission was studying the question of contraception, Pope Paul VI explained the delay by saying that the magisterium cannot propose moral norms until it is certain of interpreting the will of God. To reach this certitude the church was not dispensed from research and from examining the many questions that are proposed. McCormick drew the obvious conclusion that the teaching was from then doubtful.[11]

The Catholic world had known since 1964 that the church was studying the issue of contraception. The majority of the members of the papal commission favored a change in the teaching.[12] However, Pope Paul did not act on that recommendation. Finally on 29 July 1968, the shoe dropped. Pope Paul's encyclical *Humanae Vitae* firmly condemned all contraception for spouses and upheld the older teaching of the church. *Humanae Vitae* touched off an explosion in the life of the church.[13] As a leading Catholic moral theologian, McCormick was very much a part of the ensuing discussion and controversy. However, he did not join in any immediate public dissent from the papal encyclical, as did many other theologians in this country and abroad.

To go against the teaching on artificial contraception one could no longer appeal to the words of the pope about doubt in the church's teaching. One has to disagree directly with the papal teaching. McCormick crossed the Rubicon with regard to the legitimacy of dissent in his response to *Humanae Vitae,* but his conclusions were more cautious than his premises. Theologians and others must be docile to church teaching, but such teaching can be wrong. After much analysis the American Jesuit concluded that the intrinsic immorality of every contraceptive act remains a teaching that is subject to solid and positive doubt. He did not go so far as to say that the teaching is certainly erroneous. If other theologians agreed and if bishops and spouses arrived at the same conclusion, it is difficult to see how the teaching would not lose the presumption of certitude enjoyed by such teaching. In practice, the dissent of reflective and competent married people should be respected. Absolution in the sacrament of penance should not be refused to those who do not accept the teaching of *Humanae Vitae.* A strong case can be made for saying that individual acts of contraception are not subjectively serious sin.[14] Notice that McCormick did not say here that contraceptive acts are objectively good acts or can be objectively good acts. The principles he held at that time logically called for more venturesome conclusions. One would have expected him to conclude that there are good and intrinsic reasons why the church's teaching on artificial contraception even in *Humanae Vitae* is doubtful. Consequently, there is no certain obligation for the faithful to follow that teaching. However, one must situate McCormick's response at this time in the light of the swirling controversy that engulfed the life of the Catholic church in the United States and throughout the world.

The controversy over artificial contraception in the short period between 1964 and 1969 was the context in which McCormick changed and developed his understanding of the hierarchical teaching office in the church and the response due to it. At the meeting of the Catholic Theological Society of America in June 1969 the American Jesuit presented his most systematic and sustained treatment of the teaching role of the magisterium and of theologians.[15]

The Teaching of the Church in Moral Matters

How should the hierarchical magisterium in the Catholic church function on moral issues? Richard McCormick's 1969 paper built the basic scaffolding that he has followed since then for a proper understanding of the role of the hierarchical magisterium. In the last twenty years, our author has addressed this issue in many different contexts. McCormick's latest book, *The Critical Calling*, discusses the teaching office of the church at length in a number of different chapters that were originally written as essays dealing with particular issues.[16] This section of the chapter will develop, in a necessarily skeletal but nevertheless more systematic way, an approach to the proper functioning of the church's teaching role in moral matters; my discussion will rely heavily on insights provided by McCormick and others, but I will present them as my own.

The proper understanding of the teaching function of the church in moral matters depends heavily, as McCormick has often pointed out, on one's ecclesiology, one's theology of the church. The Second Vatican Council brought about a dramatic change in Catholicism's understanding of the church. The model of the church as a pyramid with the hierarchy on top gave way to the model of the church as the people of God or as a *communio* (communion). The newer approaches attempted to overcome the overjuridical understanding that existed in the period before the council and leaned heavily on scriptural and patristic testimonies about the church. Obviously the hierarchical role in the church is not denied but is now contextualized as a service within the people of God. The Constitution on the Church discusses the mystery of the church in chapter 1, the people of God in chapter 2, and the hierarchical role in the church in chapter 3.[17]

A second general context for a proper appreciation of the teaching role of the church in moral issues concerns the very concept of teaching itself.[18] Teaching is not primarily a juridical category and should not be understood on the basis of such a model. Its purpose being to convince by appealing to the intellect of another, teaching attempts to persuade and not to command. It relies heavily on competence and not on authority. The proper response to teaching is not obedience, for obedience is a proper response to the exercise of jurisdiction, not to the function of teaching.

The very process of teaching is not a one-way street but always involves a process of learning. Every good teacher is also a learner. The church is no exception. The teaching office in the church tries to discern the word of God and the truth. The teaching office does not make something true or good but discovers truth and goodness.

A third general perspective reminds us that truth is not something that is possessed totally and once for all. Many, including McCormick, have pointed to the significance of the shift from classicism to historical consciousness in Catholic theology and thought.[19] Classicism thought in terms of the immutable, the eternal, and the unchanging; historical consciousness gives greater importance to the particular, the historical, and the changing. Whereas classicism espoused a deductive methodology, historical consciousness employs a more inductive approach. Human beings are always searching for the truth in the midst of the changing circumstances of time and place. The church is constantly striving for the truth. This search — even with the existence of revelation and the assistance of the Holy Spirit — is a never-ending process that involves refinements, developments, and even changes.

A fourth general context for understanding the moral teaching role in the church recognizes that truths dealing with faith can never be fully possessed, for faith ultimately deals with the mystery of God. Yes, through faith we can arrive at some true knowledge, but our knowledge will always be imperfect for "we see now only in a mirror and not face to face."[20] The Catholic theological tradition has rightly emphasized that the church tries to understand, appropriate, and live the word and work of Jesus in the light of the changing historical realities. Catholicism rejects the approaches of both fundamentalism and *sola scriptura*. The church today cannot merely repeat the scripture but tries under the guidance of the Spirit to understand God's word in the changing realities of the different worlds in which we live. Catholicism has traditionally appreciated the need for the development of doctrine.

Our faith must be expressed in human concepts and words that are related to different theologies or to systematic ways of understanding reality. Different theologies mean that different ways of understanding the same faith reality can coexist. In addition, all human systems, concepts, and words are necessarily inadequate to express fully the faith reality of our deepest religious convictions. However, this is not to say that we cannot know *some* truths about God and faith. In this connection one recalls the shift in the understanding of revelation from the neoscholastic emphasis on revelation as propositional truths to the approach of the Second Vatican Council which describes God as revealing in the acts and deeds of history and especially in the life, death, and resurrection of Jesus.[21]

A fifth general perspective emphasizes that moral truths and moral teaching in the church have quite distinctive characteristics.[22] The Catholic church has traditionally insisted that its moral teaching on most specific issues is based on the theory of natural law. Such an approach stresses the rational character of such teaching. Truths of the natural law are per se intelligible to all human beings. Thus, for example, the Catholic teachings opposed to liberalistic capitalism or totalitarianism or artificial contraception are proposed as positions that should be held by all human beings since they are based on human nature and human reason. This distinctive understanding of moral truths in the Catholic tradition must affect how the church learns, teaches, and proposes its morality. In addition, all recognize different levels of moral discourse. One can and does speak about attitudes or virtues such as hope or generosity, moral principles such as the obligation to protect innocent human life, moral norms such as the condemnation of divorce and remarriage, and prudential judgments such as the conclusion that the first use of even the smallest nuclear weapon is morally wrong. Different levels of certitude attach to these different aspects of moral teaching.

Within these general perspectives and contexts the teaching function of the church in moral matters can be developed. The first and perhaps most significant characteristic of this teaching function is its pluriform nature. The whole purpose of McCormick's 1969 essay was to prove that the total teaching function of the church in moral matters cannot be identified with the hierarchical magisterium. The term *magisterium* suggests a pluridimensional function in the church in which all members of the church have varying responsibilities. McCormick spells out three distinguishable components of this magisterium: the prophetic charism understood very broadly to include the many competencies involved, especially those of the laity and of people who have experience about a particular issue; the doctrinal–pastoral charism of the hierarchy; and the scientific charism of the theologian.[23] In subsequent years the author of the "Notes on Moral Theology" often came back to this question. He frequently cites other theologians such as Rahner, Congar, Dulles, Coffy, and others to support the contention that the magisterium cannot be limited just to the hierarchy.[24] Two comments are in order here. First, in his later writings McCormick, with character-istic modesty, does not give his own position enough impor-tance; he clearly proposed his position in 1969 — before many of the people he so often quotes in later years. Second, the American Jesuit later recognized that he was not wedded to the terminology of a dual or plural magisteria in the church: all he wanted to do was to point out that the total teaching function in the church cannot be reduced to the hierarchical teaching role, and that the hierarchical role needs the inde-pendent work of theologians and others.[25] Various aspects of the total teaching function of the church will now be discussed in greater detail.

The Hierarchical Teaching Office

In keeping with the pluriform aspect of the teaching func-tion in the church I will use the term *hierarchical magisterium* to refer to the teaching role of pope and bishops in the church. This hierarchical teaching office is connected with the office of bishops in the church. Catholic theology and canon law today distinguish between the infallible and the noninfallible teaching of the hierarchical magisterium.

Debate exists within the church about the possibility of infallible teaching on specific moral questions. Comparatively few theologians hold that in theory the hierarchical magisterium can teach infallibly on specific moral matters. In particular, some scholars hold that the condemnation of artificial contraception belongs to the category of infallible teaching since it has been taught throughout the church by the pope and all the bishops.[26] Most theologians reject the infallible status of the condemnation of artificial contraception. Teaching can be infallible either through the extraordinary teaching office of the pope or ecumenical councils in defining a doctrine or through the ordinary teaching of pope and bishops. All admit there has been no extraordinary definition with regard to contraception. The vast majority of Catholic theologians think that the condemnation of artificial contraception is not infallible because it does not fulfill the three conditions necessary for infallibility: the matter must be (1) divinely revealed or necessary to explain what is divinely revealed; (2) taught with moral unanimity by the pope and the body of bishops; and (3) proposed as having to be held definitively by the faithful. The first and third conditions, and maybe even the second, are not met in the case of contraception.[27]

On specific moral questions there cannot be an infallible teaching because of the very nature of specific moral teachings. McCormick embraces the distinction between the transcendental and the categorical to prove that no categorical matter could be a saving truth and connected with revelation.[28] Perhaps this distinction does not give enough importance to inner-worldly realities and their relationship to salvation. However, specific moral teachings are removed from the core of faith, involve much complexity, and are subject to historical development so that a person cannot claim to achieve a certitude in these matters that excludes all possibility of error. Note that we are talking about specific moral norms such as divorce, contraception, no first use of even tactical or small nuclear weapons. In this light, moral theologians do not have to deal with the question of infallible teaching that is being discussed today. We are dealing, rather, with what contemporary Catholic theology and law call authoritative, noninfallible teaching. How should the hierarchical magisterium go about its authoritative, noninfallible teaching?

The hierarchical magisterium must always conform itself to the truth and serve the truth. Thus the pope and bishops must be in dialogue and contact with the sources of truth, such as scripture, tradition, reason, and experience. In the area of moral teachings reason must have great importance because of the recognition that Catholic moral teaching is reasonable, and so too experience is particularly significant because the people of God live out this moral reality in their daily lives. Dialogue must also include other Christian churches and all people of good will. The hierarchical magisterium has an obligation to use all means available to arrive at the truth in these questions.[29]

The hierarchical teaching office in the church involves both the pope and the bishops. The bishops are true teachers in the church and not just delegates or spokespersons for the pope. Bishops do not fulfill their teaching office if they merely repeat what the pope has said.[30] Bishops as individuals, as national and regional groups, and as the total college of bishops have their own teaching function and role along with the pope.

Connected with the office of pope and bishop, the teaching function enjoys the special assistance of the Holy Spirit and constitutes authoritative teaching. No individual in the church can claim to be an authoritative teacher, for this role belongs to the pope and the bishops. However, the assistance of the Holy Spirit does not dispense these teachers from human means of learning and searching out the truth. Yes, pope and bishops have a teaching office and a special assistance of the Holy Spirit, but these distinctive features of their teaching role are not substitutes for the human process of discerning the truth.[31] It is a truism in the Catholic tradition that the divine works in and through the human. McCormick associates the assistance of the Holy Spirit with the two fundamental human processes of evidence gathering and evidence assessing.[32] The Holy Spirit helps in the process of discernment, but the Spirit does not overrule or substitute for the normal ways of human discernment.

Every member of the church can appreciate the help that church teaching in general and the hierarchical magisterium in particular can provide. As individuals in our pursuit of truth we are limited by our own finitude. We see only one part of the whole. This limited vision can distort our moral analysis and conclusions. In addition, all of us must recognize our sinfulness; our sin blinds us at times and prevents our arriving at moral truth. The church as a community that exists over time and space helps to overcome the limitations characteristic of every individual human being, since each of us lives in a particular culture, a particular place, and a particular time. And through the gift of the Holy Spirit the church strives to overcome the reality of sin. To be sure, the church itself is also sinful, but God's grace helps us resist sin's power. Thus the church in general and its hierarchical teaching office can assist us in overcoming the innate human limitations of finitude and sinfulness in our search for moral truth. The church is a community of grace—not a group of individuals.

Theology, too, needs and profits from the hierarchical magisterium. By definition the theologian studies the word and work of God in a thematic, reflexive, and systematic way. The moral theologian examines Christian moral life in an analytic and critical manner using all the tools of the human search for truth as illumined by faith. The faith experience of the church community is the source of theological reflection. Theology in its attempt to understand systematically Christian experience knows the inherent difficulties that attend trying to express this experience in a coherent, adequate, and systematic way. The moral theologian realizes that human reason and human constructs can never perfectly express moral experience. Moral intuitions need, rather, to be expressed in appropriate, adequate, and coherent systematic moral discourse, and theologians are constantly looking for better and more adequate understandings. Thus by its very nature theology depends on the experience of the Christian community and the teaching proclaimed by the hierarchical magisterium.

The Christian in the Catholic community, as well as the Catholic theologian, believes in the teaching office of pope and bishops in the church and in the assistance that the Holy Spirit gives to that office. In a spirit of faith one graciously accepts and appreciates this teaching office. The assistance of the Holy Spirit does not, however, do away with the human processes of discerning truth in moral matters; nor is such a teaching function the only way in which the church is involved in the process of learning and teaching.

Perhaps the best illustration of how the hierarchical teaching office should function in moral matters comes from the process used by the United States bishops in writing their two pastoral letters on peace and on the economy. Much study and dialogue went into the process itself of formulating both letters. Experts in scripture, theology, philosophy, and all pertinent human and social sciences were consulted as were many people who had experience with the particular matters involved. Such broad and deep consultation recognizes and makes use of the competence and contributions of scholars and of personal experience.

In moral teaching one must distinguish the various levels of moral discourse such as values, attitudes, virtues, principles, norms, and judgments. Logic and Catholic theology as exemplified by Thomas Aquinas have taught that as one descends to the more particular and specific, one cannot claim the same degree of certitude as in more general matters.[33] I do not see, for example, how anyone can deny the principle that human life should not be killed is somewhat more material and specific so that almost all humans admit some exceptions. The very specific principle of hierarchical Catholic moral teaching maintains that one cannot directly take innocent life on one's own authority. Such a principle depends on a number of aspects including the philosophical theory behind the distinction between *direct* and *indirect*. Since theologians and philosophers disagree about this theory, claiming that one can have absolute or even moral certitude about the position on direct killing is very difficult. In my judgment, absolute, specific moral norms involving human behavior described in a concrete way (i.e., this very specific act is always wrong) can never claim a certitude that excludes the possibility of error or exceptions. Everyone would have to admit that murder is always wrong, but murder by definition is unjustified killing. Similarly, I would maintain that lying is always morally wrong because lying by definition is a moral term and not a behavioral term. However, telling a falsehood (a behavioral term) is not always wrong. The malice of lying consists in the violation of my neighbor's right to truth so that not every falsehood is a lie. Concrete behavioral norms are by definition so specific and involve so many possible circumstances that they cannot claim to have a certitude that excludes the possibility of error or of exception. The perennial danger is to claim more certitude on moral matters than logic and human reason allow. At times it will surely be difficult to agree on the level of certitude or probability existing in a particular case, but all people should recognize that absolute, specific, concrete behavioral norms cannot claim a certitude that would exclude all exceptions or differences.

Again, the United States bishops' pastoral letters on peace and on the economy indicate the general direction that should be taken by the hierarchical magisterium. The bishops distinguished three different levels of their teaching: binding moral principles, statements of recent popes, and practical judgments.[34] On the level of practical judgments the bishops recognized that in the midst of such specificity others in the church might disagree.

I agree with the recognition of different levels of specificity and certitude, but three comments about the approach of the U.S. bishops are in order. First, bishops should not merely repeat recent papal teaching just because it is papal teaching, for mere repetition means that the bishops have abdicated their own teaching role. Second, one might not be able to claim moral certitude even on the level of some moral principles. One of the important principles and the linchpin of much of the bishops' letter on peace is the principle of discrimination or noncombatant immunity. However, as a matter of fact there is disagreement within the Catholic church on this issue, as is illustrated by the unwillingness of the West German bishops to uphold this independent principle in their pastoral letter on peace and the nuclear question.[35] Third, the area of legitimate diversity in the church can, because of the specificity of positions held, exist on levels other than that of practical judgments. However, the approach taken by the American bishops is at least a step in the right direction.

What is the proper response of all the Catholic faithful to such authoritative, noninfallible teaching proposed by the hierarchical magisterium? By definition such teaching is noninfallible. In other words the teaching is fallible; it might be wrong. Catholic theology has traditionally spoken about a presumption in favor of such teaching. On the basis of what has been said above, one can see the fundamental reasons supporting such a presumption; but two important caveats are required. First, the presumption is weakened to the extent that the hierarchical teaching office does not properly carry out its own function in gathering and assessing the evidence. Second, attention must be paid to the different levels of moral discourse and to the fact that the possibility of certitude diminishes to the extent that one becomes more specific.[36]

The Constitution on the Church of the Second Vatican Council repeats the terminology in use since the nineteenth century in calling for a religious *obsequium* of intellect and will. The problem concerns the meaning of *obsequium*. Is it "obedience"? "Submission"? "Respect"? Along with others, McCormick maintains that the approach of the conciliar document is too juridical in tone; he understands the proper response of the faithful in terms of a "docility" to accept the teaching. The Holy Spirit assists the hierarchical teaching office; the faithful and theologians recognize their own limitations and sinfulness; all affirm the difficulty at times in properly articulating the reasons for the positions we hold. Thus in a docile spirit one hears this teaching and is open to be persuaded by it. But that such teaching might not be persuasive can and does happen. Since we are talking about teaching, the proper response cannot be obedience or submission, for these are juridical terms that describe two particular responses to the exercise of the power of jurisdiction.[37]

The Role of the Faithful

The teaching–learning process in the church involves multiple competencies, including the role of the Christian faithful. The ecclesiological shift at the Second Vatican Council reminded us that the church is not just the hierarchy but, rather, is the people of God: the entire people of God share in the process of teaching and learning in the church. The Constitution on the Church emphasizes that all the baptized share in the prophetic or teaching function of Jesus.[38] Catholic theology traditionally has maintained that through baptism all Christians share in the threefold function of Jesus as priest, teacher, and sovereign. The liturgical renewal in Roman Catholicism found its theological grounding in the priestly function of all believers. Just as there exists both the priesthood of all believers and a hierarchical priesthood, so, too, there exists the teaching or prophetic function of all Christians and of the hierarchical teaching office. The primary teacher in the church remains the Holy Spirit, but all share in the Spirit's grace, gifts, and charisms. In this context the *sensus fidelium* takes on an important significance, for the consensus of the faithful has traditionally been accepted in the church as a criterion of saving truth.

The Second Vatican Council and contemporary theology alike have affirmed an important role for the laity as a most significant part of the people of God. One must acknowledge the compromises natural to conciliar documents; nevertheless, the expanding role of the laity in Catholicism in the last few decades testifies to the changes brought about by the council. By their competence in secular fields and by their personal activity assisted by grace, laypersons must learn the deepest meaning and value of all creation so that the world is permeated by the Spirit of Christ.[39] The Pastoral Constitution on the Church in the Modern World recognizes that the church does not always have at hand the answers to particular problems.[40] The laity is urged to take on its own distinctive role and responsibilities.[41] Here too one must remember changes in the educational background and formation of the people of God. No longer can the faithful be looked upon as sheep who must be told what they are to do.

The experience of Christian people constitutes a true locus or source of theology. The whole church can and does learn from the experience of Christians. To discern such experience requires more than a majority vote, but the experience of the people of God is a source of learning and teaching for the whole church, a role explicitly recognized in the Declaration on Religious Freedom of Vatican II. Recall that the hierarchical teaching office did not accept religious liberty until 1965. The declaration, however, recognizes that the demand for religious freedom has been impressing itself more deeply on the consciousness of human beings. The document takes careful note of these desires in the human heart and mind and declares them to be greatly in accord with truth and justice.[42] When did the teaching on religious freedom become true? The moment a document was signed in Rome? The document itself admits that the teaching was already true before the document was written.

The function of the faithful in the church's process of teaching and learning has played a central role in the concept of *reception:* a teaching must be received by the whole church; if a teaching is not truly received then that teaching does not truly represent the whole church and should be changed. Again, the criteria for understanding reception are by definition somewhat vague and difficult to apply. It is always much easier to recognize in retrospect when reception did not occur. Reception involves the many different roles of the people of God in general and of theologians and scholars in particular. J. Robert Dionne has recently examined how the teaching of the hierarchical magisterium was modified, changed, and developed on seven specific issues: papal social teaching, collegiality in the church, Catholicism and non-Christian religions, church–state relations, religious liberty, the church, and membership in the church.[43] He concludes that one of the ways in which doctrine developed and changed from the time of Pius IX in the nineteenth century to the end of Vatican II in 1965 was through the interplay of two forces: the authoritative, noninfallible teaching of the ordinary hierarchical magisterium; and the modalities whereby these pronouncements were received by the rest of the church.[44] I do not see how people can deny the changes and modifications that have taken place on these and other issues in the history of the church, for example, sexual ethics and the place of procreation, interest taking, the rights of the accused, slavery, the teachings of the biblical commission, and so forth. Such changes not only underscore the role of reception in Catholic self-understanding, but they also point out again that the teaching–learning function in the church is truly an ongoing process that can never be fully achieved. In this context, too, one can see the positive reality that dissent can and should play in the life of the church—but that issue will be discussed shortly.

The Scholarly Teaching Function of Theologians

Theology and theologians have an important role to play in the teaching–learning process of the church. Theology involves a critical, reflexive, thematic, systematic study of Christian faith and life. Moral theology is the branch of Catholic theology that deals with the issues of Christian living in our world. To a certain extent anyone who reflects on Christian faith and life is involved in the work of theology, but academically developed theology uses scientific tools and methods in its attempt to understand better the realities of Christian faith.

The relationship between the role of the hierarchical magisterium and the role of theologians by necessity will always involve both some overlaps and some tensions. The hierarchical teaching function is a pastoral role connected with the office of the pope and bishops in the church, and only that office authoritatively proposes church teaching. The theologian exercises a scholarly role that ultimately depends on the research of the individual theologian and of the theological community. The role of the theologian is cooperative with, somewhat independent of, and complementary to the hierarchical teaching role.[45] Such an understanding coheres with the recognition that learning and teaching in the Catholic church are ongoing processes. On the one hand, theologians must give a proper reception to the teaching of the hierarchical magisterium since the pope and bishops are official teachers in the church; recall, however, the different levels of hierarchical church teaching and the type of response required by all the faithful. On the other hand, the hierarchical teaching office needs the work of theology; once one begins to try to explain and teach the faith one is entering into the broad territory of theology, and in discussing moral goals, attitudes, virtues, principles, and norms one must use the understandings of moral theology.

In past ecumenical councils theologians have even had official votes. At the Second Vatican Council, the importance of theologians was generally recognized. No teaching document of the hierarchical magisterium could be published without using theology. Almost always theologians have been consulted in the writing of such documents. Some scholars have suggested that documents should also be signed by the theologians who helped to write them.[46]

In this context one can better realize the role that dissent can play in the church. For our limited purposes in discussing moral theology we are dealing only with authoritative, noninfallible church teaching and the role of dissent from such teaching. Dissent rightly can involve everyone in the church, but our discussion will center on theological dissent. Dissent from such teaching is not only at times a legitimate possibility but also a positive service to the ongoing search for truth within the church.[47]

Such a positive evaluation of dissent stems from the understandings of the hierarchical teaching office and the total teaching–learning function of the church as described above. Theologians can be irresponsible in their dissent; theologians can and will be wrong. They should always maintain their scholarly reserve in proposing their findings and research. However, theological dissent has a positive role to play in the life of the church.

The Catholic faithful can and should acknowledge both the role and the limits of theological discourse in the church. Theologians are not authoritative teachers who teach officially. Their teaching is based on their scholarship and is subject to the criticism of the church and of other theologians. However, they and the whole people of God have a necessary and irreplaceable role to play in the teaching–learning process in the church.

Some have expressed uneasiness over the word *dissent*.[48] The word may have a somewhat negative ring to it, but I think it accurately describes what is taking place. By using the word one admits very clearly that one's findings and research differ from authoritative and official hierarchical teaching. The negative aspects of the term also point up the presumption that should be given to authoritative hierarchical teaching. However, dissent's reality is not primarily negative. First of all dissent is only one aspect of the work of the theologian who is constantly striving to understand better and in a more systematic way the word and work of Jesus in the light of our contemporary circumstances; most of the theologian's work will not involve dissent. But at times theological scholarship will result in dissenting positions which, however, even if at times erroneous, must be seen as something positive in the light of the ongoing process by which truth is sought within the church.

The role of the theologian is both critical and public. The theologian serves many different publics both within and outside the church. The whole search for truth today in our society and in the church is public and dialogical. However, the theologian who publicly dissents must act responsibly. This responsibility calls for both proper restraint in proposing one's positions and respect for the hierarchical teaching office in the church. All the people of God must recognize the need for such public dissent and should not be scandalized by it.[49]

This section has described the teaching–learning process in the church and three very important components of that process — the hierarchical teaching office, the role of the faithful, and the role of theologians. Tension will always attend the search for truth. Sometimes that tension can be unnecessarily exaggerated, but if there were no tensions, there would be no real people of God. The pilgrim people of God will always know and experience the tensions of trying to find and do the truth in love.

Criticism of the Hierarchical Magisterium Today

In the light of the development of how the hierarchical teaching office and the total teaching–learning function in the church should operate, this section will now criticize how the hierarchical teaching office has been operating in the contemporary church. McCormick has acknowledged in theory and in practice the need for theology to criticize how the hierarchical magisterium functions, but he has also insisted on the need for theologians to be self-critical in carrying out their role in the church.[50] Theologians should show respect for the hierarchical teaching office, recognize they are not official teachers in the church, and be conscious of their own limitations. Theologians must be more willing to enter into dialogue with all other theologians in the church, especially with those who hold opposite positions. All of us have succumbed at some time or another to the danger of dividing theologians into various camps and writing off those who belong to a different camp. Also, theologians with the same general perspective must be more willing to criticize one another and to point out deficiencies and problems. Theologians who recognize the positive aspects of dissent must also address the limits of dissent in the church. But this section, in following a schematic approach often used by McCormick, will propose seven corrective criticisms of the exercise of the hierarchical teaching office today.

1. Admit the different levels of church teaching. The hierarchical teaching office must admit clearly and publicly the different levels of church teaching. Noninfallible church teaching by its very nature cannot claim an absolute certitude but possibly can be wrong. The charge of "creeping infallibility" still rings true today because the provisional character of noninfallible teaching is not recognized. In moral issues acknowledge that the possibility of certitude decreases as specificity increases.

2. Admit past mistakes in official hierarchical church teaching. History proves the existence of some errors. An honest owning of such mistakes will not detract from the role of the hierarchical teaching office but will in fact enhance it. In my judgment the unwillingness to acknowledge mistakes in the past and especially in the present constitutes one of the greatest problems facing the church today. Most agree that Pope Paul VI's decision not to change the hierarchical teaching on artificial contraception stemmed from his inability to admit that the teaching had been wrong. Could the Holy Spirit allow the church to be wrong on such an important matter? Instead of helping people in their Christian life has the church really been hurting them all these years? People who share my positions must squarely face this question. As I pointed out in chapter 1, I think the root of the problem comes from the failure to declare publicly the provisional nature of this and all noninfallible church teaching.

3. Bishops must exercise their own independent teaching role in the church. Bishops are not mere delegates or spokesmen for the pope. Each bishop has a teaching function, and all the bishops together with the pope form the college of bishops with its solicitude for the total church. At present, bishops do not actually exercise any independent teaching role. The role of the bishop and the college of bishops as teachers in the church will not be a reality until a bishop or a group of bishops humbly and responsibly but publicly disagrees with a papal teaching. Do you think that any bishops would have publicly disagreed with Pope Paul VI if he had concluded his study of contraception by changing the teaching of the church?

4. The hierarchical teaching office must consult widely. In keeping with the understanding of the teaching–learning process as it takes place in the church, the hierarchical magisterium must be exercised in a dialogical fashion. Today too often the hierarchical magisterium, especially in moral matters, follows only one theological school, the neoscholastic, and refuses to study, consult, or utilize other legitimate theological positions existing within the church. This narrow approach is bound to skew the efforts of the teaching office. Documents that emerge from such a narrow basis will continue to meet with disapproval from many people in the church.

5. The hierarchical teaching office must admit the processive nature of the search for truth in the church. Such an understanding not only calls for a more consultative, tentative, and dialogical approach to its own role but must also recognize the positive function of dissent in the church. Theologians and the faithful will make mistakes, but the expression of dissent at times is necessary for the good of the whole church. Yes, problems will always exist in determining what is the truth in a particular moment. History helps us discern what was true a hundred years ago. However, dissent has a legitimate and positive role within the church even though dissent, like anything else, has been abused and will be abused.

6. *The process of promoting, dialoguing with, and overseeing theologians needs radical revision.* The Congregation for the Doctrine of the Faith has recognized the need to change its own procedures.[51] These processes must respect the rights of all concerned and incorporate the procedures of due process. Above all, theologians must not be judged on the basis of just one so-called orthodox type of theology. Many have recently called for changes in how the Congregation for the Doctrine of the Faith operates.[52] Above all, the hierarchical teaching office and the Congregation for the Doctrine of the Faith must adopt a positive and supportive role for the work of theologians; today most efforts seem to be negative and confrontational. Theologians will make mistakes. In the give and take of theological discussion other theologians should enter into the argument and the dialogue. At times the hierarchical church might have to disagree publicly with some theological positions. However, the primary thrust should be to encourage the theological enterprise. Richard A. McCormick has gone further than many others in his criticism of the Congregation for the Doctrine of the Faith as it operates today. The congregation is predominantly western, situated within an authority structure to which it is subordinate and sensitive, and almost exclusively negative in its approach. The congregation should be abolished and its guardian and promotive functions exercised by others.[53] McCormick's comment leads to a final corrective criticism.

7. *Significant structural change in the church and in the teaching function of the hierarchical magisterium is*

necessary. McCormick and others have pointed out the basic differences between, on the one hand, an overly juridical understanding of the church and of the hierarchical teaching office often associated with a pre–Vatican II approach and, on the other hand, a more communitarian or people-of-God model associated with post–Vatican II thinking. The danger of oversimplification may attend such a starkly drawn contrast, but the direction of such an approach is basically correct. For many people the theology and the understanding of the teaching–learning process in the church have changed, but basic church structures have not changed. The new code of canon law, which went into effect in 1983, has really not modified many of the older structures. As mentioned in chapter 1, the structural problem is in many ways today the primary problem facing the church's theology and practice. A collegial, consultative, dialogical, and differentiating hierarchical teaching office will not emerge until the structures and styles of operating in the church are significantly changed.

This chapter has attempted to discuss the teaching role and function in the church. The first part traced Richard A. McCormick's own development away from the juridical model that stressed the judgmental role of the hierarchical magisterium and tended to identify the hierarchical magisterium with the total teaching function of the church. The second part developed in a systematic but necessarily sketchy way how the teaching role should function in the church. The third section criticized the present way in which the hierarchical teaching office is exercised in the church. In the judgment of McCormick and many others, the Catholic church urgently needs to change how it exercises its teaching–learning function.

NOTES

1. Pope Paul VI, *On the Regulation of Birth* (Washington, DC: United States Catholic Conference, 1968).
2. These articles have been collected in two volumes: Richard A. McCormick, *Notes on Moral Theology 1965 through 1980*

(Washington, DC: University Press of America, 1981) and *Notes on Moral Theology 1981 through 1984* (Lanham, MD: University Press of America, 1984).

3. Richard A. McCormick, "The Teaching Role of the Magisterium and of Theologians," *Proceedings of the Catholic Theological Society of America* 24 (1969): 239-254; Richard A. McCormick, "Conscience, Theologians and the Magisterium," *New Catholic World* 220 (1977): 268-271; Richard A. McCormick, *The Critical Calling: Reflections on Moral Dilemmas since Vatican II*, (Washington, DC: Georgetown University Press, 1989), pp. 25-46.

4. McCormick, *Proceedings of CTSA* 24 (1969): 239-254.

5. Richard A. McCormick, "Conjugal Love and Conjugal Morality," *America* 110 (1964): 38-42; and "Family Size, Rhythm, and the Pill," in *The Problem of Population* (Notre Dame, IN: University of Notre Dame Press, 1964), pp. 58-84.

6. Louis Janssens, "Morale conjugale et progestogenes," *Ephemerides Theologicae Lovanienses* 39 (1963): 787-826; Josef Maria Reuss, "Eheliche Hingabe und Zeugung," *Tübinger Theologische Quartalschrift* 143 (1963): 454-476; William van der Marck, "Vruchtbaarheidsregeling," *Tijdschrift voor Theologie* 3 (1963): 386-413; Louis K. Dupré, "Toward a Re-examination of the Catholic Position on Birth Control," *Cross Currents* 14 (1964): 63-85.

7. McCormick, *Notes 1965-1980*, pp. 16-20.

8. Ibid., pp. 50-52.

9. Ibid., pp. 114-116.

10. Ibid., pp. 164-168.

11. Ibid., pp. 211-215.

12. For the story of the struggle over contraception in Roman Catholocism, see Robert Blair Kaiser, *The Politics of Sex and Religion* (Kansas City, MO: Sheed and Ward, 1985).

13. William H. Shannon, *The Lively Debate: Response to Humanae Vitae* (New York: Sheed and Ward, 1970); Joseph A. Selling, "The Reaction to *Humanae Vitae:* A Study in Special and Fundamental Theology" (STD dissertation, Catholic University of Louvain, 1977).

14. McCormick, *Notes 1965-1980*, pp. 225-231.

15. McCormick, *Proceedings of CTSA* 24 (1969): 239-254.

16. For the places outside the *Notes* where McCormick treats the teaching function of the church see above note 3; many chapters in his *Critical Calling;* and also his article, "A Moral Magisterium in Ecumenical Perspective," *Studies in Christian Ethics* 1 (1988):

20–29. Three important essays, "L'Affaire Curran," "The Search for Truth in the Catholic Context," and "Dissent in Moral Theology and Its Implications: Some Notes on the Literature," are found in Charles E. Curran and Richard A. McCormick, eds., *Readings in Moral Theology No. 6: Dissent in the Church* (New York: Paulist Press, 1988): 408–420, 421–434, 517–539.

17. Constitution on the Church, in Walter M. Abbott, ed., *The Documents of Vatican II* (New York: Guild, 1966), pp. 14–56.

18. McCormick has insisted on this in almost all his writings on the subject; see especially "The Role of Teaching," *Proceedings of CTSA* 24 (1969): 239–245; and *Critical Calling*, pp. 95–109.

19. McCormick, *Critical Calling*, p. 42.

20. For the implicit eschatological considerations in McCormick's work, see Kenneth R. Himes, "The Contribution of Theology to Catholic Moral Theology," in Charles E. Curran, ed., *Moral Theology: Challenges for the Future* (New York: Paulist Press, 1990), pp. 48–73.

21. Avery Dulles, *Models of Revelation* (Garden City, NY: Doubleday/Image, 1985).

22. "The Search for Truth," in Curran and McCormick, *Readings No. 6*, pp. 421–434. For a discussion of the meaning of *morals* in the famous phrase *faith and morals*, see John Mahoney, *The Making of Moral Theology: A Study of the Roman Catholic Tradition* (Oxford: Clarendon, 1987), pp. 120–135.

23. McCormick, *Proceedings CTSA* 24 (1969): 239–247.

24. McCormick, *Notes 1965–1980*, pp. 652–668, 768–785; *Notes 1980–1984*, pp. 42–48.

25. McCormick, *Notes 1965–1980*, pp. 783–785.

26. John C. Ford and Germain Grisez, "Contraception and Infallibility," *Theological Studies* 39 (1978): 258–312.

27. Joseph Komonchak, "*Humanae Vitae* and Its Reception: Ecclesiological Reflections," *Theological Studies* 39 (1978): 221–257.

28. McCormick, *Critical Calling*, pp. 98–100.

29. "The Search for Truth," in Curran and McCormick, *Readings No. 6*, pp. 424–434.

30. "Dissent and Its Implications," in Curran and McCormick, *Readings No. 6*, p. 543.

31. McCormick, *Critical Calling*, p. 35.

32. McCormick, *Notes 1965–1980*, pp. 262–266.

33. Thomas Aquinas, *Summa theologiae* (Rome: Marietti, 1952), $I^a II^{ae}$, q. 94, a. 4; McCormick, *Critical Calling*, pp. 131–162.

The Teaching Function in Morality

34. National Conference of Catholic Bishops, "The Challenge of Peace: God's Gift and Our Response," *Origins* 13 (1983): 2.

35. For an analysis of the position of the West German pastoral letter, see my *Tensions in Moral Theology* (Notre Dame, IN: University of Notre Dame Press, 1988), pp. 140–148.

36. "The Search for Truth," in Curran and McCormick, *Readings No. 6*, p. 425.

37. As one might expect, McCormick deals with the proper response to noninfallible teaching in just about every discussion of magisterium. His later approaches (e.g., *Notes 1980–1984*, p. 191) depend on the work of Francis A. Sullivan, *Magisterium: Teaching Authority in the Catholic Church* (New York: Paulist Press, 1983), pp. 157–166.

38. Consitution on the Church, n. 12, Abbott, *Documents of Vatican II*, pp. 29–30.

39. Ibid., n. 36, pp. 62–63.

40. Pastoral Constitution on the Church in the Modern World, n. 32, in Abbott, *Documents of Vatican II*, p. 232.

41. Ibid., n. 43, p. 244.

42. Declaration on Religious Freedom, n. 1, in Abbott, *Documents of Vatican II*, pp. 675–676.

43. J. Robert Dionne, *The Papacy and the Church: A Study of Praxis and Reception in Ecumenical Perspective* (New York: Philosophical Library, 1987), pp. 1–282.

44. Ibid., 353.

45. "In Service to the Gospel: A Consensus Statement of the Joint Committee," in Leo J. O'Donovan, ed., *Cooperation between Theologians and the Ecclesiastical Magisterium* (Washington, DC: Canon Law Society of America, 1982), pp. 175–189. For the "somewhat independent" role of theologians, see my *Faithful Dissent* (Kansas City, MO: Sheed and Ward, 1986), pp. 52ff.

46. McCormick, *Notes 1965–1980*, p. 665.

47. McCormick addresses the issue of dissent every time he treats of magisterium. For his latest discussion, see McCormick, *Critical Calling*, pp. 25–46.

48. Ladislas Örsy, *The Church: Learning and Teaching* (Wilmington, DE: Glazier, 1987), pp. 90–93.

49. "L'Affaire Curran," in Curran and McCormick, *Readings No. 6*, pp. 416–420.

50. McCormick, *Critical Calling*, pp. 142–145.

51. *National Catholic Register*, 12 August 1984, p. 6.

52. Two theologians have recently criticized the Congregation for the Doctrine of the Faith for how they were treated. See Walbert

Buhlman, *Dreaming about the Church: Acts of the Apostles of the Twentieth Century* (Kansas City, MO: Sheed and Ward, 1987); and Bernard Häring, Intervista di Gianni Licheri, *Fede, Storia, Morale* (Roma: Borla, 1989).
  53. McCormick, *Critical Calling*, p. 91.

6. What Catholic Ecclesiology Can Learn from Official Catholic Social Teaching

Ecclesiology deals with the mystery of the church, together with its structures and organization. Official Catholic social teaching refers to what the hierarchical teaching office in the Catholic church has proposed; modern official Catholic social teaching generally refers to the teaching on the social order, especially on the economic order, that had begun with Pope Leo XIII's encyclical *Rerum Novarum* in 1891. Broader than official Catholic social teaching, Catholic social ethics involves the disciplined and systematic study of Catholic social morality. Catholic ecclesiology can learn much from official Catholic social teaching.

Preliminary Considerations

Some preliminary considerations are in order. Showing that Catholic ecclesiology can learn from Catholic social teaching is necessary before explaining what, if anything, Catholic social teaching has said that is pertinent. Some people might object that Catholic ecclesiology can and should learn nothing from Catholic social teaching. The two areas—ecclesiology and social teaching—treat two very different realities of the church and the human social order. The church as a unique community founded on the grace and the call of God has a very distinctive structure that differs by definition from any human structures and especially from human political society. Since we are comparing apples and oranges, we shall find no real relationship between them.

Traditional Catholic self-understanding does not see such a dichotomy between the two areas. Catholic faith has always seen the divine as working in and through the human; the human as such never stands in opposition to the divine. This characteristic understanding of Roman Catholicism has been considered distinctive and is referred to by different names — the analogical imagination, the principle of mediation, the sacramental principle, or an incarnational approach.[1] Since the divine uses the human and is mediated in and through the human, the church can and should learn from human understandings. The church and the human political order are not the same, but important similarities can and do exist.

The fact of God's working in and through the human is very evident in Catholic ecclesiology.[2] Catholicism insists, in contradistinction to some reformation perspectives, that the church is a visibile human society with a visible human structure. The church is not an invisible relationship between one individual believer and God but is rather a visible, human community animated by the Holy Spirit. As the incarnational principle brought the divine and the human together in Jesus, so too both the divine and the human inhere in the church and do not merely exist in juxtaposition.

History reminds us of how the early church took its structural components from the contemporary human scene. As the church grew in Roman soil, the Roman Empire furnished many structures and institutions that were taken over by the church; the church's understanding of leadership borrowed more or less freely from secular models of the day. To this day the church recognizes the need for a legal and structural model to be employed in a way that best serves the needs of the people of God. One criticism of the new code of canon law that went into effect in 1983 is its reliance on Roman law more than on the tradition of common law.[3] Notice that the problem does not turn on the opposition of a divine versus a human model but on which particular human model best serves the people of God in its present circumstances.

Yes, the church differs from a secular political community, despite many similarities and agreements. Nevertheless, both theology and history show how much the Catholic church has borrowed from human models in the very structure of the church itself.

Has official Catholic social teaching ever acknowledged that the church can and should learn from the models and structures of secular governments and the political order? The modern period of official Catholic social teaching began with the papal encyclicals of Pope Leo XIII over a hundred years ago. The first explicit mention of the relationship between life in the church and life in human political society is found in the 1971 document of the world synod of bishops, *Justitia in Mundo:* "While the church is bound to give witness to justice, she recognizes that anyone who ventures to speak to people about justice must first be just in their eyes. Hence, we must undertake an examination of the modes of acting and of the possessions and life style found within the church herself." The first area mentioned is human rights, including the right of workers in the church to a suitable livelihood and social security; the right to suitable freedom of expression and thought; and the right to procedural justice, including the accused's right to know the accuser. *Justitia in Mundo* also insists on the right of all members of the church to "have some share in the drawing up of decisions" and urges that women should have their own share of responsibility and participation in the life of society and in the community life of the church.[4]

The United States Catholic bishops in their pastoral letter on the economy cite *Justitia in Mundo* and assert: "All the moral principles that govern the just operation of any economic endeavor apply to the church and its agencies and institutions; indeed the church should be exemplary."[5] The bishops then reflect in a special way on five areas — wages and salaries; rights of employees; investments and property; works of charity; and working for economic justice. Even though this particular letter deals with economic activity, the bishops in their closing paragraph of this section state clearly that the principle involves more than just the economic order and includes the cultural order: "As we have proposed a new experiment in collaboration and participation in decision making by all those affected at all levels of United States society, so we also commit the church to become a model of collaboration and participation."⁶ Thus the American bishops firmly insist that the principles of justice, collaboration, and participation that ought to exist in the political order should also be present in the church. In fact, the church should be exemplary in these matters.

The comparatively late linking of the internal life of the church with the life of human political society raises some significant questions. Why was the linkage never mentioned earlier? What explains why the connection was made in 1971?

This development coheres with the great changes that occurred in Roman Catholicism at the time of the Second Vatican Council. A pre-Vatican II understanding of the church and the relationship between the church and the human political order saw no basic bond or connection between the two. From a purely ecclesiological perspective pre-Vatican II Catholicism tended to see the church as the kingdom of God and thus as basically holy, without spot, and in no need of reform or change. A later theology characterized such an approach as *triumphalistic*.

In the relationship between the church and the state both orders were said to be perfect societies insofar as they contain within themselves all they need to achieve their purposes. These two societies are distinguished from the family, which is not a perfect society because it does not have within it everything that its members need to achieve their end; the family depends upon both the church and the state.⁷ Since the church and state are two perfect societies, little or no room remains for linkage between them. *Perfect* in this sense does not mean "morally perfect" or "holy," but especially in the light of triumphalistic ecclesiology such a connotation was also present.

The peculiar circumstances of the Catholic church in the United States and the theory that went along with such an understanding also discouraged any recognition of a direct link between the church and the political society. In the

United States, Roman Catholicism for the first time faced
in a conscious way the relationship of the church to a democratic form of government and, especially, to a religiously
pluralistic society. Before that time both Catholics and Protestants generally accepted that civic unity required religious
unity. The state thus supported and defended the church in the
system known as the union of church and state. The United
States' experiment involved civic unity without religious unity.
Could Catholics fully support this system and work in the
political and social order together with people belonging to
other religions and to no religion? In practice, American
Catholics wholeheartedly accepted the country's separation
of church and state as well as religious pluralism, but the
theory justifying such an approach had matured only in the
1950s and was finally accepted by the hierarchical church
at the Second Vatican Council in 1965.

John Courtney Murray, a United States Jesuit, was the principal architect of the theory accepting religious freedom and
the so-called separation of church and state.[8] (Note that the
acceptance of the separation of church and state did not
involve the separation of the church and society.) In the 1940s
Murray had advocated intercredal cooperation, or the working
together of Catholics with all others to bring about greater
peace and justice in the temporal society. To justify such
cooperation, Murray clearly distinguished between the supernatural order and the natural order, between the role of the
church and the role of the state. In the supernatural order
the Catholic church rightly claims to be the one true church
of Jesus Christ and does not permit any common worship,
or *communicatio in sacris,* with non-Catholics. However, in
the natural order the Catholic theory of natural law has
recognized that all people share the same basic human nature
and are therefore called to the same morality and should work
together for the common good.[9] The defense of the separation of church and state likewise began with taking note of
the distinction between the supernatural and the natural
orders, the spiritual and the temporal.[10]

In his earlier approach to justify intercredal cooperation
in the temporal and social realms and in his later defense of
religious liberty, Murray found it important to emphasize the

differences between the supernatural and the natural orders and between the church and the state. In such a perspective any direct linkage between the supernatural order and the natural order was downplayed. Murray thus stressed Catholic distinctiveness and differences in the supernatural order but common ground and the cooperation of Catholics with all others in the temporal realm. Like Catholic social teaching itself, Murray saw before Vatican II no direct link between anthropology in general, with its important call for freedom in the temporal political order, and the more specific sort of anthropology and freedom that were required in the life of the church. Only in 1966 did Murray directly connect, through analogy, freedom in the political order with freedom in the realm of the church.[11] Why did both Murray and official Catholic social teaching see a direct link between the temporal order and the spiritual order in terms of their common understanding of the human only under the influence of Vatican II?

One very significant change involved overcoming the dichotomy between the supernatural and the natural that had become almost a dualism in Catholic thought and practice. The Pastoral Constitution on the Church in the Modern World of Vatican II insisted that the gospel, grace, and the supernatural have to affect all reality.[12] Redemption is not limited only to the spheres of the supernatural and the church. The distinction between the two orders and the two realms of the supernatural and the natural had been used to prevent any direct linkage between ecclesiology and Catholic social teaching. The Pastoral Constitution insisted, rather, on the need to overcome the split between faith and daily life and to apply the gospel and God's grace to our life in the world (n. 43).

The most significant changes occurred in ecclesiology itself.[13] Vatican Council II accepted the notion of the church as always in need of reform. The principle of *aggiornamento,* "updating," included considering both the signs of the times and the historical sources. The structures of the present had developed and grown over time. The return to the sources and the needs of the present provided criteria for judging and reforming the existing structures and laws of the church.[14]

The theological basis for reform came from eschatology: the church lives in tension between the now and the future of the fullness of grace; the church is a pilgrim church. In the light of its eschatological fullness the church is never perfect and always stands in need of change and reform.

Vatican II's recognition of the church as the people of God rather than as primarily a hierarchical institutional structure thus opened the door for rethinking the role of authority in the church. The church is the community of the baptized, the people of God animated by the Holy Spirit and served by the officeholders in the church. Catholic ecclesiology before Vatican II had almost identified the church with the kingdom of God. Now the kingdom of God came to be seen as much broader than the church. A sign of the kingdom that in its eschatological fullness and even in its contemporary reality is more than the church, the church itself is now considered in terms of its service to the kingdom and to the world, not as the be-all and end-all to be identified with the kingdom of God and to be served by all others.

In addition, Vatican II accepted a sacramental ecclesiology—the church is a sign of the kingdom. The sign must point out to others the presence of the kingdom; the church must show to others the meaning, dignity, and respect of the human person. Taking the church as a sign helped pave the way for a reforming effort to make sure that the church was indeed such a sign and beacon in our world.

All these changes brought about a more direct link between Catholic ecclesiology and Catholic social teaching. This connection was made very clear in the Pastoral Constitution on the Church in the Modern World. "Everything we have said about the dignity of the human person and about the human community and the profound meaning of human activity lays the foundation for the relationship between the church and the world and promotes the basis for the dialogue between them. . . . Thus the church, at once a visible assembly and a spiritual community, goes forward together with humanity and experiences the same earthly lot which the world does. She serves as a leaven and as a kind of soul for human society as it is to be renewed in Christ and transformed into God's family" (n. 40).

Since the church and the world are mutually related, they enjoy a reciprocal relationship. One would expect the Pastoral Constitution on the Church in the Modern World to point out the help that the church tries to bring to human persons, society, and human activity. However, one paragraph (n. 44) also recognizes the help that the church receives from the modern world. "(T)he church knows how richly she has profited by the history and development of humanity. . . . Thanks to the experience of past ages, the progress of the sciences, and the treasures hidden in the various forms of human culture, the nature of man himself [sic] is more clearly revealed and new roads to truth are opened. . . . Since the church has a visible and social structure as a sign of her unity in Christ, she can and ought to be enriched by the development of human social life" (n. 44). The dialogue and reciprocal relationship between church and world link the two and openly admit that the church can and should learn from the world in its understanding, proclamation, and living as a human community.

Subsequent documents in official Catholic social teaching take up the same theme. In his *Sollicitudo Rei Socialis,* Pope John Paul II commemorated the twentieth anniversary of Pope Paul's encyclical, *Populorum Progressio* (1967) and quoted the phrase that the church is an "expert in humanity."[15] In a special way John Paul II has called attention to anthropology in both social teaching and ecclesiology. In *Redemptor Hominis,* his own first encyclical, he emphasized that "man [sic] is the primary route that the church must travel in fulfilling her mission—he [sic] is the primary and fundamental way for the church."[16] Catholic social teaching itself now recognizes a mutual relationship between ecclesiology and Catholic social teaching.

Specific Points That Can Be Learned

In the light of that direct link and relationship between ecclesiology and Catholic teaching I shall now discuss the more important values and aspects that Catholic ecclesiology can learn from Catholic social teaching. One of the most distinctive characteristics of official Catholic social teaching in the last few decades has been the development that has taken place in that realm. Within Catholic social teaching one can readily see areas of continuity and of change. At the same time, the methodology of Catholic social teaching has itself changed, even somewhat dramatically, in the one hundred years of modern official teaching. This section of the chapter will consider the most important aspects of these three different areas where Catholic social teaching can provide helpful guidance to Catholic ecclesiology: continuing emphases in Catholic social teaching; dramatic new developments in Catholic social teaching; and a historically conscious methodology.

Continuing Emphases in Catholic Social Teaching

Two important continuing emphases in Catholic social teaching that are helpful and applicable to Catholic ecclesiology are (1) the principle of subsidiarity and (2) the subordination of authority to justice and truth.

Modern official Catholic social teaching has strongly insisted on the principle of subsidiarity. The principle was enunciated by Pope Pius XI in *Quadragesimo Anno* in 1931 and described as "a fundamental principle of social philosophy, fixed and unchangeable." The principle primarily delineates the proper role and function of government. One should not withdraw from individuals and give over to the community what individuals can accomplish by their own enterprise and activity. To transfer to the larger and higher collectivity functions that can be performed by lesser and subordinate bodies is an injustice and a disturbance of right order. The government is a help (*subsidium*) that should enable individuals, voluntary groups, and smaller and more local governmental bodies to do what they can; the larger unit of government should intervene only when individuals, voluntary groups, and local governments cannot deal with the particular issue.[17]

The principle of subsidiarity coheres with Catholic social teaching's attempt to avoid the two extremes of individualism and collectivism in its approach to political society. Individualism wants to restrict the role of government as much as possible and supports the axiom that the least government is the best government. Collectivism so extols the role of the collectivity that it subordinates all to the whole and takes over the rightful role of individuals, of voluntary associations, and of more local governments.

The very phrasing of the principle of subsidiarity lent credence to the ideas of some people in the United States and elsewhere who were employing this principle in the 1950s to deny a larger role to government.[18] In 1961 Pope John XXIII, in *Mater et Magistra,* recognized the growing complexity and socialization (multiplication of social relationships) of modern life and the need for the federal government to intervene more than in the past in order to reduce imbalances in economic life and bring about justice. The common good in these circumstances requires greater government involvement because only the federal government is big enough to deal with the complexity, multiplicity, and polysemy of the issues. However, John XXIII still strongly upheld the principle of subsidiarity itself.[19]

Can and should the principle of subsidiarity be applied in the church? The answer to both "Can?" and "Should?" is "Yes." The ecclesiology of Vatican II acknowledged that too much emphasis had been placed on the universal church and on the hierarchical leadership in the church. The church is above all the community of God gathered around the eucharistic banquet table. The church is primarily the people of God, not just the universal governing function in the church. Similarly, Vatican II emphasized the importance of the local church, seeing the universal church as a community of local churches. More importance has also been given to the diocesan church and to the local bishop and the college of bishops.[20]

Especially in the light of the growing centralization in Roman Catholicism in the pre–Vatican II period, a great need exists for the principle of subsidiarity today. The functions more heavily stressed while the church universal truly exercises only a subsidiary function. The fifth principle of the 1971 Synod of Bishops' ten principles for the revision of canon law stated that the principle of subsidiarity should be more broadly and completely applied to church legislation.[21] In the judgment of many people, the subsequent 1983 code of canon law failed to put this principle into practice. The new code is basically the same as the old one, with only a few comparatively peripheral changes. The consistent application of the principle of subsidiarity would call for a much more radical change.[22] As chapter 1 pointed out, the church will always experience tension between the local and the universal; no easy or pat answers will do away with tensions. However, both the recognition of growing diversities within the Catholic church today and the ecumenical requirements of the time call for a much more thorough and complete application of the principle of subsidiarity to the life of the church.

Catholic social ethics and teaching have traditionally emphasized the primacy of justice and have seen the role of authority as discerning and ordering in accord with justice. Without doubt, Catholic social teaching accepted an important role for authority, and, for many people in the tradition, monarchy was considered the best form of government; indeed, Catholic social ethics came into existence when monarchies of some type were the most common and accepted form of government. One of the fascinating developments in the tradition has been the move toward the formal acknowledgment of democracy as the best form of government. Only beginning with the speeches of Pope Pius XII in the early 1940s in the midst of World War II did Catholic social teaching move to support democratic sorts of government as the best. An earlier approach had maintained that a particular government could be any one of a diversity of forms provided that the government brought about justice for society.[23] A later section will discuss this and other related developments in greater detail, but for our present purposes I want to raise the question, How was it possible for Catholic social ethics and its official teaching to make this very significant change when in its history it had been strongly supportive of monarchies and in the nineteenth and early twentieth centuries had condemned liberal democracy? One of the significant factors making such a development possible was the approach taken to authority: authority was never absolutized and was always subordinated to justice, human reason, and natural law.

In the Thomistic and Catholic traditions a just and well-ordered society is governed by law. The eternal law is the plan of God for the world, whereas the natural law is the participation of the eternal law in the rational creature. Human reason reflecting on human nature can arrive at ethical wisdom and knowledge. Human law is an ordering of reason for the common good and is made by the person who has charge of the community. This human law either reiterates the principles of natural law or applies the natural law in changing circumstances. As based on human nature, the natural law is universal and binding on everyone. In the changing historical and cultural contexts of time and place, human law specifies the demands of the natural law. Thus, for example, the natural law argues for progressive taxation but human law works out the precise details. The natural law would demand that people drive cars carefully and safely, but human or positive law fleshes out what is careful and safe under different conditions. The purely human or positive law thus specifies the demands of the natural law.[24]

At first glance, a model based on law would seem to give great emphasis and power to authority as what makes the law. The legislator or authority determines what is right or what is to be done by all others. However, two characteristics of Catholic natural law theory stand in the way of such an understanding: the rational or intrinsic understanding of law in the Catholic tradition; and the important role of mediation in Catholic theology and ethics.

The intrinsic or rational aspect of law is prominent in the Thomistic tradition.[25] Not primarily an act of the will but an act of reason, human law is an ordering of reason for the common good made by the one who has charge of the community. The legislator or authority must therefore conform himself or herself to reason, justice, and the demands of the common good because the will of the legislator does not make something right or wrong. The most important virtue for the ruler is not power but wisdom — knowing what is right, just, and helpful for the common good and directing all people toward it.

Voluntaristic and extrinsic approaches to law have a very different perspective. If law is primarily an act of the will of the legislator, then the source of law's obligation comes from the will of the ruler. Something is good because it is commanded. The Catholic tradition runs opposite — something is commanded because it is good. A rational and intrinsic notion of law thus emphasizes that the legislator or ruler must conform to what is reasonable and just. The legislator has neither the ultimate nor the last word.

The intrinsic and rational understandings of human law have other important ramifications. In theory the Catholic tradition has had no problem with the legitimacy of civil disobedience. Some people have maintained that the Thomistic tradition too readily and easily accepts civil disobedience by simply maintaining that an unjust law is no law at all and does not oblige in conscience. Thomistic theory not only justifies possible civil disobedience but also sees the going against the letter of the law in the light of the spirit of the law as a matter of virtue — the virtue of *epikeia*. By its very nature purely human law admits of exceptions because it is not based, as is natural law, on immutable and universal human nature (a very disputed point) but on changing historical and cultural circumstances. The legislator determines what is for the common good in the usual circumstances, but other circumstances can enter in and change the reality. In other words, the letter of the law can get in the way of its spirit. To go against the word of the law is not always wrong. In fact, *epikeia* is the crown of the virtue of legal justice which at times calls for an individual to go against the letter of the law in order to achieve true justice and right ordering.[26]

The Catholic insistence on mediation sees human law as a mediation of natural law and natural law as a mediation of the eternal law. Thus the human lawgiver is not free to decide what the law should be. Human law is determined not primarily by the will of authority but by the plan of God, the natural law, and the concrete determination of what is best for the common good.

In Catholic political ethics the will of the ruler does not make something right or wrong. For a long time Catholic social ethics favored monarchies, but the monarch was never held to be an absolute ruler. The monarch had to correspond to the demands of reason, justice, and the common good that were the true basis of just law. To be sure, the older Catholic political theory stressed justice and right ordering at the expense of the freedom of the individual; nevertheless, for the same basic reason the older theory also severely limited the freedom of the ruler, for Catholic social teaching has always insisted that the ruler or lawgiver is not supreme and that he or she must conform to the just, the reasonable, and the demands of the common good.

The same fundamental principles can and should hold for the church—a theme that was touched upon in chapter 1. Church authority does not make something true or right. Church authority must conform itself to the true and the right and the just. Church authority should be seen as a mediator and servant of God's grace and must conform itself to God's grace. Authoritarianism can never be accepted in the church. The Holy Spirit assists authority to discern more readily and surely what the call of God is and what the church community needs. Vatican Council II proposed such an understanding of the hierarchical teaching office in the church: "This teaching office is not above the word of God but serves it, teaching only what has been handed on, listening to it devoutly, guarding it scrupulously, and explaining it faithfully by divine commission and with the help of the Holy Spirit; it draws from this one deposit of faith everything which it presents for belief as divinely revealed."[27] Thus authority in the church must always be exercised in this manner, recognizing that it does not have the ultimate or the last word but is itself striving to discern and correspond to the word of God, the grace of the Holy Spirit, and the needs of the faith community here and now and in these circumstances.[28]

*Dramatic New Developments in Official
Catholic Social Teaching*

Modern official Catholic social teaching as found in official church documents tends to emphasize continuity with the past. The older rule was to cite only official church documents, scripture, and earlier writings from the tradition, such as the fathers of the church or Thomas Aquinas. Only 1 of the 167 footnotes of the Pastoral Constitution on the Church in the Modern World refers to a contemporary book—a 1964 book on Galileo published by the Vatican Press.[29] *Populorum Progressio* in 1967 makes a decided shift; 9 of the 69 footnotes refer to contemporary publications. Seldom if ever have the documents explicitly recognized a change in the teaching or contrasted the newer teaching with the older teaching. However, in reality, very significant and deep changes have occurred in Catholic social teaching in the last century or so (some of these changes were discussed in the third chapter). For our purposes here, the significant changes involve anthropology, the central criteria for judging a just social order, and the best form of government.

In *Octogesima Adveniens* in 1971, Pope Paul VI maintained: "(T)wo aspirations persistently make themselves felt in these new contexts, and they grow stronger to the extent that human beings become better informed and better educated: the aspiration to equality and the aspiration to participation, two forms of human dignity and freedom."[30] The anthropology stressing freedom, equality, and participation becomes normative for the entire letter. Subsequent documents such as Pope John Paul II's *Laborem Exercens* and *Sollicitudo Rei Socialis* continue these emphases. Karol Wojtyla's earlier major philosophical treatise, *The Acting Person* (published originally in Polish in 1969 and in English in 1979), devotes its fourth and final part to participation.[31]

The condemnations of freedom in nineteenth-century official Catholic social teaching are well known. This very negative attitude is found especially in the teachings of Pope Pius IX but is still present in the corpus of writings of Pope Leo XIII, who began the tradition of modern official Catholic social teaching with *Rerum Novarum* in 1891. Many commemorations of *Rerum Novarum* took place in 1991, and rightly so because this encyclical dealing with the rights of workers continues to ring true today. However, the contemporary church no longer celebrates or often cites the encyclicals of Leo XIII that deal primarily with the political order and the legal order. There were no centennial celebrations in 1988 of the anniversary of Leo's encyclical, *Libertas*

Praestantissimum, which dealt with freedom and strongly denounced liberalism.

In *Libertas Praestantissimum,* Pope Leo XIII condemned "the modern liberties." The liberty of worship goes against the "chiefest and holiest" duty that commands human beings to worship the one true God in the one true church. The theory that calls for the separation of church and state is an "absurdity." Liberty of speech and of the press he condemned because the authority of the law must protect "the untutored multitude" from error and falsehood just as it protects the weak from violence inflicted by the powerful. Since the truth alone should imbue the human mind, the liberty of teaching is greatly opposed to reason and tends absolutely to pervert human minds inasmuch as it claims for itself the right of teaching whatever it pleases—a liberty that the state cannot grant without failing in its duty. The liberty of conscience can be understood only as the freedom to follow God's commands and to do one's duty.[32] Recall that only at Vatican Council II in 1965 did Roman Catholicism finally accept religious freedom officially. Years earlier, Pope Leo XIII was no supporter of civil liberties and human freedom.

Leo's position on equality is very clear. His general discussions usually begin by recognizing that although a true equality obtains insofar as all human beings are children of God and called to eternal happiness, no equality exists in civil society and culture. "The inequality of rights and of power proceeds 'from the very Author of nature, from whom all paternity in heaven and earth is named.'"[33] The metaphor of the human body with its various organs and parts is used to justify the inequality that must exist in society. "But, as the abilities of all are not equal, as one differs from another in the powers of mind or body, and as there are many dissimilarities of manner, disposition, and character, it is most repugnant to reason to endeavor to confine all within the same measure and to extend complete equality to the institutions of civil life."[34]

Participation of the people in civil society and in the political order had no place in Leo's thought. The people were the "untutored multitude."[35] Authorities were called the "rulers" (*principes*). Leo's understanding of the political order was authoritarian or, at best, paternalistic. Religion "is wonderfully helpful to the state. For, since it derives the prime origin of all power directly from God himself, with grave authority it charges rulers to be mindful of their duty, to govern without injustice or severity, to rule their people kindly and with almost paternal charity; it admonishes subjects to be obedient to lawful authority, as to the ministers of God; and it binds them to their rulers, not merely by obedience, but by reverence and affection, forbidding all seditions and venturesome enterprises calculated to disturb public order and tranquility."[36]

Thus a most significant change in the anthropology found in official Catholic social teaching has taken place since the time of Pope Leo XIII in the latter part of the nineteenth century until today. Above all, these changes have seen a strong contemporary emphasis on freedom, equality, and participation as essential characteristics of the human person.

In his study of contemporary Catholic social teaching David Hollenbach refers to "an astounding development" whereby human rights has become "a prime focus" of official Catholic social teaching."[37] J. Bryan Hehir maintains that the "principal way in which John Paul II addresses the social questions is through human rights categories."[38]

In the eighteenth and nineteenth centuries official Catholic teaching strongly opposed "the rights of man" as associated especially with the French revolution. By definition human rights are intimately connected with human freedom. But recall the general opposition of Catholicism to these freedoms in the nineteenth century and the fact that only at the Second Vatican Council in 1965 did Catholics finally accept officially the right to religious freedom. In the nineteenth century Catholic emphasis fell on law and duties but not on rights.[39] In 1963 *Pacem in Terris* gave the first full-blown discussion of human rights in official Catholic social teaching.[40] Since then, human rights have become a central criterion in judging the justice of existing social systems.

The Pastoral Constitution on the Church in the Modern World of Vatican II proclaimed the "profound changes" that have occurred in the political order, and the document affirmed further the role of democratic structures. "It is in full accord with human nature that juridical-political structures should, with ever better success and without any discrimination, afford all their citizens the chance to participate freely and actively in establishing the constitutional bases of a political community, governing the state, determining the scope and purpose of various institutions, and choosing leaders. . . . Let the rights of all persons, families, and associations along with the exercise of those rights be recognized, honored, and fostered. The same holds for those duties which bind all citizens."[41] Today we may find nothing startling in such a statement, but in the eighteenth and nineteenth centuries Catholicism strongly opposed the emergence of democracies. And as late as the twentieth century the Vatican entered into concordats or treaties with the governments of Mussolini and Hitler. Catholic teaching insisted often that it was indifferent to any particular form of government. The first official praise of democracy as the best form came with the Christmas addresses of Pope Pius XII in the 1940s.[42]

Great changes in anthropology, the central criteria for judging a just social order, and the best form of government have occurred in a comparatively short period of time in official Catholic social teaching. What explains these changes?

One very significant and overarching factor for the acceptance of these particular changes was the church's response to the challenge of liberalism. Over the course of time the church came to accept many aspects of liberalism, but not all, for liberalism is too closely connected with a one-sided individualism. Thus, for example, in finally accepting human rights, Catholic teaching insists on both political and economic rights; liberalism, on the other hand, was strong on political and civil rights but weak on economic and social rights. Catholic social teaching today has accepted, obviously with some modifications, what it had strongly opposed a century or more ago. The church should not uncritically accept any movement, but we must all admit that the church has learned from liberalism even while criticizing some of its aspects.[43]

Catholic ecclesiology can and must learn from these dramatic changes in official Catholic social teaching. I admit that the church and the political order are not exactly the same, but definite similarities and congruences exist, especially in the light of the fact that the church is a sign of the presence of the reign of God and looks forward to the future fulfillment of that reign. Purposely I have spoken not only of democracy in this section but also have stressed developments in anthropology, the criteria for judging a just society, and the best form of the political order. These three dimensions of the social order are intimately connected, with anthropology being the most general of the concepts and democracy the most specific. Since the church now understands itself as an expert in humanity, this anthropology must be proclaimed and lived by the church itself. Freedom, equality, and participation must become more evident and be promoted and protected in the life of the church if the church is truly to carry out its function as an expert in humanity. Today, Catholic ecclesiology must incorporate and promote the contemporary Catholic approaches to anthropology that are found in official Catholic social teaching.

Human rights as a central criterion of justice can and should be present in the church itself. Yes, these rights will not be exactly the same as rights in the political order, but they must enshrine and defend the same basic values. Canonists in the last few decades have called for a bill of rights that would be part of the constitution of the church. The official documents guiding the work of the revision of canon law made the safeguarding of rights one of its ten guiding principles. Pope Paul VI had originally called for a first section that would have treated the "fundamental law of the church," which would have been a constitutional statement including the rights of the people of God. However, the fundamental law was ultimately scuttled.[44] The 1983 code of canon law has a section on the rights of the faithful (canons 208–223), but in my judgment the rights presented in this section are very inadequate.[45]

The Catholic church can and should learn from democratic forms of government. These forms incorporate the anthropological concerns and the emphasis on human rights mentioned above. The Church, because it is primarily the people of God, is open to learning from truly democratic societies. To point out exactly what democracy in the Catholic church should look like is well beyond the scope of this chapter. Many other authors such as Dennis McCann in the United States, Edward Schillebeeckx in Europe, and Leonardo Boff in South America have addressed these issues.[46]

The objection that these emphases on freedom, equality, participation, human rights, and democracy are attempts to Americanize the church is not true. The same stress and the same values are found in the official documents of the universal teaching authority of the church and do not come only from American documents. Many theologians and canonists from outside the United States have also been advocating a more free, equal, participative, and just church. And, on the other hand, American Catholics are not uncritical of American society. For example, Rosemary Ruether, an American who has called for a greater democratization of the church, has also been very critical of many social, cultural, economic, and political institutions in the United States.[47] To be true to its own mission, function, and purpose, the Catholic church must be more open to incorporate into its structures the anthropology, criteria of justice, and form of government mentioned here.

A Historically Conscious Methodology

As the last section has pointed out, very significant substantive changes have occurred in official Catholic social teaching. Substance, however, is intimately connected with method. Substantive changes point to an underlying methodological change in official Catholic social teaching that has developed in the last few decades.

In my judgment the more recent official documents of Catholic social teaching have adopted a more historically conscious methodology as distinguished from the classicism of earlier documents. Classicism tends to think in terms of the eternal, the immutable, and the unchanging; historical consciousness recognizes continuity and discontinuity but gives importance to the particular, the individual, the contingent, and the changing. While classicism employs a deductive approach, historical consciousness sees a greater but not absolute role for inductive reasoning.[48]

These contrasting methodologies can be illustrated readily from the documents themselves. Pope Pius XI's 1931 encyclical, *Quadragesimo Anno* ("On Reconstructing the Social Order"), proposes a general plan that the pope thought had universal validity and was to be applied to the whole world. The methodology of *Quadragesimo Anno* is decidedly deductive.[49] Forty years later, in 1971, Pope Paul VI in *Octogesima Adveniens* recognized the diversity of situations in the contemporary world: "In the face of such widely varying situations it is difficult for us to utter a unified message and to put forward a solution which has universal validity. Such is not our ambition, nor is it our mission. It is up to the Christian communities to analyze with objectivity the situation which is proper to their own country, to shed on it the light of the gospel's unalterable words, and to draw principles of reflection, norms of judgment, and directives for action from the social teaching of the church."[50] Notice how such an approach recognizes both continuities and discontinuities.

The dramatic substantive changes outlined in the previous section could have occurred only because official Catholic teaching adopted a more historically conscious methodology. In the process, Catholic social teaching was able to change its approach to freedom, equality, participation, human rights, and democratic forms of government. A truly historically conscious approach will not merely accept or canonize what is happening here and now but will also evaluate the present critically in the light of the past and the future. The Christian perspective thus finds great significance in the scriptural witness, the tradition, and the future eschatological fullness as God's gracious gift, as well as in the signs of the times. The pilgrim church and its ongoing life learn from what is happening in the world but at the same time are always ready to oppose and to criticize what stands in the way of the gospel and the reign of God.

Catholic ecclesiology can and should learn from official Catholic social teaching and from other sources to employ on a regular basis a more historically conscious methodology. In reality, the reforms of Vatican II came about because precisely such a methodology was at work. Existing church structures were criticized and reformed in the light of scripture, tradition, the signs of the times, and the coming of the reign of God.[51] Once again, historically conscious methodology will not uncritically canonize all that is occurring today. However, such an approach can and should learn from the contemporary historical realities that Vatican II referred to as the signs of the times. A more rigorously consistent historically conscious methodology in ecclesiology will share with official Catholic social teaching the importance of freedom, equality, participation, basic human rights, and democratic forms of government.

Catholic ecclesiology can and should learn from official Catholic social teaching. Some very important substantive and methodological approaches will enable ecclesiology to make the church more truly a sign and servant of both humanity and the reign of God.

NOTES

1. Andrew M. Greeley, *The Catholic Myth: The Behavior and Beliefs of American Catholics* (New York: Scribner, 1990); David Tracy, *The Analogical Imagination: Christian Theology and the Culture of Pluralism* (New York: Crossroad, 1981).

2. For a very helpful contemporary summary and overview of Catholic ecclesiology, see Richard P. McBrien, *Catholicism,* study ed. (Minneapolis: Winston, 1981), pp. 567-729.

3. Ladislas Örsy, "Title I: Ecclesiastical Laws (cc. 7-22)," in James A. Coriden, Thomas J. Green, and Donald E. Heintschel, eds., *The Code of Canon Law: A Text and Commentary* (New York: Paulist Press, 1985), pp. 34ff.

4. *Justitia in mundo,* in David M. Byers, ed., *Justice in the Marketplace: Collected Statements of the Vatican and United States Catholic Bishops on Economic Policy, 1891-1984* (Washington, DC: United States Catholic Conference, 1985), pp. 257-258.

156   *Ecclesiology and Social Teaching*

5. National Conference of Catholic Bishops, *Economic Justice
for All: Pastoral Letter on Catholic Social Teaching and the United
States Economy* (Washington, DC: United States Catholic Conference, 1986), n. 347, p. 174.

6. Ibid., n. 358, p. 179.

7. Marcellinus Zalba, *Theologiae Moralis Summa II: Theologia
Moralis Specialis, Tractatus de Mandatis Dei et Ecclesiae* (Madrid:
Biblioteca de Autores Cristianos, 1953), pp. 199ff.

8. Important studies on John Courtney Murray include the
following: Donald E. Pelotte, *John Courtney Murray: Theologian
in Conflict* (New York: Paulist Press, 1976); J. Leon Hooper, *The
Ethics of Discourse: The Social Philosophy of John Courtney Murray*
(Washington, DC: Georgetown University Press, 1986); Robert W.
McElroy, *The Search for an American Public Theology: The
Contribution of John Courtney Murray* (New York: Paulist Press,
1989).

9. John Courtney Murray, "Current Theology: Christian Co-
operation," *Theological Studies* 3 (1942): 413–431; "Current
Theology: Co-operation, Some Further Views," *Theological Studies*
4 (1943): 110–111; "Current Theology: Intercredal Co-operation:
Its Theory and Its Organization," *Theological Studies* 4 (1943):
267–286; "On the Problem of Co-operation: Some Clarifications,
Reply to Father P. H. Furfey," *The American Ecclesiastical Review*
112 (1945): 194–214.

10. John Courtney Murray, *The Problem of Religious Freedom*
(Westminster, MD: Newman, 1965), p. 28.

11. John Courtney Murray, "Freedom, Authority, Community,"
America 115 (1966): 592–593; see Hooper, *Ethics of Discourse*, pp.
184ff.

12. The Pastoral Constitution on the Church in the Modern
World, part 1, nn. 11–45, in Walter M. Abbott, ed., *The
Documents of Vatican II* (New York: Guild, 1966), pp. 209–248.
For a discussion of this development in official Catholic social
teaching, see my *Directions in Catholic Social Ethics* (Notre Dame,
IN: University of Notre Dame Press, 1985), pp. 43–69.

13. For a succinct and very helpful delineation of the new vision
of the church in society proposed by Vatican II, see Richard P.
McBrien, "The Future Role of the Church in American Society,"
in Leslie Griffin, ed., *Religion and Politics* (Notre Dame, IN:
Review of Politics, no date given), pp. 87–101. The following
paragraphs in the text summarize some of McBrien's six theses as
they are elaborated in his article.

14. John W. O'Malley, *Tradition and Transition: Historical Perspectives on Vatican II* (Wilmington, DE: Glazier, 1989).

15. Pope John Paul II, *Redemptor Hominis*, n. 14, in Byers, *Justice in the Marketplace*, p. 281.

16. See J. Bryan Hehir, "John Paul II: Continuity and Change in Social Teaching," in Charles E. Curran and Richard A. McCormick, eds., *Readings in Moral Theology No. 5: Official Catholic Social Teaching* (New York: Paulist Press, 1986), pp. 253-255.

17. Pope Pius XI, *Quadragesimo Anno*, nn. 17, 18, in Terence P. McLaughlin, ed., *The Church and the Reconstruction of the Modern World: The Social Encyclicals of Pius XI* (Garden City, NY: Doubleday/Image, 1957), pp. 246-247.

18. See Benjamin L. Masse, *Justice for All: An Introduction to the Social Teaching of the Catholic Church* (Milwaukee: Bruce, 1964), p. 77.

19. Pope John XXIII, *Mater et Magistra*, nn. 54-58, in Byers, *Justice in the Marketplace*, p. 115.

20. Patrick Granfield, *The Limits of the Papacy: Authority and Autonomy in the Church* (New York: Crossroad, 1987), pp. 107-133.

21. John A. Alesandro, "General Introduction," in Coriden, Green, and Heintschel, *Code of Canon Law*, p. 6.

22. Knut Walf, "The New Canon Law—the Same Old System," in Hans Küng and Leonard Swidler, eds., *The Church in Anguish: Has the Vatican Betrayed Vatican II?* (San Francisco: Harper, 1987), pp. 91-105.

23. Paul Sigmund, "The Catholic Tradition and Modern Democracy," in Griffin, *Religion and Politics*, pp. 3-21.

24. Thomas Aquinas, *Summa Theologiae*, I^a II^{ae} (Rome: Marietti, 1952), q. 90-q. 97, pp. 410-423.

25. For a more complete discussion of the meaning and ramifications of an intrinsic or rational approach to law, see John Mahoney, *The Making of Moral Theology: A Study of the Roman Catholic Tradition* (Oxford: Clarendon, 1987), pp. 224-258.

26. Édouard Hamel, "La vertu d'épikie," *Sciences Ecclésiastiques* 13 (1961): 35-56.

27. Dogmatic Constitution on Divine Revelation, n. 10, in Abbott, *Documents of Vatican II*, p. 118.

28. The literature on authority in the church is immense. For a very competent overview, see Thomas P. Rausch, *Authority and Leadership in the Church: Past Directions and Future Possibilities* (Wilmington, DE: Glazier, 1989).

158   *Ecclesiology and Social Teaching*

29. Pastoral Constitution on the Church in the Modern World, n. 36, fn. 100, in Abbott, *Documents of Vatican II*, p. 234. Note that the Abbott edition adds unofficial footnotes to the document. The footnote number in the official document is 62.

30. Pope Paul VI, *Octogesima Adveniens*, n. 22, in Byers, *Justice in the Marketplace*, pp. 234–235.

31. Cardinal Karol Wojtyla, *The Acting Person* (Boston: D. Reidel, 1979), pp. 261–300.

32. Pope Leo XIII, "On Human Liberty," (*Libertas Praestantissimum*), nn. 18–30, in Etienne Gilson, ed., *The Church Speaks to the Modern World: The Social Teachings of Leo XIII* (Garden City, NY: Doubleday/Image, 1954), pp. 69–76.

33. Pope Leo XIII, "On Socialism," (*Quod Apostolici Muneris*), n. 5, in Gilson, *The Church Speaks to the Modern World*, p. 193.

34. Pope Leo XIII, "On Freemasonry," (*Humanum Genus*), n. 26, in Gilson, *The Church Speaks to the Modern World*, p. 130.

35. Pope Leo XIII, "On Human Liberty," (*Libertas Praestantissimum*), n. 23, in Gilson, *The Church Speaks to the Modern World*, p. 72.

36. Ibid., n. 22, in Gilson, *The Church Speaks to the Modern World*, pp. 22–23.

37. David Hollenbach, *Justice, Peace, and Human Rights: American Catholic Social Ethics in a Pluralistic World* (New York: Crossroad, 1988), p. 87.

38. Hehir, "John Paul II: Continuity and Change," in Curran and McCormick, *Readings in Moral Theology No. 5*, p. 260. See Otfried Hoffe *et al.*, *Jean Paul II et les droits de l'homme* (Fribourg: Editions Universitaires, 1980).

39. Fr. Refoulé, "L'Eglise et les libertés de Leon XIII à Jean XXIII," *Le Supplément* 125 (1978): 243–259.

40. Pope John XXIII, *Pacem in Terris*, nn. 11–45, in Byers, *Justice in the Marketplace*, pp. 152–159.

41. Pastoral Constitution on the Church in the Modern World, n. 75, in Abbott, *Documents of Vatican II*, pp. 285, 286.

42. Sigmund, in Griffin, *Religion and Politics*, pp. 3–21.

43. Rosemary Radford Ruether, *Contemporary Roman Catholicism: Crises and Challenges* (Kansas City, MO: Sheed and Ward, 1987), pp. 1–23.

44. James A. Coriden, "A Challenge: Making the Rights Real," in Leonard Swidler and Herbert O'Brien, eds., *A Catholic Bill of Rights* (Kansas City, MO: Sheed and Ward, 1988), pp. 7–32. This book is a commentary on the "Charter of the Rights of Catholics

in the Church" proposed in 1983 by the Association for the Rights of Catholics in the Church (ARCC).

45. See my *Toward an American Catholic Moral Theology* (Notre Dame, IN: University of Notre Dame Press, 1987), pp. 161–169.

46. Dennis P. McCann, *New Experiment in Democracy: The Challenge for American Catholicism* (Kansas City, MO: Sheed and Ward, 1987); Edward Schillebeeckx, *The Church: The Human Story of God* (New York: Crossroad, 1991); Leonardo Boff, *Church, Charism, and Power, Liberation Theology and the Institutional Church* (New York: Crossroad, 1985).

47. Ruether, *Contemporary Roman Catholicism*, pp. 24–75.

48. Richard M. Gula, *Reason Informed by Faith: Foundations of Catholic Morality* (New York: Paulist Press, 1989), pp. 30–39.

49. Pope Pius XI, *Quadragesimo Anno*, in McLaughlin, *The Church and the Reconstruction of the Modern World*, pp. 219–278.

50. Pope Paul VI, *Octogesima Adveniens*, n. 4, in Byers, *Justice in the Marketplace*, p. 225.

51. O'Malley, *Tradition and Transition*, pp. 44–125.

7. Catholic Social Teaching and Human Morality

The methodology of contemporary Catholic social teaching sometimes uses Christian warrants and sometimes employs more inclusive human appeals that do not presuppose any distinctively religious beliefs. These two approaches to Christian social ethics are themselves not new, but new and different aspects are currently involved in discussing both approaches.

A traditional debate has taken place in Christian ethics between the advocates of a scriptural approach and supporters of a natural law methodology. In general, Roman Catholic moral theology strongly endorsed and exemplified the natural law approach. For the most part Catholic moral theology did not base its teaching on exclusively Christian arguments or methods. However, the natural law approach has a strong and important theological foundation that had been developed by Thomas Aquinas, among others. God's plan for the world and for the life of humankind is the eternal law, but *law* for Aquinas is primarily an ordering of practical reason. Through creation, God has given human beings their reason; human reason reflecting on human nature can discover God's plan: creation and mediation thus constitute the foundations for the traditional Catholic acceptance of natural law. The plan or law of God is discovered through human reason's ability to reflect on human nature and discover how human beings should act in harmony with the plan and work of the

160

creator. Thus natural law is the participation of the eternal law in the rational creature. Some Protestant ethicists, especially Barthians, strongly criticize a natural law approach, but other Protestants recognize at least some place for human reason in their ethics.[1]

The fourth chapter indicated how the currents of thought that are associated with the Second Vatican Council brought about some profound changes in Catholic life in general and in moral theology in particular. The council called for moral theology to be more thoroughly nourished by the scriptures. The older manuals of moral theology were criticized for being legalistic, minimalistic, individualistic, and not truly theological; the Second Vatican Council also deplored the split in the attitudes of so many Catholics between faith and daily life. The natural–supernatural distinction, or even dichotomy, in the manuals of moral theology and theology in general was severely criticized at the time of the council. Faith, scripture, and theology must be relevant to the concerns of the daily life of the members of the church and to theological reflection on social and political life.[2]

Official Catholic social teaching and its methodology illustrated this change in approach. *Pacem in Terris,* the 1963 encyclical of Pope John XXIII, was the last document to employ an exclusive natural law approach, the same methodology that had been used by Leo XIII in *Rerum Novarum* and in subsequent documents.[3] *Pacem in Terris* clearly sets out its methodological presuppositions in its introduction (nn. 1–7). The laws governing the relationships between human beings and states are written by the creator in human nature, and human beings, made in the image and likeness of God, with intelligence and freedom can discover and act in accord with God's plan. In the discussions of peace in this document no appeal is made to Christian warrants such as grace, Christian reconciliation, or the gift of Jesus and the Spirit to the disciples. However, the Pastoral Constitution on the Church in the Modern World of the Second Vatican Council, in its consideration of the human person, human community, and human activity in the world, appeals to the

Christian warrants of creation, sin, redemption, and, to some extent, eschatology (nn. 12–39). Subsequent documents have also appealed to Christian warrants and sources as well as to inclusive human appeals.

Two types of questions arise in this new context. The first never-ending discussion concerns how each of the two different approaches should be used. What is the meaning of natural law or of human reason? Should reason be used inductively or deductively? How does one move from the time, culture, and place of the scriptures to the time, culture, and place of the present? Should one employ an ascending or a descending Christology? These important, continually recurring questions lie beyond the scope of this chapter. The second type of question concerns the relationship between these two different approaches and the reasons for choosing one approach rather than another. These church documents are dealing with the question of a good and just social order. In discussing this area, one issue is fundamental and basic: Does official Catholic social teaching recognize one single social moral order that is the same for all human beings or are Christians and Catholics called to do something different from what is required of others in trying to bring about a more just society?

The question is framed in such a way as to avoid certain presuppositions which might go along with it. For example, the question under discussion does not necessarily presuppose a deductive or an inductive methodlogy. These documents of official Catholic social teaching deal with what perhaps can be called the social moral order, or *social justice* in the broad sense of the term. These are matters that admittedly affect all human beings and belong to the public forum. The challenge for all humankind is to bring about a more free, just, participative, and sustainable society. Are Christians called to do something different from others in trying to bring about change in the social moral order? In my judgment, the answer to the question is this: Only *one* social moral order exists and all humankind, including Christians, are called to work for the same social justice.

One Social Moral Order

This chapter will defend the thesis that contemporary official Catholic social teaching recognizes that there is only one social moral order for all. Christians and Catholic Christians are not called to do something other than what is required for anyone else.

Two preliminary reasons give credence to this thesis. The first is a negative argument that by itself cannot be totally convincing. Nowhere in these documents can one find an explicit statement that there is a different moral content in the social order for Catholics or for Christians. Such an argument is not totally convincing because it could well be that the documents presuppose and imply what they do not say explicitly. However, if such a position were taken, one would expect some references to it, even if oblique, since the docuents want to teach the members of the church about their social responsibilities.

Second, the documents are often addressed not only to the baptized but to all men and women of good will. Pope John XXIII started this practice with his encyclical *Pacem in Terris* in 1963. Before then, the documents were generally addressed to the Catholic church, its members, and its leaders, in keeping with the very concept of an encyclical, which is a letter that is circulated to the churches. The natural law method of the earlier encyclicals made them in principle open to all other human beings, but as a matter of fact they were not specifically addressed to all humankind. Now, even though appeals are often made to scripture and Christian warrants, the letters where applicable are addressed to all humankind. Thus, Pope John Paul II's *Laborem Exercens* (1981) and *Sollicitudo Rei Socialis* (1987) are addressed to all men and women of good will. Such an address does not necessarily prove that only one social moral order exists for all but points in the direction of such an understanding.

An examination of the most significant documents of contemporary official Catholic social teaching indicates that they explicitly and implicitly admit there is only one social moral order. Christians and Catholics are not called to do something different from others in working for the common good. *Gaudium et Spes,* the Pastoral Constitution on the Church in the Modern World, recognizes that "the social order and its development must unceasingly work to the benefit of the human person. . . . This social order . . . must be founded on truth, built on justice, and animated by love; in freedom, it should grow every day toward a more humane balance" (n. 26). Indeed, "[T]he subject and the goal of all social institutions is and must be the human person, which for its part and by its very nature stands completely in need of social life" (n. 25). For "Christian revelation . . . leads to a deeper understanding of the laws of social life which the creator has written into the spiritual and moral nature of human beings" (n. 23). *Gaudium et Spes* explicitly recognizes "the rightful independence" and "autonomy" of human affairs. Autonomy and rightful independence can be misunderstood to mean that these two created realities do not depend on their creator and have no relationship to God. However, the constitution employs explicitly the concept of mediation to explain both the autonomy of created things and their dependence on God. "[T]he autonomy of earthly affairs . . . mean[s] that created things and societies themselves enjoy their own laws and values which must be gradually deciphered, put to use, and regulated by human beings"; from the faith perspective, this is the will of the creator (n. 36). "For though the same God is savior and creator, Lord of human history as well as of salvation history, in the divine arrangement itself the rightful autonomy of the creature, and particularly of the human being, is not withdrawn. Rather, it is reestablished in its own dignity and strengthened in it" (n. 41).

The Pastoral Constitution on the Church in the Modern World clearly comes down on the side of one social moral order that is the same for all and is based on human nature and human dignity. One might maintain that this document, as the first one to bring in distinctively Christian warrants, is a transitional document that still holds on to the basic presuppositions of the earlier documents with their natural law basis. However, later documents do not justify such an interpretation. A brief analysis of the more significant later documents indicates that the same fundamental acceptance of one social moral order for all remains.

In Pope Paul VI's *Populorum Progressio* (1967) the basic criterion of a just social order is the complete development of the human being, which is expounded throughout the whole first part of the encyclical (nn. 6–42). True to the Catholic insistence on the social aspect of human existence, the second and final part deals with "the development of the human race in the spirit of solidarity" (nn. 43–80). In this section the pope refers on occasion to his visit to Bombay, where he called for mutual understanding and friendship so we can all work together to build the common future of the human race (n. 43). *Populorum Progressio* ends with a final appeal to the sons and daughters of the church, to Christian brothers and sisters, to non-Christian brothers and sisters, and to all people of good will "to achieve a responsible develop-ment of humankind in which all human beings will have an opportunity to find their fulfillment" (n. 84).

Octogesima Adveniens, the apostolic letter of Pope Paul VI on the eightieth anniversary of *Rerum Novarum,* cites *Populorum Progressio* to point out "the church's duty to put herself at the service of all, to help them grasp their serious problem in all its dimensions, and to convince them that solidarity in action at this turning point in human history is a matter of urgency" (n. 5). This letter discusses at length the new social problems that confront human society and calls for all people to work together to solve these problems and to work for a destiny that is shared by all (e.g., nn. 12, 21). The basic criterion of what should be done to solve these problems remains the nature of the human person and the human family (e.g., nn. 11, 13, 14, 15, 16, 17, 19, 20, and 21). The second part of the letter calls to mind two human aspirations that are making themselves felt in these new contexts—equality and participation, two forms of human dignity and freedom (n. 22). Political activity is to be based on the common good, for the human person is social by nature (nn. 23, 24, 46). The common good has been a central theme in Catholic social teaching. Thus, Catholics are called to recognize the problems that confront the contemporary world and to work with all others to bring about a just transformation of society that is based on the criteria of the nature of the human person, the human family, and the common good.

Justitia in Mundo, the document issued by the 1971 synod of bishops, recognizes that the forces working for bringing about justice in the world are "rooted in the awareness of the full basic equality as well as of the human dignity of all. Since human beings are members of the same human family, they are indissolubly linked with one another in the one destiny of the whole world, in the responsibility for which they all share."[4] The very title "Justice in the World" indicates one social moral order that is common to all. "The right to development must be seen as a dynamic interpenetration of all those fundamental human rights upon which the aspiration of individuals and nations are based" (O'Brien, p. 393). The church is not alone responsible for justice in the world but her responsibility is part of her mission. "Her mission involves defending and promoting the dignity and fundamental rights of the human person"; "Christians . . . testify to the power of the Holy Spirit through their action in the service of human begins in those things which are decisive for the existence and the future of humanity" (O'Brien, p. 399). The conclusion of this synodal document calls for collaboration with other Christians, other believers in God, and also with those who do not recognize the author of the world in fostering social justice, peace, and freedom (O'Brien, p. 404). Again, the implications are clear. All people must work together in trying to attain *one* social moral order and *one* social justice.

Evangelii Nuntiandi, Pope Paul VI's 1975 document on evangelization deals primarily with evangelization but sees the social mission of the church as part of the evangelizing function. The pope sees human development and liberation as part of the evangelizing mission of the church, but the gospel involves much more than this dimension. "[E]vangelization involves an explicit message . . . about the rights and duties of every human being, about family life without which personal growth and development is hardly possible, about life in society, about international life, peace, justice, and development—a message especially energetic today about liberation" (n. 29). Between evangelization and human development are profound links of an anthropological order because the human being to be evangelized is not an abstract being but is subject to social and economic questions. There are also links of a theological order since one cannot disassociate the plan of creation from the plan of redemption. And links are to be found, too, of the evangelical order because one cannot proclaim the new commandment without promoting in justice and in peace the true, authentic advancement of human beings (n. 31). Thus redemption and the gospel include true human advancement, which appears to be the same for all human beings. Talking about the specific contribution of the church, *Evangelii Nuntiandi* does not propose that Christians should do something different from what other human beings are called to do in the service of justice and true human advancement. The church provides Christian liberation with the inspiration of faith, the motivation of fraternal love, and a social teaching. But no specific mention is made of a special content for Christians that differs from the justice, human advancement, and social good for which all human beings are called to work (n. 38).

Laborem Exercens, the 1981 encyclical of Pope John Paul II, very clearly affirms the reality of one social moral order for all. "The church considers it her duty to speak out on work from the viewpoint of its human value and of the moral order to which it belongs" (n. 24). A strong point in the encyclical concerns the priority of the person and of the subjective aspect of work. "Thus the principle of the priority of labor over capital is a postulate of the order of social morality" (n. 15). The truth that constitutes the fundamental and perennial heart of Christian teaching on human work is that human work has an ethical value of its own that clearly and directly remains linked to the fact that the one who carries it out is a person—a conscious and free subject, that is to say, a subject who decides about herself or himself (n. 6). The ethical nature of work emphasizing the primacy of the subjective "should also find a central place in the whole sphere of social and economic policy, both within individual countries and in the wider field of international and intercontinental relationships" (n. 7).

One section of *Laborem Exercens* (IV, nn. 16–23) is devoted to the rights of *all* workers. Such rights must be seen within the broad range of human rights that are connatural with human beings and that constitute the fundamental conditions for peace in the modern world: peace both within individual countries and societies and in international relations (n. 16). Note again the emphasis on universal human rights that belong to all human beings and must be recognized by all human societies. *Laborem Exercens* closes with a long section (V) on the spirituality of work. Here, a specifically Christian approach is developed, in contrast to the moral teaching part of the document that proposes what is required of all.

Sollicitudo Rei Socialis, issued by Pope John Paul II in 1987 to commemorate the anniversary of *Populorum Progressio,* incorporates many of the themes already seen which point to the fact that one social moral order obtains for which all people — Christians, other believers in God, and nonbelievers alike — are called to strive and work. The human person is the basis for a just social order. All people are called to work in solidarity for the true and authentic development of human persons. The conclusion of *Sollicitudo* makes this point: "At stake is the dignity of the human person whose defense and promotion have been entrusted to us by the creator. . . . Every individual is called upon to play his or her part in this peaceful campaign, a campaign to be conducted by peaceful means in order to secure development in peace in order to safeguard nature itself and the world about us. The church too feels profoundly involved in this enterprise and she hopes for its ultimate success" (n. 47).

Documents of contemporary official Catholic social teaching acknowledge one social moral order or social justice for which all, including Catholic Christians, are called to work. There are references to the moral order and the order of social morality. The basis for this one order is the nature and dignity of the human person and of authentic human development of people both as individuals and in solidarity with others.

Universal human rights furnish an important criterion of social morality. These documents also insist on the need for all human beings to work together in order to achieve this justice, be they Catholics, other Christians, other believers in God, or nonbelievers who are people of good will.

Another way to prove the thesis of this chapter is to examine the content of official Catholic social teaching. Is the teaching that is advocated proposed just for Christians or for all human beings? Part of the problem here is to produce an accurate and succinct statement of the content of official Catholic teaching; the danger lies in summarizing this teaching so that one will propose it in such a way as to support only one's own thesis.

"A Pastoral Message," proposed by the United States bishops in conjunction with their pastoral letter on the economy, succinctly summarizes the content of Catholic social teaching on the economy. The following summary of the principal themes of Catholic social teaching will depend heavily on this pastoral message.[5] The bishops develop briefly six moral principles that "give an overview of the moral vision that we are trying to share" (n. 19). Note the universalist intention of the document. The pastoral message uses the terms *principles* and *themes* synonymously. I prefer to use the word *themes* rather than *principles*. *Themes* is broad enough to embrace the attitudes or dispositions of persons as well as the values, principles, and norms that should direct life in society.

The basis of official Catholic social teaching is the dignity of the human person. For the Christian such human dignity or sacredness is rooted in creation, but all humankind can and should recognize this fundamental dignity.

The human person is social and develops and grows only in community with others. Thus society is not foreign or opposed to the individual person, but human persons are called to live together in society with other human beings. The dignity and the social dimension of the human person constitute the twin cornerstones of the vision for society in official Catholic social teaching.

Human rights have emerged in the last three decades as the criterion often proposed in official Catholic social teaching for determining the justice of a particular society. However, this teaching insists not only on political and civil rights (e.g., freedom of religion, speech, assembly, etc.) but also on social and economic rights (e.g., rights to food, clothing, shelter, and health care).

The justice that should flourish in society in the vision of Catholic social teaching recognizes both the personal and the social dimensions of the person. Commutative justice regulates relationships between individuals; distributive justice directs the relationship of society and the state to the individuals; social or legal justice governs the relationships of individuals to society and the state. Commutative justice is blind, no respecter of persons, and involves arithmetic justice. If I borrow five dollars from you and five dollars from the wealthiest person in the world, I owe each of you the same. Distributive and social justice respect persons and involve proportional, not arithmetic, justice. Thus, for example, the wealthy should not only pay more taxes but also pay a greater percentage of their income in tax. One of the fundamental demands of social justice today is the need for all to participate in the life and direction of society and the state.

The proper role of government is directed by the principle of subsidiarity, which avoids the two opposing dangers of individualism and totalitarianism, thus illustrating the basic anthropology at work. Society exists for the common good. Government should intervene to help individuals, voluntary associations, and local governmental authorities to do what they can, and the federal government should do only what the smaller and lesser bodies cannot do effectively. Property, too, has an individual and a social aspect because from the Christian perspective the goods of creation exist to serve the needs of all. But again, nonbelievers can and should recognize this social dimension of property to serve the needs of all.

In recent years Catholic social teaching has emphasized the preferential option for the poor, a concept and way of life that originated especially in Latin American liberation theology. Although this option has strong roots in the Judeo-Christian tradition, nonbelievers can and should have this same preferential option as a value and as a hermenuetic principle or norm for what is just in society.

This synthetic summary of the major themes of Catholic social teaching indicates that such an approach is available to, and required of, all people living in a particular society. Christian motivation and intentionality definitely shape a person's approach, but all human beings are called to accept this vision and to put it into practice.

Corroboration

Other reasons can corroborate without conclusively proving the thesis that Catholic social teaching recognizes only one social moral order or social justice that all people — Catholics, Christians, believers in God, and nonbelievers — are called to work for in solidarity. First, an older Catholic social teaching in the pre–Vatican II period that extends back to Thomas Aquinas insisted that the social moral teaching was based on the natural law which is common to all humankind. Many people, including myself, have criticized the older manuals and handbooks of moral theology for their classicist, one-sidedly deductive, and physicalist view of natural law. The older Catholic understanding of one social moral order could definitely be wrong and in need of change. However, one can criticize severely the natural law theory of the manuals and still come to the conclusion that there is only one social moral order for all. In fact, in the debate in Germany in the last two decades the defenders of the natural law, or an autonomous ethic, which sees all Christian morality as open to human reason, have generally belonged to the revisionist school of moral theologians.[6] These revisionists have disagreed with many of the conclusions of the manuals of moral theology and of official Catholic teaching, especially in sexual areas. They disagree in many philosophical areas about what is meant by *human reason* and *human nature,* but they agree with the basic theological perspective that human reason reflecting on human nature can arrive at an understanding of the moral order. Thus this chapter's thesis harmonizes with the older Catholic tradition on this subject and has been affirmed even by many contemporaries who have somewhat severely criticized the philosophical presuppositions of neo-scholastic philosophy and of Thomism. While not pretending to be totally convincing, this argument adds corroborative force to the persuasive reasoning about the basis of Catholic social teaching itself.

A second corroborative argument again has its basis in Catholic universalism. The traditional Catholic teaching on the natural law and on the universal salvific will by which God calls all people to salvation illustrates catholicity or universality. In its relationship with the world and society, Roman Catholicism has not been a narrowly particularistic sect that, according to the famous typology of Ernst Troeltsch and Max Weber, sees itself in opposition to the world and withdraws from the world rather than be corrupted by compromise with the world. The church as a type, however — best illustrated by Roman Catholicism, says Troeltsch — is a universal community open to all and whose members live in the world and work together with all others for a better human society.[7] Typologies are never exact; reality rarely lets itself fit neatly into any series of simple types or categories. Nevertheless, anyone can recognize that Roman Catholicism has not been sectarian but, rather, has always seen itself as living in the world and working to bring about a more just and humane society.

One might object that for most of its history Roman Catholicism accepted a Constantinianism that called for the union of church and state. In such a unitary vision the independence and autonomy of the temporal order were not recognized. However, even in a Constantinian vision, the temporal order retained what was thought to be its own finality and purposes. By its very nature, according to the reasoning often proposed, the temporal order is subordinate to the spiritual and hence should be subject to the spiritual. The control of the spiritual order was more often acknowledged to be indirect, not direct. Even in the theoretical acceptance of Constantinianism a relative autonomy of the temporal order was acknowledged.

To be sure, Roman Catholicism has had great difficulty in coming to grips with some aspects of modernity, especially with religious freedom and religious pluralism. Again, official Catholic teaching only in 1965 with the Vatican Council's Declaration on Religious Freedom accepted religious freedom and pluralism. However, in recent times Catholic social teaching has firmly accentuated the need for all people to work together for a just temporal order.[8] The Pastoral Constitution on the Church in the Modern World does not hesitate to speak about the autonomy of the temporal order.

A third reason tending to confirm the thesis of this chapter comes from an interpretation stated by the United States Catholic bishops in their pastoral letters on peace and on the economy. In the letter on peace the bishops explicitly admit that Catholic social teaching on peace and war is directed to two different audiences. When addressing the Catholic faithful, the emphasis is on Christian aspects. When addressing wider, pluralistic audiences, the document employs a more inclusive human approach. The pastoral letter on peace points out how these two different styles and approaches have been used in past Catholic social teaching. In this context the document clearly affirms the existence of *one* social moral order or social justice for which all must work in solidarity: "The wider civil community although it does not share the same vision of faith, is equally bound by certain key moral principles. For all men and women find in the depth of their consciences a law written on the human heart by God. From this law, reason draws moral norms. These norms do not exhaust the gospel vision, but they speak to critical questions affecting the welfare of the human community, the role of states in international relations, and the limits of acceptable actions of individuals and nations on issues of war and peace."[9]

Bishop James Malone, then (1984) the president of the National Conference of Catholic Bishops, treated explicitly the same issue in a significant address. The American bishops not only want to speak to Catholic believers but they also want to make a religiously informed contribution to the public policy debate in our pluralistic society. "When we oppose abortion in that forum, we do so because a fundamental human right is at stake—the right to life of the unborn child. When we oppose any such deterrence policies as would directly target civilian centers or inflict catastrophic damage, we do so because human values would be violated in such an attack. When we support civil rights at home and measure foreign policy by human rights criteria, we seek to do so in terms all people can grasp and support."[10] Thus the American bishops recognize that on questions of public policy they are not proposing values and norms only for Catholics but for all humankind.

Further Considerations

This section will develop in greater length two significant aspects of the thesis of this chapter: a more precise understanding of the social moral order and the relationship of my thesis to the ongoing discussion in contemporary Catholic moral theology.

What does *the social moral order* mean and include? I have employed this term on the basis of its use in various official documents in Catholic social teaching. *Order* and *ordering* are important and traditional concepts in Catholic ethics. In the Thomistic tradition, law is viewed as the objective norm of morality and is seen primarily as a work of practical reason whose function is the proper ordering of things. Such a generic understanding of law applies to the different types of law— the eternal law, the natural law, and human law. Further, the different types of law are related through mediation: the natural law is the participation of the eternal law in the rational creature. Human law either makes known the requirements of natural law or makes specific what is left indeterminate in the natural law. Thus, for example, the natural law requires that one drive automobiles carefully and safely, but the human law should decide which side of the street drivers should use.[11] The moral order thus refers to how all things should be ordered; the social moral order refers to the ordering that brings about a just society.

The manuals of Catholic moral theology in the pre–Vatican II period truncated the Thomistic understanding of morality and reduced it almost totally to the role of ordering and of law. In my judgment morality and also the moral order involves more than just norms. Social morality by its very nature is always going to give more importance to ordering and to structures and institutions for these are the very foundations of the social order, of human beings living in society with other human beings. The social order does not directly deal with the private, the internal, and the invisible. However, the social moral order does depend heavily upon the attitudes, dispositions, or character of the people who comprise the society. Social morality demands two realities — a change of heart and a change of structures. In addition to the attitudes and virtues that should characterize the individual person who lives in the society, a proper understanding of the social moral order also includes the values, the norms, and the principles that should direct the life of society; finally, there is the level of the concrete structuring of social realilties and of the particular judgments that must be made: The social moral order must embrace all these three levels.

The more objective levels of values, principles, and norms, on the one hand, and particular structures, institutions, and judgments, on the other hand, are in my judgment the same for Christians, non-Christians, and all human beings in general. All human beings are called to live together in a particular political society and as part of the total human family. The social moral order thus understood is open in principle to every human being. By no means do all human beings accept the values, norms, and institutions that are proposed, but all by reason of being human are *called* to accept these values, norms, and institutions, and no insurmountable reason exists (e.g., the lack of explicit Christian revelation) that prevents the acceptance of the social moral order. From a purely pragmatic perspective, having a society requires some fundamental and basic agreement about what the society is and how it should function, but the position taken here is not just a pragmatic one.

Attitudes, virtues, dispositions, and character refer to the more subjective aspects of human morality where one can and should expect a greater degree of differences depending upon the differences of the individual. All people living in the same society must ultimately come to some agreement or consensus about the type of society that they want to live in and the values that such a society should have but each individual human being will retain his or her own dispositions, preferences, character traits, and so on. However, the fundamental attitudes and dispositions that govern life in society are the same for all. For example, concern for the poor is frequently proposed as an important attitude in Catholic social teaching and often is grounded in the Hebrew and Christian scriptures. However, concern for the poor should characterize all people in the society and not just those who accept Judaism, Christianity, or some other religious faith. Concern for the poor does not necessarily require any religious belief at all. The basic dignity of all human beings can serve as the foundation for a special concern for human beings who are in need. Intentionality and motivation will definitely differ, but concern for the poor is an attitude required of all human beings.

How does the thesis of this chapter fit into some of the ongoing discussions about similar issues? One question concerns the best way for Catholic social teaching to address its subject matter. Since Catholic social teaching is addressed not only to Catholics but to all others, the documents will at times use Christian warrants but at other times use more inclusive human warrants. The tactical question will remain. What the present thesis adds is that the tactical question is really the only question that must be addressed. One does not appeal to Christian sources and themes because some content exists that is meant only for Christians. However, I would strongly disagree with the contention that the documents should appeal only to inclusively human sources and warrants. In addressing the Catholic community the documents should appeal to the specific realities shared by this particular community. In fact, I do not think the documents in the past have appealed enough, for example, to the relationship between liturgy and social practice; the Catholic community is primarily a eucharistic community, and this sacramental reality should have an important relationship to life in human society.

The broader context of the subject matter under consideration here is the question, Is there a unique moral content to Christian morality? The question has been discussed from different contexts and in different countries. As in any ongoing debate, clarifications and developments have ensued. Norbert Rigali has recently helped the discussion by focusing on what is the precise question involved and what are extraneous questions. The debate, he thinks, is not about the distinctiveness of Christian morality, for all admit many things such as love of God and neighbor are distinctive about Christian morality. Nor does the issue concern moral theology or Christian ethics, which is the thematic and systematic reflection on Christian morality. Rather, the precise question is this: Does Christian faith add any unique material content to morality, the moral order, or the moral life?[12]

In the present issue the focus is even narrower: we are talking here about the social moral order, an order obviously more limited than the moral order as a whole. The social moral order deals only with one part of morality and does not touch the private, the purely personal, and that which does not have an effect on society. Also within the confines of any given society we are dealing only with the social moral order for all people who belong to that one society. The presupposition is that these people have to live with one another in peace, justice, and harmony despite their many differences, which often involve religious differences. One could logically maintain that faith does not add any material content to the social moral order but still hold that faith does contribute different material content in the broader moral order.

I have maintained that there is only one moral order for Christians and for all human beings alike. In trying to explain this thesis I have found helpful another suggestion made by Norbert Rigali that he later abandoned. Formerly, Rigali distinguished four different spheres: essential, existential, Christian essential, and Christian existential. Essential morality is what is required of all persons because they are human persons, or, in the narrower context of the present discussion, is what is required of all people in order to live in a just human society. Existential morality refers to the particular calls, gifts, and dispositions of individuals, such as one's profession, state in life, place of living. Christian essential morality refers to responsibilities incumbent on a person as a member of a Christian faith community and that belong to all such members. Christian existential morality refers to the particular vocation or call of a person within the faith community, e.g., to dedicate oneself to the service of peace. Rigali has rejected this earlier distinction because it is based on classicism, which sees a uniform moral order based on a universal human nature. In the name of historical consciousness, Rigali argues now for a multiform moral order based on concrete persons in history.[13]

No doubt, my position is universalist. But I do not think it necessarily has to be classicist. Part of the problem is in knowing the precise way in which historical consciousness is to be understood. I believe that historical consciousness is compatible with human universality. Universality and classicism are not necessarily opposed; in fact, they exist on two different levels. Rigali and I agree that the difference between morality and ethics is very important and significant in this discussion. *Morality* refers to a normative ordering that involves what should or should not be done. *Ethics* is a second-order discourse that reflects on morality in a thematic, systematic, and reflexive way. Rigali rightly points out that the issue under discussion is on the level of morality (whether or not there is a unique moral content to Christian morality) and not on the level of ethics. I am asserting a universality on the level of morality; the discussion about classicism and historical consciousness is not on the level of morality but on the level of ethics. One could hold to a general and an "in-principled" universality on the level of morality without necessarily embracing classicism on the level of ethics.

Rigali can be pushed from the other extreme to reply to the charge that his position tends toward sectarianism. On the narrower question of the social moral order, he needs to address the question of how people in a pluralistic society can work for justice for all its citizens. Will he admit any universal values or principles such as those proposed by Catholic social teaching? Can one have justice in human societies if people are radically incapable of agreeing on what justice is? Rigali could continue to help the discussion by responding to questions about universality. Does he admit any universality? And, if so, where? On the level of the social moral order? Of human rights? Of the dignity of the human person?

In the current discussion about the uniqueness of Christian morality, questions have arisen about what the scriptures contribute to morality. Some people with whom I share the position of affirming that there is one moral order for all claim that scripture gives only paranesis, or moral exhortation, but no normative morality.[14] I disagree, and I think Catholic social teaching also uses scripture to provide some normative content. However, the level of the normative as found in scripture is on the whole rather general because the scriptures themselves are historically and culturally limited. Thus, for example, the preferential option for the poor as found in scripture is normative. The common destiny of the goods of creation to serve the needs of all is often based on Christian warrants. Yet the normative aspects that are found in scripture are not unique to the faith community but can be accepted by all people.

This chapter has defended the thesis that official Catholic social teaching today recognizes one social moral order. Catholics, Christians, believers, and nonbelievers are called to work together for the common good of society. In accord with this thesis, Catholic social teaching will continue to address two audiences — the church and all human beings — and will appeal both to Christian warrants and to more inclusive human appeals. All human beings are called to work together in solidarity for authentic human development and liberation.

NOTES

1. For an overview of the discussion about natural law, see Charles E. Curran and Richard A. McCormick, eds., *Readings in Moral Theology No. 7: Natural Law and Theology* (New York: Paulist Press, 1991).

2. For a description of this work of renewal and for an analysis and criticism of the relationship between faith and ethics especially as it was discussed in the last two decades in Germany, see Vincent

MacNamara, *Faith and Ethics: Recent Roman Catholicism* (Washington, DC: Georgetown University Press, 1985).

3. The pertinent paragraph numbers of official documents will be given in the text. These documents can be found in a number of different sources.

4. There are no official paragraph numbers for *Justitia in Mundo*. My references will be to David J. O'Brien and Thomas A. Shannon, eds., *Renewing the Earth: Catholic Documents on Peace, Justice, and Liberation* (Garden City, NY: Doubleday/Image, 1977). This citation is from p. 391.

5. National Conference of Catholic Bishops, "A Pastoral Message," in *Economic Justice for All: Pastoral Letter on Catholic Social Teaching and the U.S. Economy* (Washington, DC: United States Catholic Conference, 1986), nn. 12–18, pp. ix–xi.

6. For this discussion in Germany, see MacNamara, *Faith and Ethics.* The theologians associated with this approach include Alfons Auer, Franz Böckle, Josef Fuchs, and Bruno Schüller.

7. Ernst Troeltsch, *The Social Teaching of the Christian Churches,* 2 vols. (New York: Harper, 1960).

8. One of the early and perduring concerns of John Courtney Murray, whose scholarship prepared the way for the official Catholic acceptance of religious liberty, was the need for cooperation between Catholics and all others in the social sphere. In the 1940s Murray justified such intercredal cooperation on the basis of natural law, which is shared by all. See John Courtney Murray, "Intercredal Co-operation: Its Theory and Its Organization," *Theological Studies* 4 (1943): 257–286.

9. National Conference of Catholic Bishops, *The Challenge of Peace: God's Promise and Our Response* (Washington, DC: United States Catholic Conference, 1983), n. 17.

10. *Washington Post,* 19 August 1984.

11. John Mahoney, *The Making of Moral Theology: A Study of the Roman Catholic Tradition* (Oxford: Clarendon, 1987), pp. 224–258.

12. Norbert Rigali, "The Uniqueness and Distinctiveness of Christian Morality and Ethics," in Charles E. Curran, ed., *Moral Theology: Challenges for the Future: Essays in Honor of Richard A. McCormick* (New York: Paulist Press, 1990), pp. 74–93.

13. Norbert Rigali, "On Christian Ethics," *Chicago Studies* 10 (1971): 227–247; "Morality and Historical Consciousness," *Chicago Studies* 18 (1979): 162–168; "The Unity of Moral and Pastoral Truth," *Chicago Studies* 25 (1986): 225–229.

14. Bruno Schüller, "Zur Diskussion über das Proprium einer christlichen Ethik," *Theologie und Philosophie* 51 (1976): 321–343.

8. Providence and Responsibility: The Divine and the Human in History

This chapter deals with providence and responsibility, the divine and the human in history, from the perspective of moral theology. Moral theology involves the critical, thematic, and systematic reflection on the life and action of members of the Christian community.

Determining how to live and act as Christian believers requires one to come to grips with this topic. The problem is perennial: How do the divine and the human come together in human action and in history? Does divine providence affect human responsibility? The immense topic touches many aspects of our understanding of God, the transcendent, history, human agency, and the world.

The first part of the chapter will consider how Catholic moral theology has historically dealt with the problem of human responsibility and divine providence. The second part will treat contemporary discussions about providence, and the third will discuss implications for moral theology in the light of the first two parts.

Historical Overview

Providence in its etymological sense refers to God's foresight. In a more specific sense, providence sums up God's relationship to the world as knowing, willing, and executing the plan of salvation and leading the world to its decreed end. More will be said later about providence, but most commentators regard providence as a mystery and strive to understand how the divine and the human work together.

On the more popular level, one senses that providence is invoked somewhat frequently as emphasizing the divine at the expense of the human and thereby downplaying human responsibility; human passivity can easily be justified by an appeal to divine providence. Most Christians today find some truth in the Marxist claim that religion is the "opiate of the masses." Not only the promise of an afterlife but also the recognition that an all-wise and powerful God has a plan for the world can contribute to the weakening of human responsibility. Anne Patrick has proposed that a literalist understanding of divine providence and of the direct intervention of God in history cashes out for some Catholics and Protestants in absolutist defenses of unborn life and passionate espousals of creationist theories of the origin of the species.[1]

An overview of Catholic moral theology indicates that providence is seldom mentioned and that human responsibility is consistently stressed and in no way lessened because of the role of divine providence. The manuals of moral theology that were in use from the seventeenth century until the Second Vatican Council do not discuss providence and generally do not refer to the direct, independent intervention of God in the world. Anyone familiar with such handbooks would agree that providence plays no role in the assessment of moral conduct. Full responsibility rests with human agents, a fact that calls for an explanation. Why do the manuals of Catholic moral theology not appeal to providence? Why do the handbooks not downplay human responsibility because of divine providence? The Catholic tradition in general, Thomistic philosophy and theology, and the very nature of the manuals of moral theology all help to explain why the handbooks emphasize the human responsibility of the agent and do not lessen or change this responsibility in the light of divine providence.

As I have often mentioned, the Catholic theological tradition has consistently and characteristically emphasized the role of the human and its significance. Protestant thought has often accused Catholic moral theology of not giving enough importance to the divine. The perennial danger for Catholicism has not been quietism or passivity but Pelagianism. The Catholic temptation has been to give too much importance to the human and to downplay the role of the divine in human action. At its best, the Catholic tradition insists on the importance of the mediation of the divine in and through the human. Thus from the standpoint of moral theology one should rightly expect that God does not act directly and immediately in the world but in and through the human. Likewise, human beings must accept full responsibility for their actions.

The Thomistic tradition explicates the meaning of mediation in areas of importance to moral theology and its understanding of providence. Anthropology, natural law, and an intrinsic understanding of morality develop the concept of mediation in Catholic thought as exemplified in the work of Thomas Aquinas. The divine is not seen as subtracting from full human responsibility. The first part of the *Summa* of Thomas Aquinas treats of God, while the second part turns its attention to human beings. Aquinas's prologue to the *Prima Secundae* spells out the Thomistic anthropology—the human being is an image of God precisely insofar as the human being is endowed with intellect, free will, and the power of self-determination.[2] The human being images God not by obeying God's law but by being the principle of her or his own action through intellect and free will. The Thomistic position on anthropology thus avoids the two extremes of a pseudo-Augustinianism that sees the human being as really moved extrinsically by God, and a philosophical Aristotelianism that sees the human being as the principle of his or her own actions without any relationship to God. Aquinas brings the divine and the human together by seeing the human being as an image of and participation in the divine to the extent that the human being is the principle of her or his own operations and actions through intellect and free will.

While not the primary ethical category for Thomas Aquinas, natural law occupies a significant position in his thought.[3] For him divine providence works in and through the natural law. The world is governed by divine providence. God's plan for the world can properly be called the eternal law because law is the dictate of practical reason in the one who governs. Human beings as rational creatures are subject to divine providence in a most excellent way, insofar as they partake of a share of providence by being provident both for themselves and for others. Since human beings have a natural inclination to their proper act and end, they participate in eternal reason. This participation of the eternal law in the rational creature is called the natural law. Providence works in and through the natural law and in no way can be seen in opposition to the natural law.[4] I think the most accurate and succinct statement of Thomistic natural law is this: Human reason directs human beings to their end in accord with their nature. God's plan for the world is mediated in and through the natural law. Human beings alone are responsible for determining how to act in this world, and the norm of their action is based on human reason reflecting on human nature. The responsibility to discover what is morally good and to act in accord with the good rests with the human being.

The intrinsic character of Thomistic ethics stands out from the very structure of the ethical discussion in the *Prima Secundae* of the *Summa*. The treatise begins with the question of the ultimate end of human beings.[5] The answer to this question is happiness, meaning that one has come to the fulfillment of one's own nature. Morality is not something imposed from outside by a divine decree or command but rather the true self-fulfillment of the human being. The principle of finality as one of the cornerstones of Thomistic ethics brings into sharp relief the intrinsic character of this moral theory. Thomistic morality has been attacked for being eudaimonistic, but this very charge certainly highlights the intrinsic character of Thomistic morality. Morality is not something imposed from the outside but rather involves what is good for the human being.

Earlier chapters have shown that Thomas Aquinas strongly opposes an extrinsic understanding of morality, according to which something is good because it is commanded. For him, something is commanded because it is good. The Thomistic understanding of law further illustrates well the intrinsic nature of Thomistic morality.[6] Not primarily an act of the will of the legislator, law is an act of reason ordering to the common good. Voluntaristic approaches tend to be extrinsicist, but the emphasis in Aquinas is on human reason and its role. Thus the eternal law is God's ordering which is made known by human reasoning in the natural law. An intrinsic morality based on human reason mediating the divine reason puts the understanding of the moral requirement squarely and fully in the hands of the human agent.

I personally have criticized a number of aspects of Thomistic ethics but not its emphasis on mediation and the general approaches that flesh out the idea of mediation in ethics. Thomistic thought lacks historical consciousness and a more historical appreciation of human development, and in connection with this problem, the ethical methodology in Thomism tends to be much too deductive; not enough importance is given to the person and to the subject. However, despite these and other criticisms, I find myself in basic agreement with the Thomistic emphasis on the human as mediating the divine. The human being has full moral responsibility for understanding the requirements of morality.

The Thomistic notion of providence likewise insists on human mediation of the divine. Providence, too, is understood teleologically and in the light of reason and not of the will: "Now to rule or govern by providence is simply to move things toward an end through understanding."[7] For providence two things are required—the ordering and the execution of the order. God is the cause of operations for all things that operate. But the basic Thomistic insistence on mediation stands out in the recognition that the execution of divine providence is accomplished by means of secondary causes. Secondary causality thus gives the human causes their proper role. God and the human must work together and God's causality is not independent of human causality.[8] Aquinas deals with three major issues that are raised perennially in discussions of providence: contingency; freedom; and evil. Again, mediation is invoked. Precisely the secondary causality of human and natural agents serves as the basis for dealing with these three issues. The basic principle about the possibility of evil is succinctly explained. A defect can occur because of a defect of the secondary agent just as the product of a perfectly skilled artisan might be defective because of a defect in the instrument used.[9] Divine providence likewise does not exclude contingency precisely because of secondary causes. God has created human beings with their freedom. God has to respect the freedom that was given to the creatures no matter what will happen as a result. If God preserves in natural things the contingency that is due to imperfections in the natural causes, all the more reason exists for God to preserve free will since free will pertains to the perfection of the human. Since the human being attains the divine likeness by acting freely, providence should not take away this freedom.[10] Thus Aquinas uses his understanding of mediation and secondary causality to deal with the problems raised against providence by contingency, freedom, and evil.

Providence thus understood as working through secondary causes does not take away from human responsibility. Again, one can and should criticize the Thomistic approach to solving some of the problems inherent in the mystery of providence, but the Thomistic notion of providence does not change, alter, or take away from human freedom and full human responsibility for action in this world. Providence works in and through the natural law.

Thomas Aquinas in his understanding of providence appeals to the consequent will of God. The consequent will of God takes into account the free response of human beings. Thomas and the Catholic tradition have always been able to avoid the danger of belief in predestination precisely because of the recognition of the freedom of human causes and the consequent will of God. God does not will eternal damnation for some human beings apart from their own free human acts. For Thomas, divine knowledge of what human beings will do does not diminish the freedom of human choice. As transcendent, God sees all things as present even though they are future to us.[11]

Within the manuals of moral theology, providence is usually not discussed and human responsibility for all human actions is assumed. The manuals departed in some significant ways from the Thomistic approach but the points made above continue to have some influence. In general, the handbooks of moral theology, which came into being after the Council of Trent, based morality on the natural law which was the same source for the morality of all humankind. The moral life was seen as the responsibility of the moral being to live in accord with the natural law. No diminishment or altering of human responsibility because of divine agency was mentioned.

Moreover human responsibility was stressed by the ecclesial contexts that shaped the manuals. These textbooks of moral theology were practical handbooks to train confessors to exercise their function in the sacrament of penance, especially their role of judging the existence of sins and their gravity. The Catholic tradition has characteristically understood sin primarily as a morally bad action and thus the responsibility of the Christian. The understanding of the sacrament of penance stressed human responsibility for one's own actions. The broader theological contexts of the manuals rested on the Catholic understanding that one's actions and life in this world determine one's eternal destiny. Without a doubt, the textbooks strongly accepted and endorsed the role of merit in the Christian life. Thus the whole theological and ecclesial contexts of the manuals of moral theology stressed human responsibility for human actions. Again, contemporary Catholic theologians have rightly pointed out the many deficiencies of the handbook tradition, but the tradition did emphasize human responsibility for moral actions and did not reduce that responsibility or do away with it in the name of divine providence or divine action.

I can recall only one relevant discussion of direct and immediate divine intervention in human affairs in the manuals of moral theology and in the earlier Catholic tradition itself. The question under consideration was the immutability of natural law. According to the traditional understanding, the natural law is necessary, universal, and unchangeable for all human beings. Questions were raised about possible changes in the natural law based on scriptural incidents such as God's commanding Abraham to kill his son, God's commanding the Israelites to take things from the Egyptians, God's commanding

Hosea to engage in fornication. In accord with the scriptural exegesis of the times, such incidents posed embarrassing problems for the Catholic moral tradition precisely because they seemed to go against the prescriptions of natural law.

The response of Thomas Aquinas in the *Summa* to this problem is fascinating. Aquinas recognizes that the natural law can change by additions being made to it, but the real problem involves subtractions from the natural law. Can something cease to be condemned by the natural law? The Angelic Doctor distinguishes the primary principles of the natural law that are totally immutable from the secondary principles. Since the secondary principles are conclusions from the primary principles, they can admit of some exceptions in a very few instances. Since God is the giver of life, the creator of all goods, and the author of marriage, the acts done in these exceptional instances under the command of God are not the forbidden acts of killing, stealing, or fornication. In this explanation God is not intervening to change the natural law or to give dispensations from it.[12]

Marcellino Zalba, one of the last manualists in the Catholic tradition, flatly denies any possibility of a proper change in the natural law, which means that the matter concerned would be the same but the obligation would cease. Such a change could not even be accomplished by a direct intervention by God who is the supreme legislator; God would be contradicting God's self by so doing. Some commentators argue that an improper change in the natural law can occur precisely because the matter involved and the circumstances can change, but such a change can only occur in the secondary principles of the natural law that concern not the end but means to the end. The scriptural exceptions I mention above are explained in this way. God could give to another being the dominion or power that God has. However, Zalba prefers to say that an improper change in natural law cannot occur if the law itself is completely and adequately formulated. Thus, for example, one cannot directly kill an innocent person on one's own authority.[13]

In the cases of scriptural exceptions and on the basis of a literal interpretation of the scriptures the Catholic tradition and the manualists did recognize that God could command individuals to do certain acts that might appear to violate the natural law. But in the *Summa* Thomas Aquinas did not want to see these resulting actions as the divine legislator's making a violation of, or dispensation from, or exception to natural law — an understanding that could readily result from a legalistic and voluntaristic approach. The manualists were undoubtedly more voluntaristic and extrinsicist in their moral theory than Aquinas, but, as Zalba's summary of the tradition and his own position show, the solution to the problem was not proposed in terms of God as legislator giving a dispensation or exemption from the natural law. The theologians in the Thomistic tradition did not want to admit that such dispensations from or exceptions to the natural law could be made by God.

Further evidence from the Catholic tradition supports the claim that a belief in divine providence did not affect the understanding of human responsibility and the moral conduct of how individual believers and the believing community should act in particular situations. For the last two decades Catholic theologians have been discussing the question that I have described as whether or not there is a unique content to Christian morality.[14] Is there one moral order for Christians and another for all others? In Germany, the question has been debated between the supporters of an autonomous ethic and the advocates of a faith ethic. I first approached the issue in the United States from the perspective of social morality and ethics in a pluralistic society, and I argued against any unique Christian morality that *per se* is not available to all others. Despite the contemporary discussions on these issues, general agreement exists that the manuals of moral theology do not propose a unique moral content for Christian morality. The moral norm was the same for Christians as for all others.[15]

The manuals of moral theology did not address the question of providence and responsibility, the divine and the human in history, in the same way as contemporary theologians discuss it. The involvement of the moral agent is described not as responsibility but in terms of knowing and acting in accord with God's law. Life in this world is ruled by natural law which is the participation of the eternal law in the rational creature. Through human reason reflecting on human nature, human beings can determine what they are to do and what God wants them to do. The understanding of natural law coheres with the understanding of providence as based on mediation and the fact that God works through secondary causes. Thus in theory providence does not by itself alter or change human responsibility to discover and act in harmony with natural law. The general tendency within the tradition denies that God could grant dispensations from or exceptions to the natural law because in so doing God would contradict God's self. Thus a belief in providence does not affect the requirements of human morality in this world, for providence in the Thomistic tradition works through the natural law.

Contemporary Discussions about Providence

Contemporary discussions about divine providence treat primarily history and the divine and the human in history. The Thomistic tradition in Catholic theology did not pay enough attention to historical consciousness and Catholic moral theology did not develop a historical sense; discussions of providence did not deal primarily with history but with the freedom and causality of natural and human agents. Providence in the Protestant tradition and in more current discussions, however, is more intimately related with the question of history: Christians believe that Jesus is the sovereign of history; divine sovereignty rules over history; divine providence sees the goodness, wisdom, and power of God using history for the divine purpose.

Much of the contemporary discussion about providence in history come from the Protestant and especially the Reformed tradition. These traditions have historically stressed the role of the divine and have often accused the Catholic tradition of Pelagianism. For example, the Reformed tradition at one time contained a belief in predestination that was never accepted in the Catholic tradition; the sovereignty and the glory of God remain important concepts for many in the Reformed churches. Similarly, the evangelical Protestant tradition shares much of the same emphasis today, but the approach is based on a more literal reading of the scriptures.

Contemporary discussions about providence and the divine and human in history continue to reckon with the three issues discussed by Thomas Aquinas — contingency, free will, and evil. Contingency has come to the fore in discussions about evolution and the prehistory of humanity. Providence often talked about a divine plan and purpose in the universe. Modern scientific theories often stress randomness and contingency in the evolutionary development that led to the emergence of human beings. Such randomness appears to deny a divine plan or purpose in history.[16]

Human free will and evil in relation to providence have been the factors most discussed recently. In the face of monstrous evil, God would appear to be either powerless or malevolent. Two historical realities in contemporary history have touched off debates about divine providence and even the existence of God — the Holocaust and the danger of nuclear destruction of the world.

The Holocaust poses great problems for a people who believes in the God of the Covenant who has chosen a people for God's own. How could such a God stand powerless as six million Jews were killed? How could any person even believe in God after Auschwitz? This event has shaken the Jewish community of faith as no other historical event.[17] Some Jews have come to the conclusion that belief in God is no longer possible; others have changed their understanding of God but still are believers. But all believers, not only Jewish believers, have had to wrestle with the Holocaust. After all, Christians were the agents in the Holocaust, so Christians must face the horror and tragedy of the Holocaust in a very involved way.

The fear of nuclear annihilation has also raised questions about providence.[18] In the earlier part of the twentieth century, science was looked upon as the engine of a progressive development of human history. Some argued against the concept of providence and even the existence of God because no need for God was found in the light of everything that science and human beings could accomplish. However, the nuclear threat has now underscored the demonic in history and in science and in technology. Now for the first time in human history, human beings have the power to destroy the world as we know it.

The Holocaust and the threat of nuclear annihilation are not the only events that call into question the meaning and existence of divine providence. The evils of famine, ecological threats, terrorism, genocide, and many of the stories we read in our daily newspaper always raise the same basic question. Is God powerless in the face of evil? What does God's silence say about God?

Such questions have raised significant issues for contemporary theology. Many of the tensions in the Catholic church today center on moral theology. However, in the question of providence under discussion here, I am happy to report that moral theology is not at the center of the discussion!

Systematic theology and the theology of God in particular are the focus of contemporary discussions about providence. Providence has traditionally been associated with God's central attributes—goodness, wisdom, power. Questions about providence quickly become questions about God. Some people can no longer believe in God after the Holocaust; Gordon Kaufmann has developed a new understanding of God in the light of the nuclear threat of annihilation.[19] Many have reconsidered classical theism to account for a God who suffers and changes in response to the sufferings of God's people. Contemporary theologies of God stress the absence, hiddenness, and silence of God in human experience and history.

Discussions about providence naturally include significant questions about the meaning and existence of God, but providence itself has also been a topic for significant contemporary thinking. Many Christian theologians today propose an understanding of providence that does not entail direct, independent, divine intervention in human history. Langdon Gilkey, for example, understands providence in a noninterventionist manner as the universal divine activity of the preservation and continuation of creaturely being over time, as the ground of self-actualizing freedom, and as the creative source of new possibilities in each situation. In addition, contemporary experience reminds us of the further role of providence as the principle of judgment or nemesis on the distorted elements of what human freedom has created. Tragedy and nemesis are not the final words. To have faith in providence is to expect new possibilities despite tragedy and suffering. However, providence must not be seen alone but requires the supplement of incarnation, atonement, and eschatology.[20]

Within the Catholic tradition, Karl Rahner continues to emphasize the Thomistic concept that God works through secondary causes. Here Rahner employs his understanding of God as the transcendental ground of the world. The distinction between the transcendental and the categorical is used to explain the mystery of God's transcendence and immanence. The distinguished German Jesuit theologian refers to divine intervention in the world in quotation marks. A special "intervention" of God can only be understood as the historical concreteness of the transcendental communication of God that is already intrinsic to the world. When we as believers believe that God hears our prayers or intervenes in history, this does not mean that what is immediately tangible in these "interventions" does not exist in a functional relationship with the world or that it could not be explained causally. Such things are not in principle removed from the causal relationships of the world.[21]

Contemporary discussions about providence create significant and important questions for spirituality. In keeping with contemporary religious experience, spirituality today often emphasizes the absence of God and the apophatic experience of God as contrasted with the presence of God.[22] Christian prayer in the face of the absence of God and the apparent powerlessness of God in the midst of human suffering often becomes a prayer of desperation or of lament.[23] Where is God while all of this is happening? In addition, much discussion concentrates on the prayer of petition and its meaning in the light of an understanding of providence that excludes the immediate, direct, divine intervention in the world. A noninterventionist theory of providence does not result in a deistic understanding of a God who created the world and no longer cares about it. The divine is always active and present in history as the persuasive lure to human activity. However, this providential and caring God accepts the freedom of secondary causes. God does care about us and works for our well being personally and corporately, but God does not unilaterally interfere in the world apart from secondary causes. Many abuses have been and are connected with the prayer of petition; often its purpose fosters the concept of an interventionist God and creates a passivity among the Christian people. Thus the prayer of petition should never be the main Christian form of prayer, but it still has a proper place even within the context of holding to the belief that God makes no direct, immediate intervention in human affairs.[24]

The practical consequences of contemporary discussions about God and providence loom large and significant. On the pastoral level, providence has often been used to support a one-sided passivity in Christian life and a failure to take responsibility for life. Much work must be done in shaping the daily life of believers to follow the old spiritual axiom: "Work as if everything depended on you and pray as if everything depended on God." This spiritual adage is quite compatible with contemporary theories of providence which deny any direct, immediate intervention of God in human history.

Implications for Moral Theology

The first part of this chapter pointed out that the Thomistic tradition in moral theology saw no opposition between providence and the human norm for moral action precisely because God's providence governs human beings through the natural law which is the participation of the eternal law in the rational creature. The manuals of Catholic theology, because of their practical purposes, did not discuss the meaning of providence but constantly stressed the role of the human in discovering God's plan and did not appeal to divine interventions to change or alter the natural law. Probably people in the manualist tradition would have accepted some direct divine intervention in history, but they did not use that notion to alter what natural law requires human beings to do in this world. Many contemporary theological explanations of providence deny any direct divine intervention in human history. Those coming out of the Catholic tradition in moral theology would find such an understanding somewhat congenial. To prove this understanding of providence lies beyond the limits of this chapter. I will simply accept such an approach to providence and the human role in history. This section will discuss the implications of such an understanding of providence for three areas of moral theology: the theology and meaning of history; understanding power; and the invocation of providence in human decision making.

Theology and the Meaning of History

One can only approach the meaning of history with fear and trembling. Perhaps no area of Christian thinking has seen more mistakes than efforts to unravel the meaning of history. From the theological perspective, the meaning of history is intimately connected with eschatology and the relationship between the present and the future of the reign of God.

In the very beginning of Christianity a mistaken view of the meaning of history appeared. Without a doubt, the early church in general expected the end of the world to come quickly. Such a view that the end-time was immanent colored much of the early church's position on questions about life in this world and about history. The expected shortness of life and brevity of history naturally disparaged and downplayed the meaning and significance of human existence in this world.

In the course of Christianity apocalyptic views have frequently appeared, according to which God is to come at the end of time to destroy the world and everything in it and usher in the fullness of God's reign. Hardly a century has gone by without many people predicting that the cataclysmic end of the world was coming at a particular time (and particularly soon).

Twentieth-century Christians in the West and especially in the United States often went to the opposite extreme in proposing a progressive view of a history that was steadily evolving to make the kingdom of God more present in this world. Liberal Protestantism is often associated with this progressive view of history, which is so often attacked today.[25]

Within Roman Catholicism, much contemporary theology, spirituality, and social ethics have rightly stressed the relationship between the reign of God and historical, political, and social human existence in this world. The Pastoral Constitution on the Church in the Modern World condemned the split or dichotomy between faith and daily life that so often permeated Catholic self-understanding until then.[26] Recall that even as late as the 1950s there continued to be a debate between so-called incarnationist and eschatological approaches to the world and to Christian spirituality. The eschatological approach imparted no importance or significance to what happened in history and in the world. At best the world and history constituted a stage on which salvation took place. To live in this world meant merely to pass the time while waiting for the fullness of salvation to come at the end of time.[27] The Second Vatican Council developed a theology of earthly realities and of history that had begun to appear in the previous decades. However, the approach of the Second Vatican Council to history is not above criticism. The Pastoral Constitution on the Church in the Modern World correctly tried to relate the gospel, grace, and the supernatural to history and life in this world. I agree with the basic direction of this correction, but the document did not avoid the danger of seeing everything as grace and failed to recognize fully the finitude, the imperfection, the sin, and the lack of completeness that exist in human history. One could charge the constitution with suffering from a chronic case of collapsed eschatology.

The first part of the constitution deals with the church and the human vocation and divides the discussion into four chapters (on the human person, the human community, human activity in the world, and the role of the church in the modern world).[28] The fundamental structure of the two chapters on the human person and the human community treats the subject in the light of creation by God and also mentions human sinfulness but ends with a Christological perspective. Christ as the new human being in the discussion of the human person and Christ as the incarnate word and human solidarity in the portions about the human community are the culminating points of these chapters. The first two chapters do not develop any ideas or teachings about the fullness of the reign of God as a future event to come at the end of time and history. The third chapter, however, thanks to revisions made on the council floor during debate, does bring in the fullness of the reign of God as future: we do not know the time of the consummation of the earth and of humanity; we do not know how things will be transformed, but the world as it has been deformed by sin will pass away.[29] One can understand how this constitution could easily succumb to the overoptimism of the times, but at least the framers of the document partially recognized the problem.

One easily admits how fraught with danger is the enterprise of developing a theology and an understanding of history. Theological, philosophical, and experiential perspectives — together with one's understanding of providence — contribute to how one approaches the meaning of history. From the theological perspective, I insist on seeing the divine working in history in terms of the many different Christian realities and symbols that are present. I believe that theological problems arise most often not so much from positive error as from the failure to consider all the aspects and dimensions that are present in a question, difficulty, or teaching. Thus I try to understand history in the light of how I have proposed to see moral theology. The Christian looks at the world and at history in light of the stance of the fivefold Christian mysteries and symbols of creation, sin, incarnation, redemption, and resurrection destiny. God is the creator and sustainer of the world and all in it. Sin affects everything human and will always be present. By the incarnation, everything human becomes associated with the work of Jesus. The redeeming power of God as manifested in Jesus and the Spirit is already operative in our world and in our history. However, the fullness of the reign of God under the symbol of resurrection destiny is not yet fully present in this world but rather is precisely the destiny to which we are called. An adequate theology of history must address all these various facets of human existence and history. If someone puts undue emphasis on any one of these symbols, the theology of history will be distorted.

In the philosophical perspective, history involves a strange combination of both destiny and freedom.[30] The individual and human communities are always affected, even limited, by the historical forces at work. Experience reminds us that often we respond to situations that we did not create and that we cannot completely change. But at the same time, people are able through freedom to change the course of history and time. Precisely because of freedom, one cannot speak about the laws of history. Yet the destiny of history limits and conditions what one can do in any given situation.

Experience seems to verify the understanding of history sketched above. Evil and horror in history are evident to all in our contemporary times; no one needs to prove the presence and the power of evil. But we also experience the power of good in history; for example, our world has become more conscious of human rights, both political and social, than at any time in the past. The eyes of faith can see redemption at work in human history. At times, evil has been changed into good. Suffering has been a redeeming experience. But at the same time we must know that sometimes evil seems to conquer. One is often amazed by the realization that history so often repeats itself with the domination of the powerful over the weak, but we are also constantly surprised by new possibilities and developments. Perhaps the U.S.A. is becoming more aware of its own problems and rationalizations. And institutional changes have taken place in many countries. But some revolutions soon falter and a power elite becomes entrenched against the oppressed. Experience thus points out the manifold dimensions and possibilities of history. However, even in this understanding, the hope of redeeming possibilities always remains. The oppressed and the downtrodden rightly can have such hope precisely because of our understanding of the power of redemption which is always present in our world despite the presence of sin. From the Christian perspective, sin never has the last word.

The understanding of providence proposed here underscores that God works through secondary causes and accepts both human freedom and evil. God does not directly and immediately intervene to do away with such freedom and evil. In the light of these presuppositions, some parameters for a theology and understanding of history can be drawn.

First, human history will never see the fullness of the reign of God. History will always involve the penultimate. The insistence on the symbol of resurrection destiny as beyond the present means that the future reign of God always lies beyond history. Also, the understanding of divine providence as respectful of human freedom means that history will never be purely identical with the reign of God. Freedom and evil will always be present in human history.

If history can never be identified with the fullness of the reign of God, history can never be seen as totally opposed to the reign of God. Creation, incarnation, and redemption are at work in history so that history shares in the good represented by these symbols.

History, then, will know both good and evil. And even in the midst of evil the possibility of redemption is always present. Experience and theology tell us of the possibility of redemption and of somewhat radical change within historical parameters. However, at the same time the greatest historical good is always threatened by the seeds of its own destruction and abuse.

But we must push the question. Is there any truly human progress in history or is history simply cyclic? A progressive view of history that emphasizes continuing evolutionary progress does not make sense. On balance, however, I propose that human history has witnessed some progress within the contexts of many reversals, in the midst of the continuing danger and threat of evil, and, at times, of evil's triumph over the good. The theological basis for my acceptance of some progress in history comes from the realities of creation and incarnation and from the fact that the redemptive power of God overcoming sin already operates even though it is far from complete. Still, I do not espouse an easy optimism about history. We are all called to work for greater historical progress as our responsibility in responding to the gifts of God to us.

As an example, take the Enlightenment. At times, many people in the First World viewed the Enlightenment as the apex of history. Today many correctly look very negatively on some aspects of the Enlightenment understanding. One can rightly disagree with many aspects of the Enlightenment, but in my judgment its emphasis on human rights took a significant step forward in history. Yes, the danger of individualism was present at the same time. Yes, women and minorities were denied rights. Yes, economic and social rights were neglected. But the insistence on human rights even in the narrow perspective of male political rights has contributed in important ways to subsequent ages. Political and civil rights are very important, but they are not enough for human beings who also need economic and social rights. In the long run, I see some progress in history, but such progress is always threatened and does not emerge or grow in a progressive, linear, evolutionary development.

Remarkable revisions and changes are possible in history, an understanding that can give hope to the downtrodden and the oppressed. The economically poor of the Third World have shown us ways of concretely overcoming their poverty despite all the obstacles against it. In our own country we have the example of the black revolution that, however, still falls far short of its full development. Changes have been made in our culture and society in the last decade or so with regard to the role of women, but patriarchical structures are still strong. Yes, there have been developments and there is always hope for redeeming the present; but imperfection, sin, and the lack of completeness, as well as the difficulty of overcoming historical destiny, will always be with us in history. Even the best movements and developments are never perfect and are always subject to the imperfection of finitude and the destroying force of evil. Some redemption and change in history are possible and inspire hope, but at the same time vigilance and watchfulness must strive to protect humanity from the propensity to evil that is ever present in human history.

A brief excursus about a related matter seems to be appropriate at this time. From the time of the Reformation to the period immediately preceding the Second Vatican Council, Catholic self-understanding not only did not accept a progressive view of history but generally opposed historical developments that had taken place. In fact, within Roman Catholicism, many people accepted an understanding of history that saw the Middle Ages as the golden age. Such a point was brought out well in James Walsh's famous book, which received wide circulation in the United States at the beginning of this century: *The Thirteenth—The Greatest of Centuries.*[31] From this perspective, the historical developments that occurred after the Middle Ages all seemed to depart further and further from the ideal. Often the danger or enemy was described as individualistic freedom. The Reformation brought this individualistic freedom to the role of religion by freeing people from the authority of the church. The philosophical revolution of the Enlightenment freed people from the law of God and made human beings the creators of their own morality. The political revolutions associated with the French revolution and the rise of democracy substituted the will of the majority for the will of God. One should also point out that in a consistent manner some people strongly criticized the economic revolution of capitalism as individualistic freedom run amok in the economic sphere; capitalism believed that individuals could accrue great profits and not worry about the rights of workers and others. A defensive, ghetto Catholicism tended to see the modern world and history as evil and protected itself against such evils.

However, in one area it seems that Roman Catholicism has uncritically accepted a very progressive view of history. I am referring to the understanding of historical developments with regard to the structure of the church itself. One must note the irony between the Catholic opposition to what was happening in human history with its very progressive view of what was occurring with regard to the history of the church and its evolving structures. Perhaps such differences can be explained by the overdefensiveness of the church itself and its failure to acknowledge at times its own sinfulness. I am in accord with the basic Catholic theological insistence on the importance of historical development with regard to our understanding of the message of Jesus and the church itself. However, the Catholic self-understanding at its best has always recognized that not every historical development has been for the good and that a critical analysis of these developments is necessary. In the first chapter I pointed out that by the middle of the twentieth century, the Roman Catholic church was more centralized and authoritarian than it had ever been before in its history. Many of the tensions in the church today that involve authority, especially the tensions between theologians and the teaching office in the church, can be explained in part by the continuing acceptance of this overcentralized and authoritarian understanding of the church. History reminds us how many developments have occurred in church structures over the years. For example, the omnipresence of the papacy in the life of the church is obviously a new tradition of development and not in keeping with the best of the Catholic tradition.

Moral theology has no doubt that the papacy has played a very increasing role in determining Catholic teaching in moral areas. Moral theology could well use studies indicating how church authority was exercised in moral matters over the years. Interventions of the papal teaching office in moral matters have become much greater in this time since the Reformation. The involvement of the papal teaching office in moral matters has never been greater than in the twentieth century. Again, one can see why we might need a more universal teaching authority to be exercised in the light of the greater consciousness of the universal world in which we live. However, such involvements by the papal teaching office and especially how the office has been exercised have created some of the unnecessary tensions in the life of the Catholic church today. However, these developments toward a centralized and overauthoritarian papal office that is frequently involved in specific moral questions have practically been unquestioned until recently. Such a view of history sharply contrasts with the view of human history that the Catholic church was developing at the same time. In my understanding of a theology of history, I think it is also important for us to apply some of the same understanding of human history in general to historical developments within the church itself. Much more needs to be said about this issue, and historical studies are badly needed in order to see how the church has exercised its teaching role with regard to moral matters in the past. My excursus here can only point to the problem and call for further study.

Understanding Power

The concept and reality of power are intimately connected with the subject of divine providence and the realtionship between the human and the divine in history.[32] God has often been described as omnipotent. Human power is important and necessary to change history. However, many contemporary approaches to providence in history stress the absence and powerlessness of God in human history. Jesus is often invoked as an example of the powerlessness of God, since Jesus was put to death on the cross. The historical problem comes to the fore from the experiences of so many people in our world who know nothing but powerlessness and marginalization in personal, political, economic, and cultural spheres.

Three significant points can be made in the present discussion about power. First, power as seen in God and in humans is not the same as the control and domination of others. Those who have power should strive to empower others. The traditional Catholic theological emphasis on mediation and provi-

dence highlights the need to use power to *em*power, and not
to control or dominate. God empowers human beings to share
in God's gracious love. By respecting human freedom and
through secondary causality, God does not seek to control or
dominate human beings. So too in human history, power
cannot be power *over* so much as power *with*. Human responsibility calls upon us to empower all human beings to participate in developing their own lives and the life of society.
Liberation theology in its many different contexts emphasizes
the need for empowerment.

Second, in the context of powerlessness and the understanding of history proposed above, great emphasis has been
placed on the powerlessness of God. Put very boldly, God is
powerless to intervene directly in human history. For many
people today, the experience of the absence and powerlessness
of God is very real. The oppressed of the world, who are so
numerous, know that God in Jesus can be present to them
in their powerlessness. However, one must be very careful not
to draw the wrong conclusions from our consciousness and
experience of the powerlessness of God. The empowering work
of God will be mediated by free human beings. The crucifixion
reminds us of the powerlessness of Jesus, but the crucifixion
cannot become the only paradigm of the divine–human relationship. The crucifixion is part of the total paschal mystery
involving Jesus' ultimate triumph over sin and death. God
permits human evil to occur through secondary and free
causes, but God always tries to overcome evil. The powerlessness of God in the face of human evil does not mean that
God is not working to overcome evil. Those who experience
powerlessness in the world must also struggle to overcome their
condition. Yes, the powerless and the oppressed can relate
to Jesus on the cross but they must also strive to redeem the
evil structures in which they find themselves.

Third, power alone cannot be absolutized in ethical considerations. Just as power is seen as only one of the attributes
of God, so too power in moral theology must be studied in
connection with other virtues such as truth, goodness, justice, freedom, participation, and so on. Empowerment of the

poor and powerless remains a crucial ethical imperative, but empowerment must be used to promote justice, truth, peace, freedom, and the participation of all people in the life of society. Power must always be carefully guided and directed.

Human power and responsibility are seen above all in questions about technology.[33] Through science and technology, human beings have achieved great power over nature and even over history itself. The terrifying power and problem of nuclear energy illustrate the human dilemma. In the area of biomedical technology, human beings now exercise more power than ever before. Think of the fact that less than a century ago human life expectancy was half of what it is today. About a decade ago the Council of the Society for Health and Human Values determined that the most significant and far-reaching advance produced by new biological technology was contraception.[34] No one can doubt that contraception has given people great power over their reproductive faculties and brought about many cultural and social changes, as well as changes in our sexual mores. Yet the possibilities available today in the area of human reproduction are breathtaking. *In vitro* fertilization is now commonly used by many infertile couples who want to have a child. Today the abortion pill is a very debated topic. Who can imagine what the topic for discussion in biomedical technology will even be in the next decade? Biomedical technology's possibilities illustrate the power and the problems that technology creates. How should we as human beings deal with technological developments? Our contemporary world in the area of technology faces many important questions concerning human power and responsibility.

Tomes have been written on technology and human responsibility. In the short space here a basic approach or attitude to technology can be developed in the light of what has already been said about history and providence and on the basis of the stance developed earlier. As in the discussion of history, two extreme positions should be avoided. The one that is associated with a progressive view of history sees technology on a progressive, always developing course bringing goods and benefits to the human condition. The opposite extreme sees technology as demonic and opposed to the truly human.

In my perspective, technology is a limited human good that is ambiguous and susceptible of abuse. Technology is the fruit of human creativity, which shares in divine insight and power. For this reason, technology in general is a good, but some qualifications must be added immediately. Technology is a *limited* human good. The human is greater than the technological. The human embraces many aspects — the psychological, the sociological, the scientific, the artistic, the hygenic, etc. In comparison with the human, the technological constitutes a narrow and partial perspective. The human must always govern and direct the technological. Sometimes the human perspective, with its broad understanding, must say "No" to technological possibilities because of their effect on other aspects involved in the human. What is technologically feasible is not always desirable. Not only is technology a limited good but it is also ambiguous and is not a good without problems. Today we are very conscious of the negative aspects of what are intrinsically a part of our sources of power. Coal, oil, and gas have enabled human beings to produce infinitely more than our ancestors, but these fuels have also polluted our environment and caused great problems. No technology is going to be without its ambiguities and negative aspects. The ambiguities of technology are further highlighted in the debate over nuclear power plants. Technology as a limited and ambiguous good can also be abused by sinful human beings. The current nuclear danger reminds us of the deadly abuse of nuclear power. On balance, I would argue that contraception has been a boon for truly human existence but contraception has also been abused. Often in our patriarchical society the woman has born the burden and the anxieties of contraception as seen, for example, in the pill. Science and technology have given human beings great power that was not even dreamed about some years ago. Christians should use their human power in and through technology but also must remember the limits the ambiguities, and the abuses to which all technology is subject. No technology is simply good without any qualification and all technology can be abused by human power acting in the wrong way.

The divine and the human in history raise the question of hope as a Christian virtue. Hope might properly be called a very significant and distinctive Christian characteristic precisely because divine power is at work in history. How we understand hope is intimately connected with how we understand history and the working of the divine power in our world.

If divine power were totally identified with human power then one would have a very optimistic view of history. If divine power were totally absent from human history, then history for the Christian has meaning only as a stage for the working-out of the history of salvation. Hope avoids the two opposite extremes of optimism and cynicism. Christian hope is based on the divine power which is present and can be redemptive within human history. Hope is hope precisely because one cannot see in the past or the present the possibilities of change and redemption. Hope is not an easy virtue or a matter of prognostication based on what has occurred. Only those who suffer know truly how to hope. The opposite side of the tension of hope underscores the fact that hope will never be fulfilled in this world. Human experience in this world reminds us that all suffering in this world is not redeemed. The fulfillment of Christian hope lies beyond history, but such an understanding cannot become an excuse for the passive acceptance of whatever exists in history.

The Invocation of Providence in Human Decision Making

In the light of the Catholic tradition and some contemporary theories of providence, I would maintain that providence, or the divine in human history, does not take away from human responsibility, does not act as a substitute for human responsibility, and does not change the content of how Christians should act. Such a position is in accord with both the older tradition in Catholic moral theology and with the contemporary understanding of providence as denying any direct, immediate intervention of God in human history. God works in and through human responsibility, not around it.

A belief in providence might supply motivation, but providence should not affect the moral content of the responsible human act of the Christian.

A belief in providence definitely influences Christian attitudes such as hope but does not change the action that Christians are called to do. Generally speaking, even today Catholic moral theologians do not appeal to providence in discussing specific Christian decision making. Those Catholic theologians who maintain that only one moral order exists that is the same for Christians and for all others would logically not appeal to providence to explain why Christians should act differently from other human beings. This section will now discuss two invocations of providence by contemporary Catholic moral theologians.

The *Lay Letter* on the American economy, associated with the work of Michael Novak and others, accepts a notion of providence very similar to the Thomistic concept developed in the beginning of this chapter. God's providential care for this world is not like a watchmaker's. Providence means that God allows contingent forces to work in all their baffling contingency and empowers human beings to act freely. God compels no one but orders all things sweetly and from within their own proper natures and liberties. This commentary on the American economy uses such a concept of providence to justify free markets and to oppose any economic planning. The letters appeals to the providence of human beings to work out what is good. Free markets are a form of rational planning whose rationality flows from the millions of acts of concrete intelligence performed by everyone who participates in free markets. Thus divine providence is used to understand human providence and to argue against economic planning.[35] I agree with the concept of providence but not with the ethical applications made in the *Lay Letter*. In accord with this understanding of providence, I believe that the ethical question of structuring the economy should be determined by what is most fair, just, and responsible. Such criteria should govern human decisions about economic planning and no recourse to an analogy with divine providence is either required or helpful.

Providence, especially understood as involving divine intervention in the world, has also been used to argue against a consequentialist theory in ethics in general and specifically as opposing a so-called realistic ethic with regard to the use of force. John Howard Yoder has consistently and coherently proposed an ethic of unwavering, suffering love.[36] One should never use violence even to attempt to kill an attacker; Christians are called to pacifism. Over the years, others have argued that violence is necessary as a last resort to prevent even greater evils in our world. Yoder argues that we have more than the two alternatives of unmitigated tragedy and the use of violence. If I choose to kill, I do not trust God to work things out. Other possibilities are martyrdom or other alternatives occurring either from natural possibilities or from God's direct intervention. Yoder sees the justification of violence as an attempt by human beings to think they can and should control history. The appeal to providence thus serves as a good argument against consequentialism and against the opposition to pacifism. In fairness, Yoder himself realizes that one could make the case against consequentialism and in favor of pacifism by pointing out that even from the viewpoint of natural possibilities there are more than the two alternatives of violence or tragedy.[37] No doubt, one can hold opinions opposed to any form of consequentialism or proportionalism and not directly appeal to an interventionist understanding of providence. Many philosophers do so.

Contemporary Catholic moral theology also has its debate about consequentialism and about war and peace. The details of these discussions cannot be proposed here. Just one group of authors will be considered—Germain Grisez, John Finnis, and Joseph Boyle, who have coauthored a book on nuclear deterrence.[38] These three thinkers are the foremost spokespersons in contemporary Catholic moral theology for a position that is strongly opposed to any form of proportionalism and is likewise opposed to the changes in Catholic moral teaching that are often supported by more "liberal" theologians and thinkers. The basic moral theory of Grisez, Finnis, and Boyle maintains that one cannot directly go against basic human goods such as life no matter what good one hopes to accomplish. Grisez and Finnis, who were trained as moral

philosophers, have published widely, and Grisez has now written the first volume of a projected four-volume treatise on
moral theology.[39] Grisez's moral theology not only in its
specific ethical conclusions but also in its theological approaches
can be called "conservative." In their discussion of nuclear
deterrence and in their opposition to proportionalism, the
authors also discuss providence, but they do not understand
providence, as Yoder does, to maintain the possibility of a
direct, divine intervention in history.

The three authors conclude that the deterrent strategy,
insofar as it involves threats of city-swapping and final retalia-
tion, is immoral. Unilateral renunciation of such a deterrent
is morally required. The authors then develop a casuistry,
in the best sense of the term, about what the different moral
agents are required to do in the light of this moral understanding. The argument throughout the book is made purely
on philosophical grounds, with only a final chapter giving
some concluding Christian thoughts.

In this final chapter involving faith considerations, the
authors recognize the need to defend their position against
the charge of realism or that they are naive.[40] Unilateral
disarmament would surrender the West to Marxist–Leninist
domination. While recognizing Christian influence in the
West as well as the failures of the West, these authors are
much more negative about Marxist Leninism. However,
Grisez, *et al.* cannot accept the argument that one can do
moral evil in order to accomplish good. Moral evil can never
be done no matter what good might justify it. Moral evil is
the greatest evil in the world. We can never do or intend moral
evil.

In this context, one could expect an appeal to divine providence on the part of those who would hold to a direct, divine
intervention in history. But these three authors do not make
such an appeal. One has to face up to the possibility and
ultimately perhaps live with the reality of Marxist–Leninist
domination. One cannot use the need to avoid such domination as a justifying reason to do moral evil. These Catholic
authors do not reason to their position primarily from the
danger of a nuclear holocaust, but such a holocaust again

does not have to be avoided at all cost and by whatever means. Our world as we know it is going to end sometime and God will bring forth the new heaven and the new earth. We believe that the death of this physical universe will not be the end, just as we believe that the death of the individual human person will not be the end. We Christians look for the resurrection and everlasting life. The argument from realism demands that we corrupt ourselves by being willing to do moral evil. Finnis, Boyle, and Grisez recognize the charge that their positions can be accused of moral purism and an attempt to keep one's own hands clean, but they defend their position because of its philosophical truth.

These authors do appeal to the Christian doctrine of providence that God permits evil in order to bring greater good out of it. However, no appeal is made to a direct, divine intervention that might prevent future domination by Marxist-Leninist forces or prevent the nuclear destruction of the world. In what might seem to be a surprising new move, the authors appeal to providence to refute again consequentialist or proportionalist reasoning in Christian ethics. Such consequentialist approaches confuse human responsibility with God's responsibility. Human beings are not responsible for the overall greater good or lesser evil, for only God knows what they are. Human beings simply carry out the part of God's plan that God assigns to each of them as his or her own personal responsibility. Proportionalists assume for the human being the type of providence that only God can have.[41]

I disagree with the theory proposed by Grisez *et al.* and with the appeal to providence to support their theory. However, for our present purposes, we should note the restricted use made of the idea of providence by these authors. They do not understand providence as entailing a direct, immediate intervention of God in history. Their use of providence differs from Yoder's. Also, Grisez *et al.* do not use providence to change or alter human responsibility in this world. Their theory rests primarily on philosophical grounds. The theological argument from providence merely gives further support to what has already been proposed in the name of human reason. Thus their use of providence still seems to be in accord with the basic thesis of this chapter that providence does not change, alter, or lessen human responsibility in this world.

Christians believe in the mystery of divine providence, but such a mystery will always need further attempts to comprehend more adequately its meaning without anyone ever totally understanding it. The Catholic tradition of moral theology has insisted on human responsibility and does not see providence as altering, changing, or attenuating human responsibility for human actions. Such an approach is quite open to accepting a noninterventionist view of providence. Moral theology will continue to deal with the mystery of providence and with specific questions of history and power. God and God's grace are present in our world and in our history, but God acts in and through the human. The major thesis of this chapter is that the Catholic tradition in moral theology in the past and also today does not and should not appeal to divine providence in any way to change, alter, or attenuate human responsibility and actions in this world.

NOTES

1. Anne E. Patrick, "Dimensions of the Abortion Debate," in Patricia Beattie Jung and Thomas A. Shannon, eds., *Abortion and Catholicism: The American Debate* (New York: Crossroad, 1988), p. 177.

2. Thomas Aquinas, *Summa theologiae, I^a II^{ae}*, prologue, 1 (Rome: Marietti, 1952).

3. Ibid., q. 94.

4. Ibid., q. 91, a. 1, 2.

5. Ibid., q. 91, a. 1.

6. Ibid., q. 90.

7. Thomas Aquinas, *Summa contra gentiles*, book 3: *Providence, part 1* (Notre Dame, IN: University of Notre Dame Press, 1975), chapter 64, p. 210.

8. Ibid., chapter 71, pp. 237ff.

9. Ibid., chapter 77, pp. 258ff.

10. Ibid., chapter 73, pp. 244ff.

11. Thomas Aquinas, *Summa theologiae, I^a*, q. 19, a. 6; q. 14, a. 13. For a summary of Aquinas's position as contrasted with

214   *Providence and Responsibility*

Augustine's see John H. Wright, "Providence," in Joseph A. Komonchak *et al.*, eds., *New Dictionary of Theology* (Wilmington, DE: Glazier, 1987), pp. 815–818. For a somewhat different perspective, see Brian L. Hebblethwaite, "Some Reflections on Predestination, Providence, and Divine Foreknowledge," *Religious Studies* 15 (1979): 433–448.

12. Thomas Aquinas, *Summa theologiae*, I^a II^{ae}, q. 94, a. 5; q. 100, a. 8 and ad 3um.

13. Marcellinus Zalba, *Theologiae Moralis Summa I: Theologia Moralis Fundamentalis* (Madrid: Biblioteca de Autores Cristianos, 1952), pp. 352–355.

14. For an in-depth discussion of this controversy, see Vincent MacNamara, *Faith and Ethics: Recent Roman Catholicism* (Washington, DC: Georgetown University Press, 1985). I disagree with some of MacNamara's interpretations, but his book remains the best study of the debate in English.

15. Franciscus Hürth and Petrus M. Abellan, *De Principiis, de Virtutibus et Praeceptis*, vol. I (Rome: Pontifical Gregorian University, 1948), p. 43.

16. Barrie Britten, "Evolution by Blind Chance," *Scottish Journal of Theology* 39 (1986): 341–360.

17. For a recent overview of some of this important literature, see Alan L. Berger, "Holocaust and History," *Journal of Ecumenical Studies* 25 (1988): 194–211.

18. Richard Bauckham, "Theology after Hiroshima," *Scottish Journal of Theology* 38 (1985): 583–601. The threat of nuclear annihilation has brought eschatological questions to the fore. See, for example, L. Shannon Jung, "Nuclear Eschatology," *Theology Today* 40 (1983–1984): 184–189; Andrew J. Wergeit, "Christian Eschatological Identities and the Nuclear Context," *Journal for the Scientific Study of Religion* 27 (June 1988): 175–191.

19. Gordon Kaufmann, "Nuclear Eschatology and the Study of Religion," *Journal of the American Academy of Religion* 51 (1983): 3–14.

20. Langdon Gilkey, *Reaping the Whirlwind: A Christian Interpreation of History* (New York: Seabury, 1981). This has been the most significant monograph on providence in Christian theology in the last two decades. For a summary of Gilkey's understanding of providence, see pp. 264ff.

21. Karl Rahner, *Foundations of Christian Faith: An Introduction to the Idea of Christianity* (New York: Seabury, 1978), pp. 86ff.

22. William H. Shannon, *Thomas Merton's Dark Path* (New York: Farrar, Straus, and Giroux, 1987).

23. Donal Dorr, *Spirituality and Justice* (Maryknoll, NY: Orbis, 1984), pp. 217–235.

24. Jack A. Keller, "On Providence and Prayer," *Christian Century* 104 (1987): 967–969. Keller relies here on Gilkey's understanding of providence (see above, note 20).

25. Mention should be made of Reinhold Niebuhr's criticism of Protestant liberalism, but even Niebuhr retained some liberal presuppositions. See Ruth L. Smith, "Reinhold Niebuhr and History: The Elusive Liberal Critique," *Horizons* 15 (1988): 283–298.

26. Pastoral Constitution on the Church in the Modern World, n. 43, in Austin Flannery, ed., *Vatican Council II: The Conciliar and Post-Conciliar Documents* (Northport, NY: Costello Publishing Co., 1975), p. 943.

27. John Courtney Murray, *We Hold These Truths: Catholic Reflections on the American Proposition* (Kansas City, MO: Sheed and Ward, 1960), pp. 175–196.

28. Pastoral Constitution on the Church in the Modern World, nn. 11–45, in Flannery, *Vatican Council II,* pp. 912–947.

29. Ibid., n. 39, p. 938.

30. Gilkey, *Reaping the Whirlwind,* pp. 91–114.

31. James Walsh, *The Thirteenth: The Greatest of Centuries* (New York, 1907).

32. Larry Rasmussen is involved in an in-depth study of power from the perspective of Christian ethics, as is exemplified in his paper delivered at the 1989 meeting of the Society of Christian Ethics, "Divine and Human Power in a New Era: Theological Reflections."

33. The bibliography on technology is enormous. For a helpful annotated bibliography, see Frederick Ferré, ed., *Concepts of Nature and God: Resources for College and University Teaching* (Athens, GA: University of Georgia Press, 1989).

34. See my *Moral Theology: A Continuing Journey* (Notre Dame, IN: University of Notre Dame Press, 1982), pp. 141ff.

35. *Toward the Future: Catholic Social Thought and the U.S. Economy: A Lay Letter* (North Tarrytown, NY: Lay Commission on Catholic Social Teaching and the U.S. Economy, 1984), pp. 76–80.

36. See especially John Howard Yoder, *The Politics of Jesus* (Grand Rapids, MI: Eerdmans, 1972); and *The Priestly Kingdom: Social Ethics as Gospel* (Notre Dame, IN: University of Notre Dame Press, 1984).

37. John Howard Yoder, "'What Would You Do If . . .?' An Exercise in Situation Ethics," *Journal of Religious Ethics* (1974): pp. 81–105.

216 *Providence and Responsibility*

John Finnis, Joseph M. Boyle, Jr., and Germain Grisez, *Nuclear Deterrence, Morality, and Realism* (Oxford: Clarendon, 1987).

Germain Grisez, *The Way of the Lord Jesus: Christian Moral Principles* (Chicago: Franciscan Herald, 1983); John Finnis, *Natural Law and Human Rights* (Oxford: Clarendon, 1980); Germain Grisez and Russell Shaw, *Fulfillment in Christ: A Summary of Christian Moral Principles* (Notre Dame, IN: University of Notre Dame Press, 1991).

Finnis, Boyle, and Grisez, *Nuclear Deterrence*, pp. 367–390.

Ibid., pp. 378–384. The same argument is proposed by Grisez, *Way of the Lord Jesus*, p. 151. In his book, Grisez deals with providence on a number of occasions but does not appeal to a direct divine intervention in history.

9. Academic Freedom: My Experiences and Reflections

I shall reflect in this chapter on the controversy between The Catholic University of America (CUA) and me over the decision of the university that as a result of a definitive declaration from the Vatican Congregation for the Doctrine of the Faith I could no longer teach Catholic theology at Catholic University. In my analysis I shall concentrate especially on the academic and legal aspects of the case, thus avoiding any attempt to reargue the case or to question the motives of anyone involved. This chapter will assume that everyone involved acted to protect and preserve values that they thought were threatened. My purpose here is threefold: to point out what happened; to interpret how and why the parties involved made the moves they did in the development of the case; and to look backward and forward from the perspective of the present. Finally, I shall consider especially the broader question of academic freedom in American Catholic higher education.

The fundamental significance of the legal case must be seen in the light of three contexts of recent developments — in Roman Catholicism, in American Catholic higher education, and in the self-understanding of The Catholic University of America. Within the context of the church great changes occurred after the Second Vatican Council (1962–1965), but some retrenchment on the part of church authorities has taken place in the last few years. In the late 1960s Catholic higher education in general changed dramatically with its acceptance of academic freedom and institutional autonomy and with the establishment of lay-dominated boards of trustees that are no longer controlled by the sponsoring religious body.[1]

The Catholic University of America made similar striking changes in the late 1960s and early 1970s, as was precipitated and illustrated by two events.[2] In 1967 a university-wide strike closed the university, and the trustees then rescinded their decision not to renew my contract and give me a promotion as had been proposed by the requisite faculty and proper academic bodies. Prodding from the accrediting association and the experience of the strike occasioned the restructuring of CUA and its board of trustees in order to bring the institution into line with American standards.[3] In 1968 I acted as the spokesperson for twenty Catholic University professors and almost six hundred other Catholic scholars in claiming that a person could dissent in theory and in practice from the condemnation of artificial contraception in the papal encyclical *Humanae Vitae* and still be a loyal Roman Catholic. The trustees finally accepted with regard to its academic propriety the judgment of a faculty inquiry committee and of the academic senate that the twenty subject professors had not violated their responsibilities as Catholic theologians by their declarations and actions in dissenting from one of the conclusions of a papal encyclical.[4] Most people thought that the changes in the university's structure and the acceptance of this instance of theological dissent proved that academic freedom was alive and well at Catholic University.

What Actually Happened?

One must be very clear about exactly what happened at Catholic University in the more recent controversy. An inaccurate impression is often given that what occurred affected only the ecclesiastical faculties of the university (which will be explained later) and did not affect the whole institution. In fact, the board of trustees decided as a matter of religious conviction and canon law that I could not teach Catholic theology anywhere at the university.[5] I was removed from teaching in my area of competency without a judgment made in the first instance by peers that I was not competent.

External sources concluded that Catholic University as a whole violated the principles of academic freedom and institutional autonomy in my case. In the legal case in the Superior Court of the District of Columbia, Judge Frederick H. Weisberg decided in favor of the university. CUA had not violated its contractual obligations to me. However, to win its case the university had to admit that academic freedom does not exist at Catholic University. According to Judge Weisberg's decision, "nothing in its contract with Professor Curran or any other faculty member promises that it will always come down on the side of academic freedom."[6]

The American Association of University Professors (AAUP) censured Catholic University because of its actions.[7] The lengthy report of the AAUP's investigating committee concluded that in the case of Professor Curran "the administration and the board of trustees of the Catholic University of America for all practical purposes deprived him of his tenure without due process and without adequate cause . . . [and] violated Professor Curran's academic freedom."[8]

One must be acquainted with the facts in the case to understand what truly happened. However, herein lies a problem. From an epistemological perspective I have to admit that pure objective facts do not exist, for people are always interpreting facts. The experience of the case, both with an academic hearing and with a long legal process and trial, proves that neither side could agree on the facts. Keeping the limitations and problems in mind, I shall strive for objectivity.

On 18 August 1986, Archbishop James A. Hickey, the chancellor of Catholic University, handed me a letter from Cardinal Joseph Ratzinger, the prefect of the Vatican Congregation for the Doctrine of the Faith, in which I was informed that I could "no longer be considered suitable nor eligible to exercise the function of a Professor of Catholic Theology." This declaration, which Ratzinger elsewhere referred to as a "definitive judgment," was approved by the pope. The declaration culminated an investigation of my writings which I was first informed about in the summer of 1979. At the same time, Archbishop Hickey, in his position as chancellor of Catholic University, gave me a letter informing me that he was initiating the process for the withdrawal of my canonical mission. I had to respond by 1 September if I wanted to avail myself of the due process hearing guaranteed to me.[9]

To understand this proposed action fully and to interpret properly the whole case one must be familiar with the structure of Catholic University.[10] In this very structure one sees the tension between being a university in the American understanding of the term and being a Catholic university. On the one hand, in 1887 Pope Leo XIII approved the foundation of Catholic University and two years later approved the statutes of the institution and endowed it with the rights proper to a lawfully constructed university in accord with Catholic canon law. Thus in this suit Catholic University claimed that it is a juridical person in Catholic canon law and a pontifical university. Likewise, Catholic University has a special relationship with the bishops of the United States.

However, in 1887 Catholic University was also incorporated in the District of Columbia as an institution of learning with the rank of a university. In 1964 Catholic University opted to accept the provisions of the District of Columbia Nonprofit Corporation Act as an educational institution. Since 1900 Catholic University has been a member of the prestigious Association of American Universities and has been accredited by the Middle States Association of Colleges and Schools since the beginning of this association in 1921.

The current bylaws of the university place "ultimate responsibility for governance and sole responsibility for fiscal affairs of the University" in a board of trustees. At the present time the board of trustees has forty elected members equally divided between clerics and laypeople. Sixteen of the clerical members are to be members of the National Conference of Catholic Bishops, and the cardinals who are diocesan bishops will normally be clerical members of the board of trustees. The bylaws also recognize that the archbishop of Washington will be chancellor of the university and "shall serve as a liaison between the University and the National Conference of Catholic Bishops, as well as between the University and the Holy See."[11]

Catholic University also has three ecclesiastical faculties, or what American terminology would call departments, that are governed by a set of canonical statutes that have been approved by the Vatican in accord with the norms proposed in official church documents.[12] According to these applicable norms, Catholics who teach disciplines relating to faith and morals need from the chancellor a canonical mission to teach in the name of the church. The chancellor may withdraw the canonical mission only for the most serious reasons and the faculty member may request the procedures for due process which *mutatis mutandis* are the same procedures used for the dismissal for cause of a tenured faculty member (V, 8). However, these faculties share the aims and goals of the entire university (II, 1 and 2). The chancellor is to "protect the doctrine and discipline of the church . . . in accord with recognized academic procedures" (III, 7 g). These norms and practices concerning appointments to the faculties are "intended to assure fidelity to the revealing Word of God as it is transmitted by tradition and interpreted and safeguarded by the magisterium of the Church and to safeguard academic freedom" (V, 11). These canonical statutes came into effect in 1981.

"These Faculties, however, are not exclusively ecclesiastical; they also have other academic programs which do not have canonical effects and to which these Statutes do not apply" (I, 1). I was a member of the department of theology which according to these statutes "has a pontifical faculty." The heading of the statutes dealing with theology reads "Statutes of the Pontifical Degrees Program of the Department of Theology." I maintained in a letter to university authorities in 1981 and throughout the case that these statutes did not apply to me since they were unilaterally imposed by the university after my tenure contract had already been entered into in 1970.

The canonical statutes were compromise documents. We as faculty members insisted that the protection of academic freedom be written into the canonical statutes and that the ecclesiastical faculties be seen as integral parts of the university. However, the chancellor insisted that canonical mission be incorporated into the statutes and that his function of protecting the doctrine and discipline of the church be spelled out. The ambiguity of the statutes enabled everyone to live with them until the crunch came.

My first decision was whether or not to accept the procedures for due process in order to defend myself against the chancellor's move to take away my canonical mission. I maintained that I had never received a canonical mission and did not need one since the new canonical statutes did not apply to me. Without waiving my rights in this matter I agreed to accept the due process procedure as a way to obtain a hearing on the case. In retrospect, much time and effort would have been saved if I had simply conceded the issue of canonical mission and retained my claims as a tenured faculty member.

My position before the faculty hearing committee emphasized the case's issues concerning academic freedom.[13] Academic freedom as accepted in the American academy means that a tenured professor can be dismissed for cause only after a judgment in the first instance by faculty peers about the professor's incompetence. The final decision is made by the governing board of the institution on the basis of this record. I based my position on the protection of academic freedom written into the ecclesiastical statutes and the decision of the 1968 faculty inquiry committee in the case of the dissenting professors — that were a canonical mission required, it had to be understood in accordance with established American academic principles and procedures. In my understanding the faculty committee had to make a judgment about my competency in order to take away my canonical mission. The declaration from the Vatican congregation could be rebutted by other academic evidence of my competency as a Catholic moral theologian.

The chancellor's position was straightforward. The canonical mission is given to a professor to teach in the name of the church. The highest authorities in the Roman Catholic church had concluded that I was neither suitable nor eligible to be a professor of Catholic theology. This definitive judgment alone constituted the most serious reasons required by the statutes to take away the canonical mission.

The committee did not enter into questions of my competency but ultimately assumed it. However, the faculty committee did not think that the Vatican declaration was the only reality to be considered in the case. The report of the faculty committee recognized the "potential conflict" between the jurisdiction of the church, on the one hand, and the institutional autonomy of the university and my tenure rights, on the other hand. The committee concluded that the board of trustees could take away the canonical mission only if I remained a tenured faculty member at Catholic University and taught in my area of competence somewhere in the university.[14]

Both the chancellor and I disagreed with the committee report.[15] The committee accepted my competency as well as the American academic principles of institutional autonomy and academic freedom in the university as a whole but recognized that such principles do not exist in the ecclesiastical faculty of theology. I had spent my career at Catholic University working for the compatibility of academic freedom and Catholic universities including theology. Now in my judgment the committee concluded that academic freedom did not exist in the faculty of theology. I said at the time that I was 75 percent satisfied with the committee report.

The chancellor and the board of trustees had greater reservations about the committee report. They claimed that the committee had exceeded its mandate in saying anything beyond the right to take away the canonical mission. Also, the committee did not give sufficient attention to the wording of the Vatican declaration that I was neither suitable nor eligible to teach Catholic theology in general and not just on an ecclesiastical faculty.[16]

After the faculty committee report I was willing to live with the conclusion of the committee and at least for a time accept a position teaching in my area of competency elsewhere in the university. The academic freedom of the Catholic University as a whole would be vindicated even though such protection did not exist in the ecclesiastical faculty of theology. And after the committee report I could not realistically expect to teach in the ecclesiastical faculty of theology.

In the spring of 1988 it became clear that the chancellor, the administration, and the board of trustees had a different position. They were determined that in the light of the declaration from the congregation I could not teach Catholic theology anywhere at Catholic University. They were willing to allow me to teach social ethics, but I would have to accept publicly the Vatican declaration as binding on me and thus I could not teach Catholic theology. I was willing to be called a professor of social ethics, but I could not accept the Vatican declaration as binding on me without denying the principles of academic freedom. In his deposition for the civil suit, Archbishop Hickey testified that it was his position from the very beginning that I could not teach Catholic theology anywhere at Catholic University. In this whole enterprise the chancellor was the principal and leading actor. The board of trustees and the administration ultimately supported him in this contention.

At its meeting on 2 June 1988, the board of trustees took its final action in my case. "The Board accepts the declaration of the Holy See as binding upon the University as a matter of canon law and religious conviction." "[A]ny assignment allowing Father Curran to exercise the function of a Professor of Catholic Theology despite the Holy See's declaration that he is ineligible to do so would be inconsistent with the University's special relationship with the Holy See, incompatible with the University's freely chosen Catholic character, and contrary to the obligations imposed on the University as a matter of canon law."[17]

The administration and trustees of Catholic University could have used other means and arguments to achieve their goal of making sure that I did not teach Catholic theology at Catholic University. Their brief use of one other approach in the spring of 1988 was ultimately replaced by the argument from religious conviction and canon law. The faculty committee had concluded that my canonical mission could be taken away only if I continued to teach in my area of competency, "namely, as a professor in the area of moral theology and/or ethics." At one time the administration maintained that it was following the faculty committee report by offering me a teaching position in social ethics while insisting that I sign a statement saying I would not teach Catholic theology at the university because of the Vatican declaration. Catholic University officials did not pursue this approach. Perhaps they realized that their argument here was quite weak. Perhaps they wanted to make another point.

In the course of the legal suit other arguments were proposed by the university, such as the nonabsolute character of academic freedom or the different nature of academic freedom for Catholic theology. However, these were subsidiary arguments at best that were developed in a different context. The primary reason for the action taken by the university remained that found in the final decision of the board of trustees. As a matter of canon law and religious conviction they could not allow me to teach Catholic theology at The Catholic University of America.

Why Did the Parties Act as They Did?

My strategy was clear. I believed that Catholic University had accepted academic freedom and this was part of my contract. According to the principles of academic freedom I could be removed from my teaching position only on the basis of a judgment of incompetency made in the first instance by peers. Such a process had not been followed in my case. Since the trustees did not accept the faculty committee report, I went to the Superior Court of the District of Columbia to pursue my claim that the university had violated my contract.

On the basis of the declarations and actions taken by the administration and trustees it is easy in retrospect to figure out what their strategy was. They were convinced that for the good of The Catholic University of America and because of its special relationship to the Holy See, I could no longer teach Catholic theology there. To achieve their goal they had to consider the different forums in which the issue would be discussed and the different means that might be used to accomplish their purpose.

From the very beginning of the case the chancellor and the trustees gave great significance to the legal forum. They knew that the New York firm of Cravath, Swaine, and Moore had offered to represent and defend me throughout all the processes of the case on a *pro bono* basis. I was willing to go to court if necessary to vindicate what I felt were my contractual rights.

What was the best legal defense for their position? The strongest possible defense and the one that might prevent the case from ever going to court involved the defense based on first amendment rights. Catholic University as a Catholic institution had the first amendment right to be free from government interference of any kind in determining who could teach Catholic theology at the institution. Such a defense was behind the final statement made by the board of trustees on my case in June 1988. Catholic University took its action against me on the basis of canon law and religious conviction. CUA's action was thus protected by the first amendment from any scrutiny by the civil courts.

The goal of preventing my teaching theology at Catholic University and the first amendment defense of it would create some problems for the trustees and administration that any prudent person would have to consider. The first problem concerned the faculty committee. The strategy adopted by the trustees meant that they could not accept the faculty committee's report. They remanded the report to the committee with their disagreements. From a statutory viewpoint the chancellor and the trustees were not legally obligated to follow the report, despite strong moral suasion. By not following the faculty committee's report the trustees put themselves in opposition to the committee, but the committee could do nothing about it. From a strategic perspective, the trustees apparently thought that they could disagree with the report without causing disproportionate problems for themselves and the institution. The faculty as a whole would probably take no drastic action, but some dissatisfaction and even resolutions might be expressed by the academic senate. Time will tell if the trustees and administration were correct in their apparent judgment that faculty reaction would not cause too many problems in the long run.

The second problem concerned the broader academic community and the standing of Catholic University within that community. The prudent actor had to decide what risks were involved in the contemplated action.

From past experience all concerned knew that the AAUP would follow the case very closely. The AAUP both works for the acceptance of the norms of academic freedom and institutional autonomy and as a last resort censures institutions that violate these principles. The officials at Catholic University had to know that if I were not allowed to teach in my area of competence without a due process hearing by faculty peers, the AAUP would probably censure Catholic University. The AAUP insists above all on the need to follow the requisite procedures, and the association ordinarily does not enter into the validity of the judgments made in accord with the established procedures. A censure from the AAUP was all but inevitable.

Another aspect of the academic forum involved the general standing and reputation of the institution within the academic world. Would Catholic University's reputation be so tarnished by accepting the Vatican declaration as binding on the university that it would lose face and rank in the academic world? A more tangible problem concerned the accreditation of the institution by the Middle States Association of Colleges and Schools. If Catholic University violated the principles of academic freedom and institutional autonomy, the institution might lose its accreditation. A loss of accreditation would constitute a grave threat to the survival of Catholic University as an American institution of higher learning.

Eligibility for government aid and grants raised another potential problem that faced the administration and trustees in their action. Earlier Supreme Court rulings had declared that federal aid to certain Catholic colleges was constitutional because, unlike grammar schools and high schools, Catholic colleges did not proselytize and did accept academic freedom.

Perhaps federal funding for Catholic University would be jeopardized by the position taken in my case.

In retrospect, the officials of Catholic University were willing to run all of these risks. Why? The simplest and most radical response to the question rests on what ethicists call a strict deontological approach. In conscience the officials were convinced that their understanding of Catholic University and their commitment to the Catholic church called for them to take this action against me no matter what the consequences; one must do the right thing no matter what happens. Perhaps some did take this position, but others, conscious of their role as prudent trustees and administrators, would also want to examine all the possible consequences of their action. In this interpretation the actors concluded that the risks to Catholic University in the academic forum would not be proportionately harmful.

Why did the risks in the academic forum not deter the officials at Catholic University from taking the action that they did? First of all, academic interests were not primary. The evidence points to the fact that the primary actors were Archbishop James A. Hickey, as the chancellor of the university, and the more senior cardinals and bishops on the board of trustees. None of these hierarchs had much association or experience with the academic world and did not feel a true commitment to the principles of the American academy. They were and are primarily church persons. Their main source of advice did not come from academics but from civil lawyers who were involved from the very first moment in August of 1986. The only person involved with any true academic experience was Father William J. Byron, S.J., the president of the university. Thus the academic forum was not the primary concern or interest of the principal decision makers. In addition, academic standing or reputation is a rather nebulous concept that is hard to pin down.

However, prudence would call for some discussion of the risks involved in the action taken. An AAUP censure would not be fatal to the institution. Other Catholic colleges and universities, such as Marquette and Detroit, have been censured by the AAUP and have not been greatly affected by it. Surely institutions could live with a censure from the AAUP, which, in fact, the university has had to do.

What about the threat of losing accreditation? A prudent and realistic judgment could conclude that Catholic University probably would not lose its accreditation. The action in my case was a single act involving one person and did not directly affect other faculty members. History points out the reluctance of accrediting associations to take away accreditation. In 1966 St. John's University in Jamaica, New York, fired thirty-two faculty members, including six with tenure, without any due process; but the institution never lost its accreditation. One of my advisors compared the decision to take away accreditation with statements by so-called realistic politicians about decisions to use the nuclear bomb. People are and should be reluctant to use ultimate weapons.

My advisors and I concluded very early on that CUA would probably not lose its accreditation over this issue. However, I was somewhat surprised that the accrediting evaluation team "differed on their perspectives of the issue of academic freedom at CUA in the light of the Curran affair."[18] In the end, the evaluating committee report did not even slap CUA's institutional wrists in this regard.

The loss of government aid and grants would definitely constitute a serious problem for the university. Catholic University was represented in this case by Williams and Connolly, whose lawyers had been intimately involved in these cases and the discussions surrounding them. Loss of funding could come about only if someone sued Catholic University in court. However, the university had a fall-back position. The president had told faculty members that if necessary the university would separately incorporate the three ecclesiastical faculties and perhaps all religious studies on campus. These entities receive little or no government funding at this time, so separate incorporation would allow the church to maintain direct control over these departments and schools without jeopardizing government aid to the rest of the institution. Again, the academic concern of the standing of these separated entities was not of primary importance for the decision makers. Academics in general and academics in religious studies in particular would be seriously concerned about such a second-class categorization of these departments, but such concerns did not greatly affect the trustees and their lawyers.

One must appreciate the risks that were run by the officials at Catholic University. They were unwilling to accept and live with the position that I had lost my canonical mission and could not teach in an ecclesiastical faculty but would teach social ethics in the department of sociology and continue to have academic contacts with theology students not in the ecclesiastical degree programs. By accepting such an outcome the trustees would have avoided opposing a faculty committee, receiving an AAUP censure, possibly having its academic reputation diminished, and perhaps losing major government aid and grants. At one time in early April 1987 I thought that the administration and trustees were willing to accept this position. However, they did not.

Retrospect and Prospect

Judge Frederick H. Weisberg issued his decision on 28 February 1989. I lost the case. The judge rejected the first amendment defense and ruled that he had a right to hear the case based on my contract with the Catholic University of America which is civilly incorporated in the District of Columbia. However, according to the decision, I was bound by the 1981 canonical statutes and hence had a canonical mission that had been taken away according to canonical procedures. The university had no obligation to allow me to teach theology in the nonecclesiastical parts of the university since my tenure was to the department of theology. The court pointed out the ambivalence of Catholic University. The university wanted to have its status both ways—as being a full-fledged American university and as having a unique and special relationship with the Holy See. "[N]othing in its contract with Professor Curran or any other faculty member promises that it will always come down on the side of academic freedom." The judge also declared that even if I had won the case he would not have granted specific performance.[19]

In retrospect the court did not accept my contention that I was never given a canonical mission and also was not bound by the canonical statutes of 1981 that added a substantial new element to my contract. More significantly, neither my contract nor any contract at the time of my tenure (1970–1971) included the guarantee of academic freedom. I had relied on many statements made by the academic senate and sent in the name of the university to official bodies such as the Middle States Association, but only those statements made by the board of trustees are part of the contract. As for specific performance, my lawyers had always known how difficult it would be to win specific performance in this kind of contract case.

As for the future, I cannot teach Catholic theology at Catholic University. A number of colleagues from Catholic institutions of higher learning have admitted that their institutions will not hire me. Apparently they are afraid of offending Rome, the American bishops, and some of their own supporters.[20] I have found a very congenial academic home at Southern Methodist University as the Elizabeth Scurlock University Professor of Human Values.

Before going to SMU I became embroiled in another academic freedom case at Auburn University. I had been offered and accepted the Goodwin–Philpott Eminent Scholar Chair in Religion at Auburn in April of 1990 with the understanding that the appointment was to a tenured position. However, James E. Martin, the president of Auburn, changed his mind and refused to give me tenure. The university senate of Auburn censured President Martin "for violations of academic principles and policies as they relate to the issue of tenure for Professor Curran." Among the particulars was the president's being pressured by persons outside the tenure process, specifically certain members of the Auburn board of trustees, to influence unduly a tenure decision.[21]

I will probably never know accurately the full story of what transpired at Auburn. At various times the question of the involvement of the Catholic church arose. I am convinced that church authorities and/or individual Catholics did not and could not alone block my tenure. However, it seems that the question would never have arisen unless Catholics had first brought up the fact that I was controversial. Other people then used this fact to achieve their own purposes.

Back now to *Curran v. Catholic University*. Catholic University won the case, but the judge did not accept the university's first amendment defense. In retrospect, the university did not have to go as far as it did to prevent my teaching there. However, the insistence on religious conviction and canon law could have contributed to the judge's decision that contracts at Catholic University do not guarantee academic freedom for the faculty. As for the future, Catholic University will have to live with the consequences of its declarations and actions. Only time will tell what the faculty of Catholic University will be willing and able to accomplish and how the higher education community will regard and react to what has occurred.

The case has not broken any new legal ground. The court rejected the argument that the action of Catholic University was immune from court scrutiny because of the religious freedom guaranteed by the first amendment. In my nonexpert opinion, religious freedom should protect certain actions of churches but not institutions that are incorporated as institutions of higher education. Catholic University still might be vulnerable to a suit challenging its right to government aid and grants.

This case also has broader implications for Catholic higher education in the United States. The core issue has been the nature and identity of a Catholic university or college. Catholic University has some unique characteristics but still claims to be an American university. Are both identities compatible?

Can what happened to me at Catholic University also happen at other Catholic institutions of higher learning? Yes. The board of trustees at Catholic University, on the basis of its religious conviction, said that the Vatican declaration was binding on them. Boards of trustees at other Catholic institutions could make the same decision. By making the decision based on its religious conviction and free choice the board tried to defend its own autonomy. No one is telling the board what to do. This brings up a significant ambiguity in the concept of institutional autonomy in relation to academic freedom. Autonomy could be invoked wrongly in order to violate academic freedom. A board is not free to accept a position that violates the academic freedom of one of its professors.

The more precise question is whether the boards of other Catholic institutions of higher learning would as a matter of fact make the same decision as the board at Catholic University. I have some doubts. Catholic University's board consists of sixteen American bishops including the most prestigious Catholic hierarchical leaders in the United States. On issues such as this one, the other members of the board tend to follow the lead of the cardinals and bishops. Depositions taken from two lay board members in my case corroborate this understanding.[22] Most other Catholic college and university boards probably have only one or at most a few bishops on the board. Many other board members would have a strong commitment to the principles of academic freedom. I doubt if such boards would easily make the same kind of decision as did Catholic University's board.

The reaction of the leadership of the mainstream of Catholic higher education in the United States to my case has been fascinating. This group has strongly endorsed academic freedom for Catholic higher education. In response to a reporter's question about the reaction of such persons to my case, I replied that they are either like Pilate or Nicodemus: they either washed their hands and had nothing to do with the case, or they came by night to tell me of their distress. To my knowledge, none of these leaders has explicitly and publicly defended Catholic University, but neither has any one of them explicitly and squarely condemned it. Some have pointed out (in my judgment erroneously) that what happened to me could occur at Catholic University because it is a pontifical university but could not happen at their institutions.[23]

Rodger Van Allen, a professor at Villanova University who has written on academic freedom and is a former president of the College Theology Society, pointed out early on in my controversy that the best thing for Catholic higher education would be my being hired by a major Catholic university.[24] However, as Richard McBrien and Richard McCormick, two distinguished theologians from Notre Dame University, have shown, this did not happen, despite attempts by some faculty members of these institutions. "We regard this exclusion as a continuing complicity in the original injustice done to Father Curran and as harmful, not only to him, but also to Catholic higher education in this country and to the church."[25]

The issue of academic freedom for Catholic higher education in the United States is still up in the air. On 26 September 1990, Pope John Paul II issued *Ex Corde Ecclesiae,* an aposolic constitution on Catholic universities that culminated twenty years of conversations and negotiations.[26] The leadership of the mainstream of Catholic higher education in the United States (the presidents of Catholic University, Fordham, and Notre Dame as well as the executive secretary of the Association of Catholic Colleges and Universities) warmly received the document.[27] *America* editorialized: "The constitution also unequivocally affirms two basic qualities that must be possessed by any school aspiring to be a university: institutional autonomy and academic freedom."[28] On the other hand, Archbishop Rembert Weakland said about this constitution and subsequent events: "I'm sure if I were president of any Catholic university, I'd be nervous at this point. I'd want some clarifications."[29] I, too, have expressed grave reservations about the constitution.[30]

Such a difference in evaluation by people generally committed to the principles and practices of academic freedom for Catholic higher education highlights the ambiguities in the apostolic constitution. Those warmly accepting the document point out that this new document incorporates important changes from its earlier drafts. The Vatican congregation listened to and often accepted the comments of Catholic higher educators in the United States. In addition, the pope insists that "a Catholic University is distinguished by its free search for the whole truth about nature, man, and God" (n. 4). Institutional autonomy and academic freedom are mentioned and defended (n. 12). Theology is a legitimate academic discipline and theologians enjoy academic freedom so long as they are faithful to theology's principles and methods (n. 29).

However, the constitution also reveals another position — and probably even a stronger and more fundamental one — that limits institutional autonomy and academic freedom. The institutional fidelity of the university to the church requires an adherence to the teaching authority of the church in matters of faith and morals (n. 27). Bishops are not external agents to the university but participate in the life of Catholic institutions of higher learning (n. 28). Academic freedom is limited by the "confines of the truth and the common good" (n. 29). Those who teach theological disciplines in these institutions must have a mandate from the competent ecclesiastical authority (part II, a. 3).

My personal experience makes me very wary of ambiguous documents. I had thought that the 1981 canonical statutes for the pontifical faculties of the Catholic University could be tolerated because they contained a strong defense of academic freedom and academic procedures. However, in the crunch such statements were undermined by other statements in the document. One can only conclude that logically this present document and its official interpreters would not, in a conflict, come down on the side of academic freedom.

Leaders of Catholic higher education in the United States rightly point to the document's insistence that Catholic universities do not have to be established officially by church authorities or by a public juridical person in the church, which would thus make the institutions subordinate to church authorities (part II, a. 3). However, such institutions can call themselves Catholic only with the consent of the competent ecclesiastical authority (part II, a. 3). Catholic institutions that do not have a direct juridical tie to the church (the vast majority of those in the United States) "with the agreement of the local ecclesiastical Authority, will make their own the General Norms and their local and regional applications internalizing them into their governing documents, and, as far as possible, will conform their existing Statutes both to these General Norms and to their applications" (part II, a. 1, 3). Also, these norms must take into account the statutes of each university or institute, and, as far as possible and appropriate, civil law (part II, a. 1-2).

Supporters of academic freedom for Catholic higher education who warmly receive the constitution correctly put heavy emphasis on these provisions. The norms for each country are to be drawn up locally and are to recognize and respect existing statutes, customs, and, even as far as possible and appropriate, civil law. Nothing in the constitution would prohibit Catholic institutions of higher learning in the United States from continuing to function as they have in the past. Adaptation to local conditions, customs, and civil law is acceptable, and in the past the American Catholic bishops have supported leaders of Catholic higher education in their insistence on academic freedom and institutional autonomy.

However, there might be some problems. First of all, another official document does not recognize full academic freedom and institutional autonomy. Second, in the last few years many Catholic bishops in the United States have come out against full academic freedom.[31] In these more conservative days of contemporary American Catholicism, it will be much more difficult for the American Catholic bishops as a whole to accept and defend academic freedom. Supporters of academic freedom for Catholic higher education should be worried and concerned.

This chapter has focused on personal reflections. In these reflections I have accepted the good will and good intentions of those who are in favor of academic freedom as well as those who oppose academic freedom and institutional autonomy for Catholic institutions of higher learning. My own personal experience and reflection on the broad range of recent events concludes that the issue is far from settled. Supporters of academic freedom should be worried and ought to work in theory and in practice to prove that academic freedom is good for Catholic higher education — and ultimately for the church itself.[32]

NOTES

1. Neil G. McCluskey, ed., *The Catholic University: A Modern Appraisal* (Notre Dame, IN: University of Notre Dame Press, 1970).

2. The Catholic University of America, Self-Evaluation for the Middle States Association, January 1970.

3. Albert C. Pierce, *Beyond One Man* (Washington, DC: Anawim Press, 1967); Robert Townsend, "At the Cultural Crossroads of American Catholic Higher Education: The 1967 Strike at The Catholic University of America" (M.A. Dissertation, The Catholic University of America, 1990).

4. John F. Hunt, Terrence R. Connelly *et al.*, *The Responsibility of Dissent: The Church and Academic Freedom* (New York: Sheed and Ward, 1967).

5. Resolution of the Board of Trustees of CUA, 2 June 1988.

6. Frederick H. Weisberg, Opinion and Order, CA 1562-87, *Curran v. Catholic University*, 28 February 1989. The full opinion is also published in *Origins* 18 (1989): 664–672; the quotation is found there on p. 671.

7. "Reports: Seventy-Sixth Annual Meeting," *Academe: Bulletin of the American Association of University Professors* 76/5 (September-October 1990): 28.

8. "Reports: Academic Freedom and Tenure: The Catholic University of America," *Academe: Bulletin of the American Association of University Professors* 75/5 (September-October 1989): 27–40.

9. Ibid., pp. 29–32. See also my *Faithful Dissent* (Kansas City, MO: Sheed and Ward, 1986).

10. For a short, uncontested summary of the structure of CUA, see "Academic Freedom and Tenure," *Academe* 75/5 (September-October 1989): 27–28. For a complete history of CUA, see C. Joseph Nuesse, *The Catholic University of America: A Centennial History* (Washington, DC: The Catholic University of America Press, 1990). See also John T. Ford, "'A Center of Light and Truth': A Century of Theology at The Catholic University of America," *Catholic Historical Review* 85 (1989): 566–597. The briefs and court record in *Curran v. Catholic University* explain the positions of both parties in the dispute.

11. Bylaws of the University, June 1985, in The Catholic University of America Faculty Handbook, (Washington, DC, 1980), pp. 17–25.

Academic Freedom

12. Canonical Statutes for the Ecclesiastical Faculties of The Catholic University of America, 1981.

13. A transcript of the hearing was made — Before the Ad Hoc Committee, in Re: Professor Charles Curran, 20 April, 4-6 May 1987.

14. Report to the Chancellor From the Ad Hoc Committee of the Academic Senate of The Catholic University of America in the Matter of Professor Charles E. Curran, 9 October 1987.

15. For a fuller explanation of this hearing and its aftermath, see my *Catholic Higher Education, Theology, and Academic Freedom* (Notre Dame, IN: University of Notre Dame Press, 1990), pp. 220-234.

16. Statement of the Board of Trustees of The Catholic University of America to the Ad Hoc Committee of the Academic Senate, sent under a cover letter from Cardinal Joseph Bernardin, chair of the board of trustees, 27 January 1988.

17. Resolution of the Board of Trustees of The Catholic University of America, 2 June 1988.

18. Report to the Faculty, Administration, Trustees, Students of The Catholic University of America by an Evaluation Team Representing the Commission on Higher Education of the Middle States Association of Colleges and Schools, p. 34.

19. *Origins* (1989): 664-672.

20. Richard A. McCormick and Richard P. McBrien, "L'Affaire Curran II," *America* 163 (1990): 127-132.

21. Auburn University Called Meeting of the University Senate, 15 January 1991, Resolution: Censure of President James E. Martin. See also "Auburn University: A Supplementary Report on a Censured Administration," *Academe: Bulletin of the American Association of University Professors* 77/3 (May-June 1991): 34-40.

22. Deposition of William Franklin Baker in *Curran v. The Catholic University of America*, 9 August 1988; Deposition of Susan DeConcini in *Curran v. The Catholic University of America*, 9 September 1988.

23. E.g., Joseph O'Hare, "Faith and Freedom in Catholic Universities," in William W. May, ed., *Vatican Authority and American Catholic Dissent* (New York: Crossroads, 1987), 160-167.

24. Rodger Van Allen, "The Implications of the Curran Case for Academic Freedom," in May, *Vatican Authority*, pp. 156-157.

25. "L'Affaire Curran: II," *America* 163 (1990): 127.

26. Pope John Paul II, *Ex Corde Ecclesiae: Apostolic Constitution on Catholic Universities* (Vatican City: Vaticana, 1990). The

document is also published in *Origins* 20 (1990): 265-276.

27. James W. Sauve, "Pope John Paul II and Catholic Colleges and Universities," *America* 163 (October 1990): 260ff; Charles E. Curran, "Point of View," *Chronicle of Higher Education,* 30 January 1991, p. A48.

28. "Editorial: A Charter for Catholic Universities," *America* 163 (1990): 259.

29. Archbishop Rembert Weakland, press conference, 12 November 1990.

30. "Point of View," *Chronicle of Higher Education,* 30 January 1991, p. A48.

31. E.g., Oscar H. Lipscomb, "Faith and Academic Freedom," *America* 159 (1988): 124-125; Daniel E. Pilarczyk, "Academic Freedom: Church and University," *Origins* 18 (1988): 57-59; Donald W. Wuerl, "Academic Freedom and the University," *Origins* 18 (1988): 207-211. In 1988 the bishops conference in the United States generally supported the position of the Association of Catholic Colleges and Universities in objecting to some of the proposals in the proposed draft of the document on Catholic higher education. However, the congregation's summary indicates that seven American bishops strongly supported the proposed norms. See Congregation for Catholic Education, "Summary of Responses to Draft Schema on Catholic Universities," *Origins* 17 (1988): 697. Note also that the episcopal trustees at Catholic University came out against academic freedom for that institution.

32. For my defense of academic freedom, see *Catholic Higher Education, Theology, and Academic Freedom,* especially chapter 5, "Rationale in Defense of Academic Freedom for Catholic Higher Education."

10. Military Force and the New World Order

Politicians, pundits, political scientists, and the public at large have been talking about "the new world order," a phrase made popular by President George Bush. To be sure, significant changes have occurred in the geopolitical order. Most people agree and resonate with President Bush's description of the challenge of the new world order—to build a world based on shared commitments among nations large and small to a set of principles that undergird our relations—peaceful settlement of disputes, solidarity against aggression, reduced and controlled arsenals, and just treatment of all peoples.[1] However, once one becomes more specific and concrete many disputes remain about what the new world order will look like.

The most significant aspect of the new world order, especially from the perspective of the United States, is the end of the cold war, which had dominated American foreign policy and much of its domestic policy since the end of World War II. A united Western Europe and the continuing economic clout of Japan and Germany will be important factors. Many of the aspects of the present world will continue to exist. On the plus side, the United States can plan to live at peace with its immediate neighbors on this continent. On the negative side, the problems of the Third and Fourth Worlds will still be present and the lack of unity, justice, and peace will continue to exist within many countries in all parts of the world—Asia, Africa, Latin America, and Europe.

What will be the role of military force in this new world order or, if one prefers less grandiose terms, in future geopolitics? This chapter will consider the current discussion of the new world order to reflect on the use of force from the perspective of Catholic moral theology. Since this is primarily a theological–ethical essay, it will not enter into the particulars of policy decisions. Two theses will be developed: First, nations today are not called to be pacifist; second, we have too readily and too quickly resorted to the use and threatened use of force and thus have failed to see that at the present time the use of force must truly be very limited and a last resort. The focus of these reflections is on nations in general and the United States in particular and not on individual persons. I believe society has a very legitimate place for individual persons who are committed pacifists and opposed to all use of military force.

Thesis 1: Nations Are Not Called to Be Pacifist

The negative statement of the thesis is the most clear — nations today are not called to be pacifist. Such a position means that one adopts some form of the just war theory. The recent debates about the Persian Gulf War contained much discussion about the theory and general agreement about the criteria involved.[2] This chapter presupposes a general knowledge of the just war theory and concentrates on the justification of the theory itself and the very significant limits that are built into this theory. Not only official Catholic social teaching as coming from the pope and bishops but also Catholic moral theology in general have acknowledged that nations are not called to pacifism.[3] The present section will explore some of the more significant theological and ethical bases for this position.

One significant theological factor involves eschatology. Contemporary Catholic theology generally proposes an eschatology that embraces the tension between the present and the fullness of the reign of God; the fullness of the reign of God

242 *Military Force and the New World Order*

is not yet here and will never be present in this world. Peace is a most significant attribute of the reign of God, but the tension of this eschatological position acknowledges that the fullness of that peace is not here. The lamb and the lion have not yet laid down in perfect peace and harmony. However, this eschatological understanding insists on the tension between the now and the future. The future of the reign of God gives a negative criticism on every existing human structure and calls for continual change and conversion. Such an eschatology not only serves as a basis for recognizing the legitimacy of force in this world, which falls short of the fullness of God's presence but also calls for as many limitations on force as possible.

A related theological basis for recognizing a possible resort to military force concerns the presence of sin in the world. In the early church Augustine defended the possible use of even killing force primarily because of the presence of sin in the world.[4] How can an ethic based on love of God and neighbor ever justify killing? The Christian is called to love one's neighbor and even one's enemies. But what happens when neighbor A attacks neighbor B? Love for neighbor B might require using force to repel the attack. Force at times might even have to be so severe as to kill the attacker. The presence of sin very much affects how we must act in this world. In the fullness of the reign of God, neighbors will not attack one another; in this world, history reminds us that attacks do occur.

Sin is only one part of the reality that surrounds us. The Catholic tradition insists rightly, in my judgment, on the goodness of creation and on the saving presence of God's reign even now. This anthropological approach avoids the two extremes of naive optimism and negative pessimism. The possible legitimacy of resort to force and even killing is only one part of the story; possible uses of force must be limited and criticized.

Catholic ecclesiology and its understanding of the role of the church in the world also support the nonpacifist position. On a number of occasions this book has insisted that the Catholic church is a church in the sociological sense of the term and is not a sect which withdraws from the world because it fears that life in the world is incompatible with the gospel.[5] The Catholic church as the primary example of a church urges its members to accept responsibilities for the world in which they live. Individuals in the state must do what is necessary for the common good. At times in this imperfect world this responsibility might call for the use of force to defend the nation or prevent a proportionate injustice. Such an understanding of the church and its relationship to the world undergirds the acceptance of some use of force and even military force, but the church also aims at transforming the world. Force and violence are never given a carte blanche.

In general, the Catholic tradition is unwilling to reduce all morality to only one value or virtue. Official Catholic social teaching insists that a just society includes truth, justice, charity, and freedom.[6] Catholic thinking never absolutizes peace but often links it with justice. The whole just war theory by its very name shows the close relationship that exists between peace and justice. Sometimes justice can demand that one go to war. War can be an instrument of justice.

The fact that the Catholic tradition does not absolutize peace also reminds us of the many different meanings of peace. Peace can mean anything from the absence of war to the perfect harmony and justice of beatitude. A very imperfect peace can at times impede justice. Discussions about just war usually treat of peace in the minimalistic sense, which is one more reason why peace cannot be absolutized. On the other hand, we are all called to work for a true and better peace that is much more than the mere absence of war.

The traditional Catholic insistence on not absolutizing peace coheres with the theory currently proposed by revisionist Catholic moral theologians in personal, sexual, and medical ethics — the theory of proportionalism.[7] Proportionalism distinguishes between moral evil and nonmoral evil. Nonmoral evil can be done as a means provided it is truly proportionate to the end in view. In this way force or war is a nonmoral evil that at times can be justified on the basis of proportionality. However, the traditional Catholic insistence on not absolutizing peace has its own validity independent of the theory of proportionalism.

Catholic social ethics and official Catholic social teaching in more modern days have pointed out the structural problem that prevents the outlawing of war. Within each individual state the central authority has the responsibility and the power to enforce justice and preserve order. The Pastoral Constitution on the Church in the Modern World recognizes that the goal of outlawing war requires the establishment of some universal public authority acknowledged as such by all and endowed with effective powers to safeguard and protect the security, justice, and the rights of all.[8] In the absence of such a reality many other things can and should be done to avoid war, but no possible human structures can absolutely provide for the total outlawing of war.

That states cannot be pacifist is thus firmly rooted in Catholic theology and ethics. A glance at our world reminds us of the reality of force, killing, and violence. Unfortunately, we Americans on the whole are not all that familiar with what is happening in our world. One great advantage of belonging to a universal church is its challenge to open up our own horizons. Pope John Paul II, for example, in his annual talk to diplomats in January of 1991 gave what a press agent might call a state of the world talk mentioning what has been occurring in the last year throughout the globe.[9]

In terms of military force and violence, one can distinguish three different kinds of wars — wars involving the superpowers, wars across the borders of other countries, and internal wars or revolutions within existing countries and boundaries. The end of the cold war and *glasnost* and *perestroika* in Russia have occasioned a collective and global sigh of relief about the danger of war between the superpowers. However, incursions across national boundaries continue with too much regularity. We are all familiar with Lebanon, Cyprus, Afghanistan, Grenada, Cambodia, Panama, Vietnam, and Kuwait. Internal uprisings and revolutions are even now occurring in many parts of Latin America and Africa. The rise of nationalism in Eastern Europe and the former Soviet Union is also bringing increasing unrest to many countries there. The empirical reality is very clear: we do not live in a world without war and without the use of military force.

The existing reality can never become ultimately normative and must always be criticized, but this empirical understanding supports the position that nations at the present time are not called to be pacifist.

Thesis 2: Nations Resort Too Readily to the Use of Force

The contemporary empirical situation can also serve as the starting point for developing the second thesis — a perennial danger exists of resorting to military force too quickly. In my judgment the United States was not justified in its use of military force in Grenada, Panama, and the Persian Gulf. Even those who disagree with such practical judgments can and should readily admit the danger of resorting too quickly to military force. Many reasons in the Catholic tradition and in our contemporary world help to support the thesis of there being a danger of too readily resorting to military force: the limitations of military force; the increasing devastation of modern weapons; distortions of social priorities; and the many temptations that escalate the appeal to military force.

The Limitations of Military Force

Peace is more than the absence of war. Pope Paul VI in *Populorum Progressio* developed the thesis that "development is the new name for peace."[10] Pope John XXIII described the ideal social order as built on truth, justice, freedom, and love.[11] The basic reality is simple — war does nothing positive to achieve true peace but can enable us to remove some of the obstacles in the way of peace. Hence the limitations of war should be much more widely appreciated and recognized. War is strictly limited in what it can accomplish in terms of bringing about true peace.

In all human affairs, force can only play a minor, subservient, and instrumental role. Catholic moral theology considers the human person to be an image of God because, like God, the human person is endowed with intellect, free will, and the power of self-determination.[12] To move and change human beings one must appeal to reason and free will. Physical force alone might bring about external compliance, but it can never by itself truly bring about human change. Human change must appeal to what is distinctively human. Yes, power plays a significant role in human reality, but many kinds of power are more significant and important than physical force: the power of truth, of beauty, of love, of exemplary living . . . Physical force at most can bring about external compliance with justice, but it can never bring about true justice, true human change, and true peace.

The Catholic understanding of the state sees it as a natural society based on human nature. Human beings are social by nature and called by God to live together in political communities so that all people may live in peace and justice. Political authority rests primarily on justice and not on force.[13] The Catholic theory of the state probably does not give enough importance to human sinfulness and tends to be too optimistic at times. However, experience in the last few years reminds us that physical force alone will not be able to keep a human community subjugated over a long period of time. Force alone, or even the predominance of force, can never bring about even a minimally just and lasting human community.

The limitations of war and of the use of military force must be seen in the light of the limitations of force in general. Military force can do nothing in a positive way to bring about true peace. Military force at best has the negative function of preventing and stopping what according to the just war theory would have to be seen as the injustice involved. Military force can prevent the evil from happening but it cannot of itself positively contribute to the building up of true peace and justice.

The Persian Gulf situation shows in a stark and acute way the limitations of exerting military force. Problems in the region were not solved by the war. One injustice was done away with, but the real work of peace and justice must now begin. We are learning the sorry and difficult lesson that war is much easier to win than justice and peace.

American rhetoric fuels a false anticipation of the good that might be accomplished by war. The Catholic ethical tradition has always seen war in relationship to justice, as is evident from the very name of the *just war theory:* war is an instrument of justice. What is the reason proposed for war in our usual national rhetoric? Without doubt we have always gone to war "for the sake of freedom." Justice does not usually enter into our ethical considerations or even the cause or reason for our going to war. I believe this rhetoric shows once again too great an emphasis on freedom and individualism and not enough importance to justice. The rhetoric is telling. Freedom from the oppressor is much easier to obtain than justice; such freedom of itself does not bring about justice or true peace. War and military force can bring about some forms of freedom from oppression, but they cannot build up the reality of justice and true peace. If we align war more with justice than with freedom, then the limitations of war become more apparent. What war can positively accomplish is quite limited.

The Increasing Devastation of Modern Weapons

A second source limiting the recourse to war today comes from the increasing devastation that can be wrought by modern weapons. Weapon development has changed dramatically in this century. Think of the changes made by air power and missiles. We now live under the mushroom cloud of two atomic bombs that have been dropped by us, and the whole world lives under the threat of nuclear annihilation. We human beings now have the power in our hands to destroy our planet.

Escalation in military power affects both the principle of proportionality and the principle of discrimination, or non-combatant immunity, in the just war theory. Proportionality means that the evils involved in the war must be compensated for by the good to be attained. However, the evils of war are now magnified and multiplied by the increasing power of our arsenals. Modern war by its very nature involves much more killing — and much more damage to the physical infrastructure of society and to the earth itself. The greater evils perpetrated by war, the greater the reason must be for justifying the resort to military force.

Consider the damage that has been done to Iraq in the Persian Gulf War. The war was very short, and American leaders claimed that they did not target civilians and nonmilitary objectives; nevertheless, the devastation and desolation were great. Without doubt, the United States will have to help rebuild in Iraq some of what our military destroyed. However, much of what the U.S. destroyed can never be rebuilt. The human toll of hunger, homelessness, migration, and fear can never be calculated. Recall that after World War II the United States helped to rebuild the German and Japanese cities that we had destroyed. Very great evils and afflictions necessarily accompany war fought with modern weapons. Accepting the just war theory means admitting that the greater the destructiveness wrought by war, the more difficult is finding proportionate reasons to justify it.

Modern weapons can easily be unjust in the light of the principle of discrimination. As a matter of fact, modern war has violated the principle by directly attacking nonmilitary targets. In World War II both sides bombed entire cities. The United States dropped the atomic bomb on two major centers of civilian population. Modern warfare can readily exceed the limitations imposed by the principle of discrimination. The Nuremburg trials did not indict anyone for killing civilians with air power because the court recognized that the allies had done the same as the Germans.[14]

Modern weapons have thus wrought new and very significant limitations to the traditional just war theory. Especially in the light of this escalating power, Vatican Council II pointed out the need to undertake an evaluation of war with an entirely new attitude.[15]

Distortions of Social Priorities

Military force is quite limited in what it can contribute to peace, and resort to it must always be an ultimate and last appeal. However, in terms of priorities, military force often ranks very high. The amount of money that is allotted for military forces throughout the world is egregiously out of proportion to the funds assigned to alleviate the many human needs of society. All recognize the problem of using statistics for one's own purposes, but statistics quoted about the United States indicate that military spending has gone seriously awry. Richard J. Barnet maintains that more than one-third of our federal budget in 1990 went to pay for wars past, present, and future.[16] Archbishop Raymond Hunthausen points out that whereas the military budget increased 50 percent over the last decade, federal programs aimed at reducing poverty were cut 54 percent.[17] The budgets of the United States and the rest of the world indicate that military force has been given a much greater share of our available resources than it should have.

One could object that the position I describe above is guilty of idealism. We live in the real world and the United States has the obligation and the duty in this real and imperfect world to protect its own interests and to promote global peace and justice. However, in my view the need to reduce dramatically both military spending and the dependence on military force is, in the last analysis, in the long-term best interest of the United States.

Catholic ethics has never shied away from recognizing a legitimate and important role for self-interest properly understood. The problem is to determine what is truly good for the individual and/or society. In terms of both, the primary problems are two — the danger of seeing the good only in terms of the short run and the danger of individualism which sees the person or a particular society as isolated from the total human community.

A major reduction in military spending is both politically and morally good and right for the United States as well as for other countries. Even in terms of being a superpower, the emphasis on military spending is self-defeating. Military force is only one type of power and by no means the most important; many other kinds of power are more significant and effective in bringing about justice and peace in our society. Our hopes that as a nation we might learn an important lesson from the cold war. The Soviet Union could not maintain its heavy commitment to the military and still provide for all the truly human needs of its people. However, we in the United States should not gloat because we could face the same reality. In the last decade we have become the number one debtor nation in the world. Economic power should never be the most important type of power either but is an instrument necessary for accomplishing many other more human tasks. We have been so strapped by our military expenditures that we have actually harmed and lessened the real power that we can and do exercise. Germany and Japan have emerged as important economic powers, but both refuse to invest heavily in military power. The irony is that by defining superpower status primarily in military terms we as a nation have actually weakened our overall position in the world. The point can and must be made in season and out of season: good morality and the long term political well being of the United States call for us to reduce drastically our military budgets.

*Temptations That Escalate
the Appeal to Military Force*

The first danger that can escalate the appeal to military force comes from the problem of self-deception. What is true for individuals can occur even more readily for nations. Every nation always claims to have justice on its side. At the very minimum, history reminds us that not all nations who have gone to war have had justice on their side. Our society needs to be self-critical and to make sure that its institutions are free to play the critical role. For example, in the Persian Gulf War the restrictions on the press were too severe and prevented any objective evaluation of what was occurring. Bureaucracies and governments have an innate wish to manage the news and to impose their own interpretation on events. True patriotism can take the form of challenging a too-quick resort to military force by the government. No iron law says that justice will always be on our side. We would be the first to dispute that claim were it made by others.

The powerful are always tempted to use their power to accomplish their purposes and, in the process, of oppressing the weak and the powerless. We as a so-called superpower must constantly be vigilant in this regard. History is strewn with examples of how the powerful have exploited the powerless, and we Americans have our place on that long list.

The temptation to overglorify the military is omnipresent. Some people claim rightly that the United States, with its emphasis on civilian control of the military and the separation of the military from the political, is less susceptible to this danger than some other countries. However, the problems about overglorifying military power and military exploits are endemic to all political societies. The military truly needs an esprit de corps; the morale of troops is very important: civilian support for the military is essential, but too often the limitations of the military are glossed over and forgotten. We can never forget that the ultimate power and strength in the nation must be judged by much more than just its military power and hardware.

The temptation to resort to military force is often appealing because it is comparatively more simple and less complicated than other possible strategies. Part of the problem in the United States comes from the fact that we want a quick and easy solution for all our problems. Often the military option appears more simple and quick than other possible approaches, but a military victory does not ensure true justice and true peace. In the Persian Gulf, for example, I believe we should have allowed economic sanctions to do their work. The truth of the matter is that most often there are no quick and easy solutions to the political problems we face.

The danger of absolutizing our own cause in war is perennial. Believers in God invariably want God to be on their side in war, so we too readily identify God with our cause and the enemy too often becomes evil incarnate. Believers are not the only ones who face this temptation. A nation at war wants a united and common effort against the enemy; all means are used to drum up popular support for the cause. Such a mentality readily identifies the cause of good with "us" and the cause of evil with "the other." In this regard consider the statements that were made during the Persian Gulf War. Saddam Hussein became evil personified. Our missiles were "Patriots"; their missiles were "Scuds." Such a tendency toward absolutizing one's own position and totally identifying it with God's will and work leaves no room for self-criticism or for the gray areas that envelop so much of human existence.

The siren of technology often lures us into a treacherous trap. I am not opposed to technology; it is a good—but a limited good—that must always be at the service of the human. The human is much broader and more inclusive than the technological. At times the human must say "No" to the technological. The limitations of force, of military force, and of technologically sophisticated military force are all interrelated. History proves that superior military technology is not always able to win a war, to say nothing of achieving true peace. Many other factors are very significant. Again, what is most distinctively human can ultimately overcome the overwhelming power of technology.

The technological imperative has created the most havoc in terms of the arms race. Bigger and better weapons and military hardware always seem to be "needed." This technological imperative fuels an inexhaustible need for weapons and thus makes military expenditures disproportionate. We do not always need new and better weapons; we need to be able to control our technology.

All of these dangers and temptations contribute to the tendency of war to exceed the moral limits of *just* war both with regard to the *ius ad bellum* (justice in going to war) and the *ius in bello* (justice in waging the war). All these factors point out why we are always tempted to resort too quickly and too readily to military solutions, to war. In this world all use of military force cannot be outlawed, but we are constantly resorting too readily to military force.

The two theses developed in this chapter—nations are not called to be pacifist and we resort too readily to the use of military force—form a general perspective on and a basic guideline to how we should approach the multiple policy questions that we face as a nation and as a world. In my judgment both theses help to explain, ground, and clarify the statements of Pope John Paul II about the Persian Gulf War. The pope wrote to President George Bush and expressed his "firm belief that war is not likely to bring an adequate solution to international problems. . . ."[18] Speaking before the Persian Gulf War began in January 1991, John Paul II claimed that "war would be a decline for all humanity."[19] So negative were the pope's remarks about the Persian Gulf War that he spontaneously felt the need to point out that he was not a pacifist and was not calling for pacifism in today's circumstances.[20] The pope is, rather, challenging us today in our contemporary circumstances to limit resort to war as much as possible and to work for structures that will enable us to outlaw war entirely.

NOTES

1. *Washington Post,* 14 April 1991, p. A27. For a negative assessment of President Bush's more specific understanding of the new world order, see James Petras, "The Meaning of the New World Order: A Critique," *America* 164 (1991): 512–515.

2. See, for example, President George Bush, "Address to National Religious Broadcasters Justifying Persian Gulf War," *Origins* 20 (1991): 570–572; Archbishop John Roach, "Senate Testimony (Dec. 6) on the Persian Gulf Crisis," *Origins* 20 (1990): 457–460.

3. Archbishop Jean-Louis Tauran, "The Pope's Approach to the War," *Origins* 20 (1991): 670–671.

4. George Weigel, *Tranquillitas Ordinis: The Present Failure and Future Promise of American Catholic Thought on War and Peace* (New York: Oxford University Press, 1987), pp. 28–32.

5. Ernst Troeltsch, *The Social Teaching of the Christian Churches,* 2 vols. (New York: Harper, 1960). Troeltsch distinguishes three main sociological types—the church, the sect, and mysticism.

6. Pope John XXIII, *Pacem in Terris,* n. 35, in David J. O'Brien and Thomas A. Shannon, eds., *Renewing the Earth: Catholic Documents on Peace, Justice, and Liberation* (Garden City, NY: Doubleday/Image, 1977), p. 132.

7. For one view of the matter see Bernard Hoose, *Proportionalism: The American Debate and Its European Roots* (Washington, DC: Georgetown University Press, 1987).

8. Pastoral Constitution on the Church in the Modern World, n. 82, in O'Brien and Shannon, *Renewing the Earth*, pp. 264-266.

9. Pope John Paul II, "Address to Diplomats Accredited to the Vatican," *Origins* 20 (1991): 525-531.

10. Pope Paul VI, *Populorum Progressio*, n. 76, in O'Brien and Shannon, *Renewing the Earth*, p. 340.

11. Pope John XXIII, *Pacem in Terris*, n. 35, in O'Brien and Shannon, *Renewing the Earth*, p. 132.

12. Thomas Aquinas, *Summa theologiae* I^a II^{ae}, prologue (Rome: Marietti, 1952).

13. Two classical explanations of the state in the Catholic tradition are Heinrich Rommen, *The State in Catholic Thought* (St. Louis: B. Herder, 1945); and Jacques Maritain, *Man and the State* (Chicago: University of Chicago Press, 1951).

14. Drew Christiansen, "The Ethics of U.S. Strategies in the Persian Gulf," *America* 163 (1990): 451-452.

15. Pastoral Constitution on the Church in the Modern World, n. 80, in O'Brien and Shannon, *Renewing the Earth*, p. 262.

16. Richard J. Barnet, "Reflections: The Uses of Force," *New Yorker* 29 April 1991, p. 92.

17. Archbishop Raymond Hunthausen, "Waging Peace in a Decade of Power," *Origins* 20 (1991): 712.

18. Pope John Paul II, "Letter to President Bush Urging the Avoidance of War in the Persian Gulf," *Origins* 20 (1991): 534-535.

19. Pope John Paul II, "Address to Diplomats," *Origins* 20 (1991): 530.

20. Pope John Paul II, "We Are Not Pacifists," *Origins* 20 (1991): 625.

Index

255

20, 39, 83, 105, 203; canon
law and, 17; papal office and,
204; present hierarchical
insistence on, 65; subsidiarity
and, 8, 143
— contemporary tensions in, 6,
10, 12, 53–54, 58, 125–29,
204; dual role of Vatican and,
71–72; factors aggravating,
13–24; inevitable, 1–2; sexual
ethics and, 18, 20, 27, 28, 88,
89; theodicy problem and,
193. *See also* Ecclesiology,
Roman Catholic.
Ruether, Rosemary, 153

Sacraments, 4–5, 7, 19, 32, 39,
47–48. *See also* Marriage;
Penance
St. John's University, 229
Schillebeeckx, Edward, 23, 61,
153
Secondary causality, 186–87, 191,
194, 195, 200, 205
Sect-Church distinction, 23–24,
62–64, 172, 242–43
Self-Defense, 74, 99, 242
Sensus Fidelium, 78 n. 2, 105,
117, 121–23, 125
Sexual ethics (Catholic), 27, 28,
35, 39–40, 88, 122; dualism
in, 29–33, 48; historical
studies, 51–52; positive aspects
of, 43–54; proportionalism
and, 96, 243. *See also*
Marriage
Sexual teachings, official
Catholic, 2, 23, 27–29, 88;
defended, 35 42–43, 77, 115;
hierarchical interventions, xi,
39, 40–42, 53; marriage and,
32–34, 38; methodology, ix,
x, 41, 42–43, 45–46, 73,

77–78; revisionist objections,
171; virginity, 34–35. *See also*
Contraception
Social ethics (Catholic), 8, 10,
34, 174–76, 177, 247;
democracy and, 144; defined,
134; law in, 145–47, 174;
McCormick and, 95–96; Murray on Church/state in,
138–39; organic view of society in, 73–74, 75; option for
the poor and, 88–89; social
conflict, 74–75; transcendental
method, 77–78; warrants for,
160
Social justice, 2, 166, 168, 169,
173. *See also* Justice
Social moral order (single), x,
63, 86, 162, 163–79, 190, 209
Social teaching (official
Catholic), 74, 75, 144,
147–48; anthropology, 58–59,
60, 61, 77, 150, 152;
Christology and, 60–62; corporatism and, 66, 73; defined,
134; development in 122, 138,
148–53, 173; ecclesiology and,
58, 62–72, 134–44, 145, 147,
151–55; eschatology and,
58–59, 60, 77; historical
consciousness and, ix, x, 76,
77, 142, 153–55; moderately
reforming, 58; natural law
method in, 161–62, 171–72;
social mission of church as
constitutive in, 91; social
moral order, 163–71, 173–74,
176, 179; subsidiarity and,
8–9, 142–43, 170; unresolved
issues, 78; use of force and,
241, 243, 244, 245
Society of Jesus, 40, 41, 92, 97,
98–99, 100

DATE DUE

GAYLORD			PRINTED IN U.S.A.